ADVANCE PRAISE FOR
AROUND THE WORLD IN (MORE THAN) 80 DAYS
BY LARRY ALEX TAUNTON

"America—the freest, most tolerant and inclusive nation on earth—is under siege by radicals who make no effort to conceal their determination to destroy it. Larry Alex Taunton has provided patriotic Americans with a powerful weapon to defeat our enemies. Buy this book to arm yourself for the defense of your freedoms. Buy a second copy for a friend."
—David Horowitz, author of *Dark Agenda:
The War to Destroy Christian America*

"To truly understand how and why America is exceptional you could travel to country after country and see for yourself. You might even want to write a brilliant book about it! But lucky for you my friend, Larry Taunton has done all the traveling for you—think of the money you've saved!—and has written that brilliant book, making the case so clear that you owe it to yourself to grab a copy and read it! Please do!"
—Eric Metaxas, host of *The Eric Metaxas Show*;
author of *Bonhoeffer* and *If You Can Keep It*

"The problem with being an American is that familiarity too often breeds contempt because we see our faults up close and take our virtues and blessings for granted. Larry Alex Taunton has provided a cure by lifting us up out of America, and taking us on a long and insightful tour of the world to see how other places actually stack up. Take the tour with him, and gain some very much needed perspective. You may find—as he did—there's no place like home."
—Benjamin Wiker, Ph.D., author of
10 Books That Screwed Up the World

"Larry Taunton—historian, columnist, and a man of abiding Christian faith—traveled (often at great risk to himself) to twenty-six nations in order to hold a mirror up to the United States of America and ask: Is America Good and is America Great? Mark Twain did much the

same more than a century ago. Twain's and Taunton's conclusions are identical: There is no place—literally No Place—like home. *Around the World in (More Than) 80 Days* is fabulous. It's going on my shelf next to *The Innocents Abroad*."
—Paul Reid, co-author with William Manchester, *The Last Lion: Winston Spencer Churchill: Defender of the Realm, 1940-1965*

PRAISE FOR LARRY ALEX TAUNTON 'S PREVIOUS BOOKS

"A literary gem."
—*FrontPage Magazine*

"Taunton's smooth and accessible prose brings to life what seems to have been a dear and lively friendship between two thinkers at odds politically and religiously, but not intellectually."
—*Publishers Weekly*

"The book's overall genius is that it's a story. An immensely compelling, page-turning, cannot-put-down kind of story. With its unique combination of superb storytelling, intellect, and passion, *The Faith of Christopher Hitchens* achieves—and deserves— the rare status of instant classic."
—The Gospel Coalition

"Beautifully written. Everyone should read this book."
—Chris Matthews, *Hardball*

"But now I do know what I think of this book, and I am concerned that I might exhaust my supply of superlatives. This book is simply outstanding. There, my first superlative…. I still have some superlatives left, so I will simply conclude by saying that I wish more Christian books were like this one. Top drawer."
—*Christianity Today*

"*The Faith of Christopher Hitchens* is a fascinating exploration and explanation of a very important figure. It describes and models the kind of friendship that Christians can and should have even with the most formidable opponents of their faith. It is a story worth telling and one that Taunton tells with great skill."
—Tim Challies

"The social elites want evangelicals to be as dumb as they suspect they are. But when a person comes along who proves that tale false, which Taunton clearly does in his exemplary book, they simply don't know what to do."
— *The Federalist*

"What Taunton accomplishes here is marvelous, equally for what it is not as much as what it is. *The Faith of Christopher Hitchens* is that most difficult, and most valuable, of memoirs: A record of virtue and of vice, of faith and faithlessness. Perhaps that is Taunton's greatest achievement: He makes us want, zealously, for Christopher Hitchens to believe."
—Mere Orthodoxy

"If atheist activists want to be taken seriously, they must be willing to engage the facts. The fact is that Mr. Taunton has simply said that Hitchens late in life was 'not certain' of his atheism. Unable to tolerate this crack in the atheist facade, Mr. Taunton's critics reacted hysterically."
— *Wall Street Journal*

"Taunton enjoys the cerebral process and has a quick, ironic wit."
– *Weld Magazine*

LARRY ALEX TAUNTON

AROUND *THE* WORLD

· IN **80** DAYS ·

Photo by Heather Durham

AROUND THE WORLD IN 80 DAYS

MORE THAN

DISCOVERING WHAT MAKES AMERICA GREAT AND
WHY WE MUST FIGHT TO SAVE IT

LARRY ALEX TAUNTON

FIDELIS
BOOKS

A FIDELIS BOOKS BOOK
An Imprint of Post Hill Press
ISBN: 978-1-64293-592-9
ISBN (eBook): 978-1-64293-593-6

Around the World in (More Than) 80 Days:
Discovering What Makes America Great and Why We Must Fight to
Save It
© 2020 by Larry Alex Taunton
All Rights Reserved

Cover Design by Cody Corcoran

All people, locations, events, and situations are portrayed to the best of the author's memory. While all of the events described are true, many names and identifying details have been changed to protect the privacy of the people involved.

FIDELIS BOOKS Post Hill PRESS

Post Hill Press
New York • Nashville
posthillpress.com

Published in the United States of America

To Stewart –

Fellow traveler,
Adventurer,
Lover of life,
And possessor of a heart of gold.
Your friendship has never wavered.

"Perhaps there has been, at some point in history, some great power whose elevation was exempt from the violent exploitation of other human bodies. If there has been, I have yet to discover it. But this banality of violence can never excuse America, because America makes no claim to the banal. America believes itself exceptional, the greatest and noblest nation ever to exist … I propose to take our countrymen's claims of American exceptionalism seriously, which is to say I propose subjecting our country to an exceptional moral standard."

—Ta-Nehisi Coates in his *New York Times* bestseller *Between the World and Me*

"In 32 years of living in this country, the United States has never once failed me. Becoming an American citizen was the greatest privilege of my life. Your book reads like an American horror story because you have damned to hell the noblest and most endearing trait of those who come to this country and who love it: the Dream. You declare: 'This is the foundation of the Dream—its adherents must not just believe in it but believe that it is just, believe that their possession of the Dream is the natural result of grit, honor, and good works.' Well, it is. And we, the Dreamers and achievers who continue to make this country the exceptional wonder that it is, will never capitulate to your renunciation. The world we desired has been won. It exists. It is real. It is possible. It is ours. And it should be yours, and your son's."

—Jason D. Hill, professor of philosophy at DePaul University, who immigrated to the United States from Jamaica at age twenty, in "An Open Letter to Ta-Nehisi Coates: The Dream is Real," *Commentary Magazine*

TABLE OF CONTENTS

Prologue   America on Trial 1

Chapter 1   The Criteria: What Defines a Great Country? 9

Chapter 2   Singapore: OCD? Tired of Democracy?
               This Country Is for You!................................ 20

Chapter 3   Hong Kong: "One Country, Two Systems" 32

Chapter 4   Japan: A Postwar Miracle and Model 41

Chapter 5   New Zealand: Welcome to Seattle................... 56

Chapter 6   Australia: A Day with Peter Singer 61

Chapter 7   South Korea: The Line Between Good and Evil .. 65

Chapter 8   Vietnam: The War America Lost? I Don't
               Think So 77

Chapter 9   Thailand: One Night in Bangkok.................... 86

Chapter 10   Malaysia: "Muddy Junction" 94

Chapter 11   India: "Tea and Cricket" 98

Chapter 12   Russia: The Mother of All Socialist Countries ... 109

Chapter 13   Britain: America Fast-Forwarded.................. 118

Chapter 14   Nigeria: The Most Dangerous Country in
               the World.. 132

Chapter 15   South Africa: The Power of One..................... 160

Chapter 16   Argentina: Like Whitney Houston and
               Bobby Brown.. 171

Chapter 17   Brazil: Apocalypto..................................... 177

Chapter 18   Chile: South America's Most Stable
              Democracy? 185

Chapter 19   Peru: "The Strangest, Saddest City Thou
              Can'st See" 192

Chapter 20   Panama: Where America Did the Impossible .. 196

Chapter 21   Norway: The Best Country in the World? 203

Chapter 22   Sweden: Where No One Is Special 214

Chapter 23   Switzerland: A Great Country for Swiss 223

Chapter 24   Germany: Ideas Have Consequences............... 237

Chapter 25   Egypt: "Wonderful Things" 249

Chapter 26   France: Living in the Ruins 262

Epilogue   The United States of America:
              "The Last Best Hope on Earth" 275

Acknowledgments... 293
Endnotes 295

PROLOGUE

America on Trial

"How can you stand for the national anthem of a nation that preaches and propagates freedom and justice for all, that's so unjust to the people living there?"

—former NFL quarterback Colin Kaepernick

Colin Kaepernick was born in 1987 in Milwaukee, Wisconsin. He is the biological child of a single white mother, Heidi Russo, whose partner, an African-American, fled the relationship when he learned she was pregnant. Russo, then nineteen, decided to allow Rick and Teresa Kaepernick, a white couple, to adopt the newborn boy. In their care, young Colin would be given a life and opportunities that almost certainly would have eluded him otherwise.

Raised in a Christian family, Colin was baptized as a Methodist and confirmed as a Lutheran. Quiet and good-natured, it soon became clear the boy was a talented athlete, too. In high school, he excelled in baseball, basketball, and football, and eventually received numerous scholarship offers to play collegiate baseball. But Kaepernick had big dreams of playing football. "I hope I go to a good college in football," he wrote in the fourth grade, "then

1

go to the pros and play on the Niners or the Packers, even if they aren't good in seven years."

America being what it is, with his hard work and talent, his dream came true. In 2007, Kaepernick accepted the football scholarship and free education offered him by the University of Nevada. He took his Christian faith seriously, attending a Baptist church during this time and adding his now-famous tattoos illustrating verses from the Bible and a Christian cross. With faith in his God, Kaepernick won the starting job as quarterback for the Wolf Pack, and in 2010, he led them to a 13-1 record and their first Top 25 ranking in sixty-two years.

True to his dream, Kaepernick was selected by the San Francisco 49ers in the second round of the 2011 NFL Draft. After a rookie year where he was the backup to quarterback Alex Smith, Kaepernick earned the starting job and led the 49ers to Super Bowl XLVII. Although they lost to the Baltimore Ravens 34 to 31, Kaepernick played well. The following year, he steered the 49ers back to the playoffs and an NFC Championship Game berth where they lost to the Seattle Seahawks. During the offseason, Kaepernick signed a six-year contract extension worth up to $126 million. Life was good.

Then came injuries, bad play, and a benching. In 2015, Kaepernick was replaced by Blaine Gabbert, as clear a sign as any the San Francisco 49ers no longer believed in his ability to lead the team to a championship. Still, were he to never complete another pass, Colin Kaepernick succeeded wildly in the only country on earth where one could become a millionaire playing the game he loved. He was young, rich, and a world of possibilities remained open to him.

It is here that Kaepernick's story takes a dark turn.

It is not uncommon for adopted children to struggle with identity, and Kaepernick often struggled with his. The impression one gets of the young Colin Kaepernick is that of a man with a genuine social conscience but whose Christian faith, while replete with platitudes, tattoos, and sincerity, was lacking in theological substance. Ideological deserts are fertile ground for propagandists and in the summer of 2016, the likable kid who wrote in elementary school enthusiastically of his American dream, fell under the influence of radical social justice warrior (SJW) Ameer Hasan Loggins, a Muslim convert and hip-hop icon-cum-Berkeley professor.

With Loggins's encouragement, Kaepernick audited Loggins's course on popular culture at Berkeley. Loggins characterizes Kaepernick as a hardworking, earnest student who was eager to learn. What, exactly, was Kaepernick learning under this new mentor? In sum, Loggins, who styles himself as an intellectual and a modern-day Malcolm X, teaches, among other things, Islam as a religion of black liberation, capitalism as a system of oppression, and American history as one act of violence and exploitation after another.

According to *The New York Times*, Loggins introduced the NFL quarterback to Nessa Diab, an olive-skinned beauty of Egyptian parentage who has made her name as a Muslim-American activist and Bay Area shock jock. Diab is California-born but spent many of her childhood years in Saudi Arabia where, she says, her sense of social justice grew. Outspoken in her support for Black Lives Matter and in her respect for such champions of social justice as Fidel Castro, her views mirror those of Loggins. She and Kaepernick soon began a romantic relationship and under the influence of Loggins's teaching and her sweet nothings, the radicalization of Colin Kaepernick was well underway.

It seems hardly coincidental that in Kaepernick's social media posts, there now appeared indications of a new identity. This Colin Kaepernick was an angry political activist. He tweeted of lynching, murder, and bodies in the streets of America. Unsurprisingly, he expressed his admiration for Fidel Castro and Malcolm X. The oppression of black people at the hands of white police officers was a theme. "We are under attack!" he wrote. "It's as clear as day!" Worse, he increasingly sounded like the black equivalent of a white supremacist, assuming the language of the violent revolutionary complete with the Black Panther black power salute. It is not hard to see the influence of his new handlers in all this.

When Kaepernick decided to take a knee during the national anthem of a preseason game in 2016, he became the symbolic leader of The Resistance, a kind of domestic anti-Americanism that deems this country the root of all evil. Perhaps due to the distraction, perhaps due to the accumulated injuries, Kaepernick was a shadow of his former self, and facing release from the 49ers, he opted for free agency. When no team picked him up, Kaepernick, the man who was an overcomer his whole life, who lived the American Dream, became a victim, accusing the NFL of collusion. But *America being what it is*, the NFL settled out of court—some estimates put the settlement as high as $80 million—and Kaepernick signed a lucrative endorsement deal with Nike. Soon, they were marketing his image on billboards and television as something like an American Che Guevara to those foolish enough to think either is worthy of emulation.

Let's recap:

Colin Kaepernick was born in a country where adoption is not only possible, but where the prevailing moral attitudes made his adoption likely.

He loved sports, and because his talents were valued, he enjoyed a free university education and a highly profitable career.

When that career failed, he blamed others, and the American legal system rewarded him handsomely as if a deep and genuine wrong was done to him *even though* no wrong was ever legally established.

And since this is a country where people are free to profit by any legal means whatsoever, he was even able to parlay his twin roles of victim and SJW into a major corporate sponsorship worth, millions.

By any measure, Colin Kaepernick has flourished and profited under an American sky.

What a country, eh?

Colin Kaepernick's story is instructive for my purpose in this book. He is one of the faces of a discontented demographic who would put America on trial. Indeed, with all the statues being toppled these days, one wonders if the next one to fall might not be that of Lady Liberty. A lynch mob gathers at her feet to punish her for her sins, past, and present, real and imagined. But this mob is not, as one might suppose, led by the likes of Vladimir Putin or Ji Xinping. Nor is it led by ISIS or al-Qaeda. Rather, this mob consists of homegrown radicals like Colin Kaepernick, Alexandria Ocasio-Cortez, and Richard Spencer, and groups with names like Black Lives Matter, Antifa, or those who fall under the broad banner of the alt-right.

Fringe elements all, these groups see themselves as social justice personified but are, in fact, the embodiment of anarchy, violence, and the politics of hateful reaction. Yes, Michael Moore-style America bashing is in vogue. Whether it is Ashley Judd shouting hate on the Washington Mall, George Soros-funded protests, Barack Obama apologizing for American "arrogance," or Rose McGowan tweeting, "I am a conscientious objector to the USA, its policies, lies, corruption, nationalism, racism, and deep misogyny." These are one side of a battle raging for the heart and soul of America. President Donald Trump's White House has become the flashpoint in a winner-takes-all contest featuring two very different visions for America.

One group sees America's wealth, power, and influence as an accident of history. For them, the idea of American exceptionalism is not only dead, it is offensive. These people never tire of lecturing us about how out-of-step America is with the rest of the world and how she needs to get with it. America, they say, is *bad* for the world. Moreover, where America is exceptional—a deep suspicion of socialism and environmentalism, strongly Christian in a post-Christian world, and alone patriotic among Western nations swept up in a globalist dream—is where America is at her worst and *must* change.

Others want to preserve America's uniqueness, her exceptionalism that is anchored in a Judeo-Christian heritage that has given rise to her laws, art, literature, culture, and place in the world as a refuge from just the types of governments the Left idealizes. Proponents of this vision would readily acknowledge that America's global influence has, at times, been evil, but this is, they would argue, the result of an agenda that has nothing whatsoever to do with the principles upon which America was founded. On the contrary, that agenda—championed by the Left and epitomized by America's bullying of third world countries to adopt permissive abortion and LGBTQ policies—is at odds with those principles.

The war between these competing visions is played out every day in local and national government, in our courts of law, in schools and universities, in media, and even in families. Listening to this cultural debate—it is not only inescapable, but it is also tearing our country apart—it occurred to me the vision advocated by those who would burn America to the ground Ferguson, Missouri-style presupposes there are better places in the world to live.

Are there?

Were Colin Kaepernick—or Alec Baldwin, as he once promised—to move to another country, where would he go? If they think there are better options, they have forgotten (if they ever knew it in the first place) what the rest of the world is like.

Earlier, I included a quotation from Ta-Nehisi Coates's *Between the World and Me* encapsulating his indictment of America. For the uninitiated, Coates is an atheist SJW agitator/author who is the intellectual version of Colin Kaepernick. While Coates is in many ways my ideological opposite, as a writer I nonetheless often admire his writing for its beauty and honesty. Unfortunately, it is too often laden with the author's insistence that he, and all people of color, are victims. He ends the aforementioned quotation with this: "I propose to take our countrymen's claims of American exceptionalism seriously, which is to say I propose subjecting our country to an exceptional moral standard."

Well, I propose to take the Left's claims of America-as-an-evil-exploiter/oppressor very seriously, which is to say I propose subjecting other countries to an exceptional moral standard, too. It seems a little perspective might be in order here.

To that end, in this book I hope to provide that missing perspective, but not from the comfort of the armchair. No, I will take you around the world, to twenty-six countries in all, on a great expedition to see if the American Left and their media allies are right. Along the way, we will answer several pressing questions:

Is America's prosperity merely an accident of history (the Islamic narrative) and a result of the exploitation of the weak (the Left's narrative), or are some cultures superior to others by virtue of their religion and political philosophy?

Do reasonable people around the world hate America or are they unsettled by our current identity crisis?

Is Europe's open borders policy bringing cultural enrichment we should model, or is it laying the foundation for the gradual overthrow of Western culture as we know it?

Is America exceptional in ways that matter and should she remain so, or should America—the last holdout in the West against globalism, militant secularism, and climate change panic—tap out and become a socialist democracy like those of Europe?

An expedition like this promises to reveal a great many things, not the least of which is all we risk losing—and what we risk becoming—if we join a Western world hellbent on suicide.

At the end of our journey, we will have discovered one of two things: The Left is right, and America really isn't so great after all, or we will see she remains, as Abraham Lincoln put it, "the last best hope of earth."

So, get your passport, a sturdy backpack, and activate your SkyMiles account. Oh, and some Handi-Wipes. You're going to need *lots* of Handi-Wipes. The world is a very dirty place.

CHAPTER 1

The Criteria:
What Defines a Great Country?

"He who would defend all, defends nothing, because defense lines cover more ground than available troops can defend. Little minds want to defend everything; sensible men concentrate on the essentials."[1]

—Frederick the Great

In 1831, French political philosopher Alexis de Tocqueville came to America. What started as a review of American prisons became a travel log of a man determined to search out the source of America's strength. He crisscrossed the country, scribbling notes of his observations as he went. The result was his classic and remarkably still relevant *Democracy in America*. Tocqueville hoped his book would give the people of his native France perspective for the turbulent times in which they lived. (If subsequent French history is any indication, they didn't read it.)

Now, roughly two centuries later, I, along with my twenty-two-year-old son Zachary, set out to do what Tocqueville did—*but in reverse*. That is, rather than traveling across America to see how it compared with Europe and France in particular, we were instead planning to circumnavigate the earth to see how America *really* stacks up against those countries that would serve as a model for the America some wish to create. Such an expedition is no easy undertaking.

Fortunately, international travel today is easy, safe, and efficient. Even so, extensive planning is required for a trip like this. The first order of business was to make sure our passports would not expire during our odyssey.[i] Which countries would require visas? This meant a bit of research. Then we needed to plan a tentative route. I say tentative because while we knew what countries must be included in such a survey, we wanted to maintain a degree of flexibility. What if someone got sick or the political situation required us to leave in a hurry? Rigid travel plans are a recipe for a miserable experience. Besides, we knew some countries would prove more interesting than others, so we wanted to be free to linger or move on.

Booking flights for an around-the-world trip is easier than you might think. Most airlines offer a little-known Round-the-World (RTW) ticket. While the rules vary from one carrier to another, they generally work like this:

- You can create your own itinerary, but you must remain within that airline's network. If none of their carriers fly, say, to Singapore, you'll have to skip it or pay for it separately.

- The ticket allows for continuous eastbound or westbound travel, the choice is yours. But once you start, you have to keep going the direction you've chosen. There's no going back. (Unless you pay for the off-course trips. We had to do this several times.)

---

i   Most countries will not allow entry to travelers unless their passports are valid for a minimum of six months after their declared exit dates.

- You are allowed to cross the Atlantic and Pacific Oceans only once.

- There is typically a limit on mileage and/or stops.

- The ticket is good for one year.

Having purchased tickets, all that remained was to pack. Author Susan Heller wrote, "When preparing to travel, lay out all your clothes and all your money. Then take half the clothes and twice the money." That is good advice. People, Americans most of all, tend to overpack. This was particularly tempting for us simply because we would be gone so long, would be settling down nowhere, and would travel from baking countries on or near the equator to countries stretching to the polar extremities. One day might find us in shorts and t-shirts sweating in tropical heat, the next we might be bundled in down trying to stay warm. This made packing complicated.

Taking Heller's advice, we made sure we had sufficient financing. You can always buy another pair of socks or shoes, but if you don't have money, you are in trouble. Beyond the obvious reasons for this, any trip including a third world country is going to involve "informal" expenses. By this, of course, I mean bribes. They aren't always called that. They might be called gratuities, service fees, ngein chā (Thailand, "tea money"), hurmat (Azerbaijan, "respect"), dash (Nigeria, "gift"), graisser (France, "grease"), um cafezinho (Brazil, "a little coffee") or any of a number of other things, but make no mistake about it, they are bribes, and your trip will go much smoother if you are prepared to pay them.[ii]

[ii]   I am not advising you to pay all bribes or any sum that might be demanded. Like almost everything in the third world, bribes are negotiable and there are times when I do not pay them. But whenever it involves my safety or that of the people with me, I pay—but not until the thing I am paying for is done.

Thus armed, we would take one piece of checked baggage and one carry-on each.

On Sunday, August 27, 2017, I kissed my wife Lauri goodbye, gave my daughter Sasha a hug, and Zachary and I headed to the airport. We decided to circumnavigate the globe via the west-bound route. So, beginning in Birmingham, Alabama, we flew to Los Angeles, our launching point for Asia/Oceania.

On long-haul flights, I come prepared. I immediately change into loose-fitting clothes, put on socks or slippers, put on my noise-canceling headphones, and settle in with a book or a movie before trying—usually without success—to sleep.

Now that we are somewhere over the Pacific Ocean, it seems like a perfect time to establish some criteria for what is, in effect, an expedition to find the world's greatest country. In such a search, how will we define greatness?

A simple internet search of "best state" or "greatest country" will yield very different results. Those results are based on the criteria used by those answering the question. What was important to them? Access to affordable healthcare? That country's carbon footprint? Social mobility? My criteria will differ substantially from most of the lists I have consulted. That is because these rankings, which are all over the internet, usually rely heavily on data and have a hidden agenda.

Take, for example, this recent list. It was produced by Condé Nast Traveler[2] and is typical of the genre. Here is their ranking of countries:

1. Norway
2. Australia/Switzerland (tie)
3. (Due to the tie for number 2, there is no number 3)
4. Germany
5. Denmark/Singapore (tie)
6. (No number 6)

7. The Netherlands
8. Ireland
9. Iceland
10. Canada/The United States (tie)

People seeing these rankings often accept them as authoritative without looking at the criteria those compiling them employed and wonder why the United States scored so low. Let's drill down a bit in this one.

The list is based on the United Nations Development Program's annual Human Development Index.[3] Reading the report, I soon discover why Condé Nast—a media behemoth that owns *Vanity Fair*, *GQ*, *Allure*, and *Vogue*—likes it. It is precisely the sort of data and social agenda-laden report the Left employs to declare life's winners and losers. A simple word search of the document yields these results:

Gay: 34 times

Transgender: 30 times

Bisexual: 29 times

Lesbian: 27 times

LGBTI: 8 times

I then looked at every instance where these words were used in the report. Each time, they were used favorably or in defense of these lifestyles. So concerned was the United Nations that this "human right" be legalized and promoted in every country, the report said, "awareness campaigns need to be launched in *households...*" (Italics mine.)

But what about Christians? Christians are the world's largest religious group,[4] numbering 2.2 billion people. According to Spectator (UK),[5] they are also the most persecuted, dying for their faith at a startling rate of one hundred thousand per year. That translates to eleven *per hour*. So, given these facts, how many times were Christians mentioned in the UN report?

Christian: 0 times

What about the Christian religion?

Christianity: 0 times

What about the persecution of Christians? Persecution was mentioned three times but not once in this context.

"Religion" was mentioned seventeen times, but six of those were in a single footnote. Religions were lumped together and often unfavorably. Yet, when it came to LGBTI issues—I have no idea what the "I" refers to—those generating the report made a great distinction between an apparent multitude of sexual identities and preferences. What percentage of the world's population are the "Ts" and "Is"? More than, say, Hindus and Buddhists, who also netted zero mentions in this study?

What this tells us, of course, is that religion is unimportant to those generating this report, and, for that reason, they weren't qualified to produce such a study in the first place. Perhaps they are unaware of it, but religion is *very important* to the vast majority of the world's population. Yet, the gurus over at the UN, in a weighty study that essentially ranks the quality of life in 185 countries, didn't think it merited a substantive discussion. LGBTI activism, however, was of great importance to them and that is what the above countries all have in common. In each of them, LGBTI people are practically a protected species. The UN might have saved themselves some time and money by just consulting Tripadvisor.

As I have said, a given ranking will be determined by the criteria used, and that criteria will be determined by what is important to those doing the survey. I find little in rankings of this kind reflecting my values and those of many people I know, be they American or otherwise. And that is because these studies generally place a premium on things that, although important to those committed to a progressive agenda, are of little importance to most people. Globally, most people aren't losing sleep over the polar icecap and paid paternity leave. They are, however, preoccupied with concerns of safety, provision for themselves and/or their families, and the ability to live their lives freely.

My criteria have such people in mind. I am reacting *against* the strictly statistical approach to determining national greatness. The Left *loves* data because it can be manipulated to justify dubious agendas. Twain was right when he said, "There are lies, damned lies, and statistics." Besides, surely a nation is more than the sum of its economic, demographic, and governmental parts. The quality of life—of *a single life*—cannot be reduced to a number. Advocates of abortion and euthanasia employ that kind of thinking with devastating effect. In using statistics on income, intelligence, and education, they have judged the lives of millions to be unworthy of living. Planned Parenthood has made an industry out of it. Iceland celebrates it.[6] Yes, I am convinced the Devil is a bureaucrat and a statistician.

This is not to say, however, data is irrelevant. It isn't. The cost of living, life expectancy, access to clean water, murder rates, number of regime changes, and so forth offer insight into a culture, but they cannot tell you the quality of it. And this brings me to my criteria. For a country to be considered great on our list, certain characteristics *must* be present:

- Freedoms—political, economic, and religious—are nonnegotiables.

- A nation's history is also a factor. Why? Because it is the best predictor of the future. Historically, France has a penchant for strikes, uprisings, and revolutions; Russia and China have little regard for personal liberties and a habit of genocide; we know Islamic states create cookie-cutter societies and oppress non-Muslims; Switzerland has demonstrated a commitment to pragmatic peace and commerce. Those histories matter.

- How is a country trending? Toward greater freedom, increased regulation, or tyranny?

- Social mobility is a key component. Can people, through hard work and talent, flourish? Or do social, economic, or governmental conditions actively conspire against it?

- What is life like for ordinary people? If it isn't good, what chance do they have of improving it?

- And what are the things most valued by that society?

What I say about other national characteristics—e.g., cuisine, climate, landscape—is merely reflective of my preferences and is not, therefore, a determining factor in my assessment of a given country. I am, after all, offering you my opinion of these countries. That said, statistics and opinions aside, there is, I believe, an absolute standard. The Preamble to the U.S. Constitution is a pithy summary of what we are looking for in the governments of the countries we are visiting on this trip:

We the People of the United States, in Order to form a more perfect Union, establish Justice, insure domestic Tranquility, provide for the common defense, promote the general Welfare, and secure the Blessings of Liberty to ourselves and our Posterity, do ordain and establish this Constitution for the United States of America.

Some will say this is unfair because it is an American standard. But the values expressed in the Preamble are not exclusively American. On the contrary, the framers of the Constitution were appealing to what they understood to be an absolute, universal standard of human rights. To quote the late Forrest McDonald, an American Constitutional historian of some eminence and a professor of mine, "The Declaration [of Independence] refers to God-given rights to life, liberty, and the pursuit of happiness. The Preamble [of the Constitution] introduces a document whose stated purpose is to secure the rights of life and liberty."[7]

Please bear in mind our country reviews are necessarily brief and therefore by no means comprehensive. I quoted Frederick the Great at the beginning of this chapter for a reason. A danger for any author is to write with his critics in mind. If he does, a good two-hundred-page book that defends the essentials and informs the interested risks becoming a dull, ponderous five-hundred-page tome as the author attempts to anticipate every objection to his thesis. This book was not written for critics.

I naively attempted to do that with my previous book *The Faith of Christopher Hitchens: The Restless Soul of the World's Most Notorious Atheist*. Knowing they would be looking for me to claim Hitchens made a deathbed conversion, I wrote an entire chapter outlining why I was making no such claims. I was emphatic on the point. That book, named the Arts & Culture Book of the Year (2016) by the Gospel Coalition and glowingly reviewed by *Publishers Weekly, The Wall Street Journal, Christianity Today, The Times* (of London), and even Chris Matthews of MSNBC's *Hardball*, was nonetheless savagely attacked by the atheist mafia who accused me of making the deathbed conversion claim anyway.

No, I won't do that here. Rather, it is my hope that this little book will educate and entertain the intelligent laymen who share my deep concern for where America is headed and want to do something about it. My perspective is that of an American. But that's okay, because my target audience is American, too. (Though I would be delighted if my book became a bestseller in, say, China.)

Finally, it is important to understand that there is a big difference between visiting a country on vacation and living there as most of the population lives. This is what I call the "Traveler's Fallacy." Vacationing in a Jamaican resort should not be confused with life for the average Jamaican. Likewise, many of the world's great cities are lovely places to live if you can afford to live in the high-priced city centers—*but almost no one can afford it.* Indeed, any country can seem tolerable if you are a one-percenter. Louis XIV, surrounded as he was with mistresses and courtiers to satiate his every desire, seems to have been happy enough. So were Genghis Khan, Chairman Mao, and Saddam Hussein. But that is in no way an indication of life in those countries. While we are citizens of none of the countries in our survey but the United States, we weren't typical tourists either. We hope to give you a glimpse of the reality of life in the countries we visited.

Before we begin our expedition, let me show you a different statistical ranking, one that is, I think, much more telling than what activist-academics at the UN are writing. It is a de facto ranking of the world's countries by ordinary people around the world. In a global poll conducted by Gallup, 14 percent of the surveyed global population said they would like to migrate permanently to another country—that's roughly seven hundred million people. Of that number, a whopping 21 percent—or 147 million people—would like to move to the United States of America. The next highest country was Germany, with 6 percent. Norway, number one on the UN's ranking, didn't even make the list.[8]

This raises some very interesting questions. Chief among them is this: Why do these people want to come to America? What makes America—dare I say it?—"exceptional"? To answer that question, we need to know a little about the rest of the world. To that end, Zachary and I will take you to six continents and twenty-six countries.

Let the journey begin.

CHAPTER 2

Singapore: OCD?
Tired of Democracy?
This Country Is for You!

"Whoever governs Singapore must have iron in him. Or give up. This is not a game of cards. This is your life and mine."

—Lee Kuan Yew, Singapore's founding father

Our plan was to visit twenty-six countries. In reality, the number of legitimate contenders for the title of the world's greatest country is rather small, with perhaps ten countries in the running. So, why, then, were we including more than double that number? We believed it necessary to give you the bigger picture of what the rest of the world is like as well as to understand America's global influence.

According to a report by Verisk Maplecroft, a socio-economic and political analysis firm, 40 percent of the world's countries will experience political unrest in 2020.[1] That translates to a mindboggling seventy-five countries. We would be hitting about five on this list in our circumnavigation of the earth.

Circumnavigating the earth has long captured the public imagination. Perhaps the most famous circumnavigator of them all is the fictitious English gentleman, Phileas Fogg, who completed the journey with his faithful valet, Passepartout, in Jules Verne's classic 1873 novel *Around the World in 80 Days*. That story has been retold in one form or another in no less than twenty films starring the likes of Conrad Veidt, David Niven, Pierce Brosnan, and Steve Coogan. But long before Verne immortalized the idea of such an adventure, others actually accomplished the feat.

The Portuguese explorer Ferdinand Magellan is credited with being the first to do it. But that isn't actually true. Magellan only *semi*-circumnavigated the earth. He was killed by Filipino tribesmen on the island of Mactan in April 1521, being the unfortunate recipient of a bamboo spear to the face. However, after more than three years, what was left of his starving crew did finish the journey, reaching Spain in September of 1522. A fleet consisting of five ships and 270 men was reduced to one ship and eighteen men.

Circumnavigation became much easier with the opening of the Suez (1869) and Panama (1914) Canals, allowing ships to avoid the treacherous route around South America's Cape Horn and Africa's Cape of Good Hope. With these advantages, Frenchman Francis Joyon and a crew of eight sailed around the world in forty days, twenty-three hours, and thirty minutes in 2017, setting a new record.

Then came the invention of the airplane. The first to circumnavigate the earth by air was the United States Army Air Service in 1924. With aviation still in its infancy, it took them a whopping 175 days. By 1949, the United States Air Force trimmed that time to an astonishing ninety-four hours and one minute when a B-50A Superfortress named *Lucky Lady II* was refueled in-air, enabling it to complete a nonstop flight. In 1992, an Air France

Concorde[i], streaking at supersonic speed, set the all-time record for a suborbital flight at thirty-two hours and forty-nine minutes.[ii]

But what about people like you and me? That is, those of us who don't own yachts built for this purpose or have access to air force fleets and state funding? In 2018, New Zealand's Andrew Fisher provided an answer when he set the world record for circling the globe on scheduled commercial flights, doing it in fifty-two hours and thirty-four minutes. With planning and a little bit of luck, you could do it, too.

Of all of these, Zachary and I reckoned our trip would be more like that of Phileas Fogg than any of the others. We weren't out to set any records and I certainly had no intention of confronting hostile tribesmen. And while we wouldn't be using a hot air balloon as had Fogg and Passepartout, we did plan to use just about every other form of transportation: short and long-haul flights; city trams and intercontinental trains; ships and boats; sports cars and four-wheel drives; tuk-tuks and rickshaws; and probably even bicycles and horses.

After a series of lengthy flights, we were in Singapore. There is no better place to start our journey than here, a country hailed by many as the model for the rest of the world. Hypermodern, hyper-clean, and hyper-rich, Singapore is the supermodel of countries. So much so, America by comparison looks like the frumpy, corpulent spinster who is past her prime but doesn't yet know it. Keeping with the metaphor, one Singaporean writer[2] has compared this country to a date with a beautiful woman who just happens to have a bit of the psycho about her:

"If you steer your conversation and curiosity the right way," he says, "your time with us will be unforgettable. But if you touch on a sore spot, we'll fly off the handle…"

---

i At the time of writing, the Concorde is no longer in service despite efforts to bring it back.

ii Occupants of the International Space Station orbit the earth every ninety-two minutes.

Unforgettable is right. The distinct guttural rumble of Lamborghinis, Ferraris, Porsches, and others of that species are as common as F-150s in America. No wonder Formula 1 is racing there now. And almost everything looks shiny and new. Even the people. The only other place on earth I've seen like it is Shanghai. Flying back into Atlanta after a visit to that city felt like I was returning to a third world country. So it is with Singapore.

Yes, Singapore is a remarkable place. And, yes, it does overwhelm the senses, full as it is with eye candy. Night is a special time in this country that is smaller than Orange County: Searchlights paint the stainless-steel buildings populating the skyline like pieces of art; music fills the botanical gardens; people do the things fashionable, moneyed people do, whether eating at a trendy Michelin-starred restaurant (there are more in Singapore than in Paris), shopping at high-end boutiques, or attending outdoor concerts. The streets and sidewalks are *so clean* I wondered if the Singaporean Department of Transportation employed an army of scrupulous maids wielding feather dusters rather than the hard-hatted guys you see in America. Trash, even gravel, along roadsides is so uncommon we started looking for it. You'll sooner find money on the ground than debris.

But, as the writer said, there are "sore spots" with the woman that is Singapore, seductive though she may be. And it doesn't take much to reveal the Jack Nicholson-in-*The Shining* side of her. Her sore spots, the parts of her that remind you she's a psycho, after all, include:

- Chewing gum. Unless it is a special gum prescribed by a doctor, it is illegal. And if you spit it out? Oh, let's not even go there.

- Leaving a toilet unflushed. Unpleasant, for sure, and I have, admittedly, felt the victim of a crime when my senses were assaulted by these stealthy hit-and-run offenders. But is a fine necessary when a bottle of Febreze will do?

- Walking around your house naked. I don't even want to know how they know you're doing this.

- Eating or drinking—even water—on public transportation. My heavens, we are on the equator here in Singapore. Not even a sip? Nope.

At this point, perhaps you're wondering as I did, *has this country any boys in it*? I mean, were these American laws—especially number two, so to speak—my entire college dorm (and my three boys) would have accumulated fines equal to that of their college tuition. How would you like to make monthly payments on that?

There are, however, more interesting laws and corresponding punishments:

- Smoking an illicit (untaxed) cigarette. I saw this warning on televisions—yes, televisions—in taxis: "It only takes one cigarette to be marked a criminal." Penalty? Up to six years in prison.

- Using someone else's Wi-Fi without their permission. Called "piggybacking," it is considered hacking and can land you in prison for up to three years.

- Graffiti or posting signage without a permit. Do you remember the American student Michael Fay? Thinking he was in East Los Angeles, he vandalized two cars and stole a road sign in Singapore. That was a mistake. He was arrested, imprisoned, and caned.

- Drug trafficking. Violate this one and you will get the death sentence. "You will be hanged," as one Singaporean told me, "and no one can save you, man." I'm cool with this one—or am I?

Draconian punishments are not typically created because the government in question is sadistic and longs for an opportunity to cane or hang its citizens. Sadistic governments just do that stuff anyway regardless of the law. No, harsh legal penalties are generally meant to prevent the very thing for which punishments like caning and death are the consequence. In Malaysia and Indonesia, the two countries bracketing Singapore, drug trafficking is a *major* problem. To prevent it from infesting Singapore, the government sent a clear message to would-be traffickers with these laws. That makes sense, right?

"Don't want to be caned or hanged?" people will say. "Then don't violate the law!"

That sounds simple enough—only it isn't so simple. Arguments like this are frustratingly stupid because they legitimize surrendering broad, sweeping powers to governments and the people who run them, and if history teaches anything, it is that people and governments are not to be trusted with broad, sweeping powers. Civil rights don't exist in Singapore. A few days ago, the country "elected" a president—without voting.[3] So much for democracy. Furthermore, Singapore has the second-highest execution rate in the world. And why wouldn't it when drug trafficking brings a *mandatory* death sentence?

Seeing "Warning: Death to Drug Traffickers Under Singapore Law" stamped boldly on the immigration card the flight attendants handed out to passengers just before landing in this, the Brave New World, I was momentarily gripped by panic when the thought "What about prescription drugs?" crossed my mind.

A few years ago, I suffered a life-altering accident when I was hit by a car while cycling. Suffice it to say I broke *a lot* of bones—nineteen vertebrae, twelve ribs, multiple skull fractures, my neck, and so on. I spent quite some time in an intensive care unit and still suffer lingering effects. Before leaving the States, my physicians—I have a stable full of them now—prescribed several medications for pain. One was oxycodone.

"You're fine, Dad. That's a prescription," Zachary said with perfect rationality. But I have had experience with irrational governments before.

"I am not so sure," I replied, whipping out my smartphone like a gunslinger. A quick internet search revealed this medication to be outlawed without a permit—for which you must apply well before entering the country—and possession of more than twenty pills constituted trafficking.

Suddenly, I felt caught in the world of *Midnight Express*, and, worse, I was Billy Hayes: "Son, you ever been in a Turkish prison?" No, and I didn't want to be hanged in a Singaporean prison, either. A couple of flushes down the toilet later, I was in the clear.

Do you begin to see the problem? Please bear in mind, as anyone who knows me can tell you, I don't even drink and, by a strict definition of the law—are there any other definitions in a country like this?—I was possibly a violator of one of their most severe laws. Like many, I was initially sympathetic with Singapore's stiff punishments for drug trafficking—*hang'em!* you say to yourself—but now I was getting a crash course in what it might mean to fall afoul of a government whose definition went well beyond types like Al Pacino's powder-nosed *Scarface* and where innocent until proven guilty isn't a legal concept.

And hanging alleged drug traffickers is one thing, but criminalizing chewing gum because you don't like getting it on your shoe? This is not only a surveillance state[4]—and as Edward Snowden revealed,[5] it is *definitely* a surveillance state—it is also a state where apparently those doing the surveilling have an obsessive-compulsive disorder.

Sheesh.

"It's like *The Truman Show*," Zachary said, making a typically astute observation. He was spot-on. Singapore is a kind of model society very conscious of the fact that others look to it as a model,[6] especially governments that want to combine free markets with dictatorship. That's why the country is so neat and tidy. Singapore is akin to a young family anxiously awaiting a visit from the in-laws: the lawn is freshly mowed, the house is cleaner than usual, and the kids have all been threatened within an inch of their lives to be on their best behavior. Had my wife and I employed Singaporean discipline in our home, who knows? Maybe the kids would've made their beds and flushed the toilets.

Whatever my opinion of the country, people in Singapore seem happy enough. That was also true of my experience in Shanghai. And why not, when it is so modern, so beautiful, and so wealthy? The problem lies in the shadows, the what-ifs, of life under an undemocratic regime of this kind. Chiefly, *what if* you end up innocently on the wrong side of the law? There's no real due process because there's no freedom of speech, freedom of the press, freedom of assembly, or any other freedom the government doesn't, at that moment, want you to have.

Interestingly, many on the Left love Singapore. This is not entirely surprising given the Left's historic fascination with totalitarian regimes. Walter Duranty, Moscow bureau chief for *The New York Times*, famously extolled the virtues of Stalin's Russia and was given a Pulitzer Prize for it. George Bernard Shaw, another classic liberal, did the same thing. They saw in that society precisely what they wanted to see.

HuffPost, in an article titled, "Why Singapore is the World's Most Successful Society,"[7] essentially declared the city-state "the most successful society since human history began." *Since human history began.* Really? Does *HuffPo* really know what life was like for the Sumerians or the Egyptians of the Middle Kingdom? Hyperbole aside, Singapore scores high in rankings of this type because it scores high in categories like per-capita income, education, and healthcare. It is as if freedom of *anything* just doesn't matter in this analysis. Calling it "a benevolent dictatorship," the piece is a typical lovefest. Call me a cynic, but I prefer leaders who are held accountable by the people.

Modern Singapore is the result of the creative vision of Lee Kuan Yew. The longest-serving prime minister in history, he served from 1959–1990. Lee is alternately portrayed as a despot and a visionary. I think he was both. Lee led Singapore from third world poverty to independence from Malaysia (1965) and spectacular wealth. He also ruled as he wished.

Let me be clear on this point: We liked Singapore. We really did. It is (currently) a marvelous place. We very much enjoyed the people we met. We were deeply impressed—as I have been generally in Asia—with the work ethic and service. Both are superior to anything I have experienced in America. And, architecturally speaking, it is a very beautiful country.

Singapore is a remarkable rags-to-riches story. Wow! Were we going around the world in search of the planet's most improved country, Singapore would certainly win the prize. But that is not the standard we are employing here. We are going around the world in search of greatness and, should we find it, to dissect the ingredients of that greatness so we might replicate it. I am looking for the country that would be a successor to what America has been.

That country is not Singapore.

No, regardless of its wealth, celebrated educational system, and glittering skyline, Singapore does not fall into that category. Singapore is an advanced surveillance state. Worse, according to *Foreign Policy*,[8] the United States helped them build it and now wants to model it. As with Western Europe, in the name of safety, cameras are watching people everywhere and the data of private citizens is being gathered unfettered by the government for who knows what purposes. That apparently doesn't bother Singaporeans. It bothers me.

However, this isn't my central reservation with Singapore. This is merely a symptom of a much larger problem. Singapore has beaten the odds by crawling out of the third world quagmire, and today, its citizens enjoy a high standard of living, life expectancy, and just about everything else. All of this is true. But it is also beside the point as far as my critique is concerned.

According to Jack Tsen-Ta Lee,[9] assistant professor of law at the School of Law of Singapore Management University, "If you define a democracy as requiring broad freedom of speech and freedom of assembly [as I think most do], then it might be said that Singapore is somewhat lacking in this regard as there are various restrictions on these rights." Somewhat lacking?

If surveillance doesn't bother you, perhaps the recent "election" of a president in the absence of an actual election might. There are virtually no civil rights in Singapore: no free speech (on the grounds it causes civil unrest); no freedom of assembly (the government must grant a permit—and they don't, as a rule, grant such permits); no freedom of the press (all agencies are state-owned); no freedom of information (the internet is very carefully and strictly controlled); no real opposition party (the People's Action Party maintains strict control of elections and has done so since 1959); and, most of all, there is no transparency in government. Who are these shadowy people who, on the eve of an election, disqualify all candidates but the one who just happens to represent the ruling party? This alarms me deeply and I think it should alarm Singaporeans, too.

My guess is these things don't trouble them because they are, as one Singaporean woman told me, "generally happy." In other words, since the surveillance, lack of civil rights, and lack of authentic democratic institutions haven't been an impediment to their personal happiness, they aren't greatly troubled by this aspect of Singaporean life. After all, they are prosperous. But this gets at the heart of what so alarms me about governments like Singapore's. They aren't the Big Brother governments like that of Orwell's *1984*—that is, controlling the masses through fear (though that aspect is certainly a part of Singapore)—they are closer to Huxley's *Brave New World*, controlling the masses through prosperity and pleasure, they create an apathetic citizenry who sleepwalk through their government's dubious political activities.

Singapore is not a constitutional government; it is a government with a constitution, and there is a big difference. Constitutional governments are governments ruled by and subject to their constitutions. By contrast, governments with constitutions alter or ignore their constitutions at will, as Singapore just did with the recent nonelection of a new president. America is increasingly tilting in this direction with an opposition party's unprecedented effort to remove, by whatever means necessary, a lawfully elected president. We have witnessed a very similar effort in Britain to reverse a lawful vote to break with the European Union. Not only does this demonstrate a contempt for the will of the people, but it also demonstrates a startling disregard for the rule of law. This dismays those Americans who value the protections a constitution like ours is meant to provide.

In the article I mentioned earlier, *Foreign Policy* described Singapore as a "curious mix of democracy and authoritarianism, in which a paternalistic government ensures people's basic needs—housing, education, security—in return for almost reverential deference. It is a law-and-order society, and the definition of 'order' is all-encompassing."

That strikes me as spot-on. Life in Singapore is, for most people, very good. The government keeps the many happy while denying the rights of the few who are unlucky enough to fall afoul of it. And while this current regime is, as *HuffPost* described it admiringly, "a benevolent dictatorship," who's to say it will remain so? I mean, the mechanisms are all neatly in place for a dictatorship of an altogether different kind. The founding fathers of the United States, deeply influenced not by the philosophy of Confucius, as Singapore was, but by the teachings of Jesus Christ and the Judeo-Christian values of the Bible, generally accepted the idea that human nature is fallen and, as a consequence, those with power cannot be fully trusted to wield it honorably. To guard against abuses, checks and balances were built into the government they established.

That is precisely what is missing in Singapore. Does the absence of this reflect the influence of Confucius' teaching, which was, at best, ambiguous about human nature? I don't know, but it certainly reflects the absence of Christian teaching on a critical point of human behavior and the preservation of good government.

Singapore is, indeed, a model. But a model of the wrong sort.

CHAPTER 3

Hong Kong: "One Country, Two Systems"

"Hong Kong has created one of the most successful societies on earth."[1]
—Prince Charles

After a short flight, we were in Hong Kong. Fittingly, Hong Kong was one of Phileas Fogg's stops on his journey. The name of the city is derived from Cantonese and means "fragrant harbor." Perhaps Hong Kong smelled like potpourri when, in 1841, the English first amputated this city of more than 230 islands from China's Manchu dynasty.

But not now.

The fragrance is that of a locker room full of big sweaty men who've spent their afternoon doing kung fu. Entering our hotel lobby, we were greeted with an overpowering Old Spice-like aroma meant to counter the smell of the city just outside the doors. It is the same everywhere in Hong Kong. Going in and out of buildings is to alternate between the warring scents of air fresheners and the inside of a dumpster, or, as author P. J. O'Rourke aptly puts it, between "Sh*t and Chanel."

This is all very much in keeping with the city that is Hong Kong. Alternately rich and poor, free and increasingly undemocratic, British and Chinese, Hong Kong is full of contradictions. A local told me Hong Kong has much in common with Singapore. Having just come from Singapore, I had to disagree. Both are hyper-capitalistic, but the comparisons don't go much further. Singapore is beautiful, clean, and orderly. (Only they do it without Singapore's draconian laws.) Hong Kong is none of these things. It is a chaotic mess of buildings, poor city planning, and smelly, crowded streets. The air pollution alone is enough to kill you. Do a quick Google Images search of Hong Kong. I'll wait. Got it? Now, here's how you can tell the real from the fake photos: any showing a crisp, clear skyline are as phony as Pamela Anderson's, uh, lips. You *never* get a crisp, clear skyline in Hong Kong due to the thick air pollution that hangs over the city as if it were the permanent host to Grateful Dead concerts.

"We will be lucky to get out of this city without getting sick," Zachary observed with a note of resignation. He was onto something. This was pre-Chinese coronavirus pandemic, and yet so many of the city's residents wore surgical masks that you'd think it was full of surgeons. The cab driver, receptionist, waiter—they are all wearing them. You start to feel left out.

The sidewalks serve as a nice metaphor for the chaotic nature of this extraordinary place. Seemingly designed like a malicious Chinese puzzle, they often twist and turn pointlessly or, worse, take you nowhere. Anyone who has walked them knows what I am talking about. Add to them the people, and Hong Kong has *a lot* of people. This city is twelve times more densely populated than New York, so walking on these sidewalks is a close approximation to running with the bulls in Pamplona, but with old ladies and their pushcarts playing the role of the bulls, and they are no less dangerous. Not only are you dodging the veritable human avalanche, but you are also dodging the water dumped indiscriminately onto pedestrians from the air conditioner condensation

tubes that seem to pour and drip from every window of this city—
and that's a lot of windows since Hong Kong has *twice* the number
of skyscrapers as New York. A travel guide says: "Women in Hong
Kong carry umbrellas even on sunny days. This is to protect their
skin." Nonsense, I say. Five minutes on these sidewalks and you
know precisely why they carry them.

And, yet, somehow it all works. The warring cultures, sights
and sounds, and even the chaos. Hong Kong is the New York of
the East.

Zachary's dislike of this city was almost immediate. I get it.
It is, as I say, chaotic. But I like it. No, wrong word. I *respect* it.
I mean, I would never want to live here. I am used to hills, trees,
clear skies, wide-open spaces, and, well, I prefer to speak to people
who don't look like they are about to remove my liver. It is also
my nature to avoid crowds. Post-accident, I am sensitive to noise,
and the noise of a Manhattan wears on me. Hong Kong is worse.
I go to such places only when I must. Even so, I recognize that in
this I am expressing a preference, not making a moral judgment.
My preferences aside, Hong Kong is a remarkable city of industry,
prosperity, and, for much of its history, freedom. Were we scoring
Hong Kong as an independent country, I think we would have to
give it a seven out of ten.

But it isn't an independent country.

In 1997, the British government officially transferred the
sovereignty of Hong Kong to the People's Republic of China.
Uh-oh. According to the terms of that treaty, the life and economy
of Hong Kong were to remain essentially unchanged for fifty years.
There was to be one country, two systems. Twenty years on, there
is one country and an effort to impose one system. As I write this
book, headlines of protests in Hong Kong appear intermittently in
my news feed. I admire these people who are endeavoring to maintain Hong Kong's independence from China. Thus, any evaluation

of Hong Kong must include an evaluation of China, just as we can no more separate California from the United States.

Originally, our country survey included mainland China *and* Hong Kong. Unfortunately, the Chinese refused to grant me a visa *unless* I signed a document promising not to write negatively about the country. Apparently, they expected a bad review. I can't imagine why. This was, I suppose, better than granting me a visa and slipping heroin or some other contraband into my bag and sending me to rot in a gulag.

Fortunately, I have already been to China. In 2010, I went to both Beijing and Shanghai as part of a US business delegation. To say I was impressed is an understatement. Shanghai, as I have said, makes *any* US city look third world. The service and work ethic are models of efficiency. The common people I met were friendly, hospitable, and generally proud of their country. As for communism, you soon realize China is no more communist than Singapore. The Chinese dumped faith in Marx and Lenin a long time ago because *they know* socialism doesn't work. The people who believe in that naïve, unworkable, utopian ideology no longer live in Beijing, Moscow, or Hanoi. On the contrary, socialism's modern advocates reside in such places as London, Paris, Brussels, Berlin, and, increasingly, Washington (and Pyongyang, of course.) No, China isn't communist; it's *fascist*, combining a hyper-capitalistic economy with a dictatorial regime, proving false the idea that free markets automatically mean free societies.

And like Singapore, it *seems* to work.

Take, for example, a perpetual problem in my hometown of Birmingham, Alabama, where there is an ongoing debate about the rush hour congestion of Highway 280, a central artery running through the heart of the city. I cannot recall a time when there wasn't some debate or plan to fix the problem. Politicians have campaigned on it. Town hall events have been held to discuss it.

Decades have gone by and *nothing* has been done. That's because democracy is slow and messy.

By contrast, the Chinese would solve the problem inside of six months. They would throw thousands of workers at the project, double the number of lanes, and annihilate everything standing in the way—houses, businesses, trees, historic properties—*everything*. Now, if you are one of those people who are regularly stuck in 280 traffic, this is good news. But if your house or business is in the way, *too bad*. This is the way life is in modern China. There are no civil rights and, surprisingly, little sense of the past if that past gets in the way of what the Party deems to be progress. I'm as capitalistic as Donald Trump, but it was with horror I watched from the thirtieth floor of my hotel as an entire city block of historic homes was demolished to make way for a new high rise. *Boom!* Gone. No doubt the Great Wall will receive similar treatment if it's in the way. This is what the *Federalist Papers* would call the "tyranny of the majority." But it's really the tyranny of the Communist— which is actually fascist—Party. Civil rights just aren't a thing in China.

China isn't a free society, even if it is a *freer* society than it was, say, fifty—or even twenty-five—years ago. In a moment that is the stuff of a dramatic movie, I grossly misjudged the degree of this new freedom. Attending a lecture given by a Chinese economist at the University of Beijing, I was pleasantly surprised when he was somewhat critical of the policies of Chairman Mao. This was, I thought, an indication we were speaking freely, honestly, about the past. As the lecture continued, he said something like: "Critics of Mao's reforms point out that his measures for implementation were excessive."

This irritated me. Genocide is more than an "excessive measure," and Mao was unquestionably a bloodthirsty, genocidal maniac. Over the years, I have heard similar statements regarding the Holocaust, minimizing it subtly, as if it wasn't so bad after all. I couldn't let this go.

"Excessive?" I said so that the full room of students and business executives could hear me. "I'll say! Let's be clear, Mao killed between forty and seventy million of his own people."

Silence. Total silence. I felt like Ann Coulter at Berkeley. One Chinese student sitting next to me, a fellow who had been quite friendly while touring me around the campus, literally backed away from me. The economist paused, looked around the room and at the doors, and then continued nervously. No one argued the point. It was as if I said *nothing*. They were afraid. This is what societies with a history of violence and repression look like even after they've liberalized a bit. The lingering cultural memories of Chairman Mao, the Cultural Revolution, and Tiananmen Square are not just things of the past. They shape the present—unless, of course, you want to read about them on the heavily censored internet. In that case, they simply never happened.

But I have great hope for China and it comes from an unexpected quarter and in surprisingly large quantities.

During that same trip, I attended a church service in Beijing. The church was Chinese rather than one of those ecumenical international churches composed of expats. Before entering, police inspected my passport and scribbled a few notes. They did the same with all other attendees. It was Palm Sunday and, despite the intimidation tactics, the place was utterly packed. What I shall never forget is the character of their worship. The fervency of it was unlike anything I ever saw in an American church. No one left. No one slept. No one looked bored. People leaned in when the preaching began. They all knew the government was taking careful note of who they were, and, yet, they came anyway. I am in awe of such people.

Since that visit in 2010, the Chinese government has cracked down on Christians, destroying their churches, imprisoning or fining some Christian leaders, and denying travel visas to still others. I remind you this is the same country that denied my visa application. A friend who does business regularly in China theorizes they were less concerned with what I would write than with whom I would associate. "People in China can't access your website. They control that. The government doesn't want you engaging Christians in China as you did last time."

What is it about Christianity that makes the government so nervous?

"No totalitarian authority nor authoritarian state," wrote the late Francis Schaeffer, "can tolerate those who have an absolute by which to judge that state and its actions."[2] This goes far to explain the antipathy of communist and fascist regimes for Christianity. They well understand Christians do not recognize the power of the state as absolute. Moreover, where temporal law and eternal law are in conflict, the Christian may, in good conscience, violate the former while clinging to the latter. It is much for the better of us all that many have done so. History is full of examples of courageous Christian men and women who, at the risk of their own lives, sought the destruction of evil laws and regimes. By contrast, socialism exalts the state *in the place of God*.

And that is why Christians are so dangerous to regimes like this one. It is also why I have hope for China. At the grassroots level and reaching up, Christianity is spreading through China like it once did through a rotten and corrupt Roman Empire. Hong Kong is a launching point for missionaries into the mainland and for a democratic movement led by Christians. They are pushing back against Beijing's increasing restrictions on the freedoms the people of this city have enjoyed for so long.

According to the *Wall Street Journal*:

Christian institutions have become part of Hong Kong's civil sensibility. While the protests are specifically for democratic elections in Hong Kong, some see a broader struggle to protect that culture from China's communist government as it increases its influence on the city. Christianity has been a visible element of the demonstrations, with prayer groups, crosses, and protesters reading Bibles in the street....

The involvement of Protestants and Catholics in Hong Kong's protest movement is an added concern for Beijing. Protestant pastors based in Hong Kong have helped propagate the evangelical brands of Christianity that have alarmed the Chinese leadership in Beijing with their fast growth.

If the growth of Christianity alarms authorities in Beijing, and it does, then they should be very alarmed indeed. Officially, Christians number roughly 4 percent of China's population. *Unofficially*, that figure is as high as 20 percent—because no one believes the government's figures, not even the government.

"It is growing fastest in the provinces," one government official told me on the condition of anonymity.

"Are you a Christian?" I asked her.

She offered a sly smile. "Yes. And there are many more of us. The government knows the data on our numbers is grossly inaccurate. That is why they are so panicked."

Grossly inaccurate is right. According to *Foreign Policy*, China is set to become the largest Christian nation in the world by 2025. And, as we know, a little leaven leavens the whole lump of dough.

To put an anecdotal exclamation on this point, one Sunday Zachary and I were Ubering our way up to Hong Kong's Victoria Peak when, at a traffic light, dozens of pedestrians, almost all women, crossed in front of our car.

"Why is this crowd mostly women?" I asked the driver.

"Church. They are coming from church."

Later that afternoon we went back to this church. Hundreds of people were gathered around the facility, almost all of them, Filipino women. There are some one hundred and seventy thousand Filipinos in Hong Kong, one hundred and forty thousand of them women who are working as domestic servants. Here, on this hot and humid Sunday afternoon, they were singing, drinking tea, eating a quick meal, and enjoying the fellowship of others who shared their faith and their culture. They were waiting their turn to get into an already packed church. So busy is this church on Sundays that they have *ten* services. We watched in amazement when, as the umpteenth service ended, hundreds of these women entered one end while hundreds exited from the other orderly and efficiently. It was clearly a well-rehearsed routine. And this was a Catholic Church, a faith all but dead in the Western world.[i]

Protestantism, by far the largest Christian element within China, is growing much faster and because it is decentralized in a way Catholicism is not, it has proved much harder for Beijing to control. Christianity has been in Hong Kong since 1841. As of 2014, there were about eight hundred and seventy thousand Christians in Hong Kong or 11.8 percent of the total population. Having reached and surpassed critical mass, efforts to suppress the church in China are Sisyphean.

So how does one score a country like China? Any country with an opaque, undemocratic, and absolutist regime cannot rate high. But China has that elusive and essential quality so many other countries with governments like it lack entirely—hope.

★ ★ ★ ★ ☆☆☆☆☆☆

---

i   I am aware that approximately 41 percent of Europeans self-identify as Catholics, but this is more of a cultural identity than a religious one. Churches are overwhelmingly empty.

CHAPTER 4

Japan:
A Postwar Miracle and Model

"Travel is fatal to prejudice, bigotry and narrow-mindedness, and many of our people need it sorely on these accounts."[1]

—Mark Twain, *The Innocents Abroad*

It was time to leave Hong Kong. But we would be back. Five times. With so many of our flights routed through that city, Hong Kong felt like the Atlanta of Asia when it came to air travel. I was excited for the next country on the agenda.

I had never been to Japan. Research for the trip indicated it was an essential stop. Would this be the greatest country in the world? Crime rates, the standard of living, education, healthcare, life expectancy—all common measures for the typical "best" or "top" country rankings—indicated it might be.

Beyond all the signs announcing that Tokyo was then planning to host the 2020 Summer Olympics, one of the first things you notice upon arrival in this city of thirteen million people is its cleanliness. The airport, bathrooms, cars, streets, hotels—they are typically very clean. Even the toilet seats are sophisticated devices meant to convince us all that nothing, uh, *malodorous* or remotely unpleasant ever takes place in the bathroom. They warm and squirt your backside, spray the air with sweet fragrances, and even play music. Indeed, one forgets why he or she is even sitting there. It's tempting to receive guests and host dinners where everyone sits on one of these. Yes, Japan is clean (and apparently, the people are, too).

American travelers are often told to "try to blend in." World Nomads says:

"Do your best to blend in. Try not to look lost—even if you are—don't speak in English too loud, and put your best poker face to use. Martina says, 'A little bit of a badass look could help, I do this all the time, even in cities like Rome or Paris.'"[2] Although I'm sure Martina's "badass look" is very intimidating, this advice, for all its good intentions, is usually given with safety in mind. The idea being that if you appear to be just one of the locals, you'll be less vulnerable to those of nefarious intentions. Some of us know better. Americans are usually easily identifiable when we travel to other countries. This remains true even if we share an ethnicity with the indigenous population. Why? Because our "American-ness" is more than just our appearance. Yes, Americans are usually big, colorfully dressed, and well-heeled, but there is something in our manner that gives us away.

Americans are loud, friendly, and open to the point of naïve. We make eye contact with strangers when passing them on sidewalks. We tend to walk with our heads up, not down as much of the world does. "Americans carry themselves like people who are proud to be Americans," says one British friend of mine. "They like their country and want you to like it, too. We used to be like that but not anymore." Americans are, by the standards of most of the world, trusting and generous. They also have a reputation for being arrogant, ignorant of international affairs, and uninterested in the world beyond their borders. Like many stereotypes, there is a measure of truth in all this.

These qualities have been the subject of much mockery, from Eugene Burdick's influential political novel *The Ugly American* (1958) in which Americans are depicted as naïve, loud, and obnoxious, to National Lampoon's eighties romp *European Vacation*, in which Americans are likewise depicted as—well, you know. But these qualities have also produced a steely resolve to confront and defeat totalitarianism; the Marshall Plan, the most generous postwar program in the history of civilization; and a global reputation for being a fair-minded people.

Whatever America's reputation and that of its people, my Americanness is not easily disguised. At six feet, three inches tall, and of decidedly European descent, blending in is something I don't try to do. Even in Europe. It's hopeless. As a French acquaintance once told me, "For the French, everything in your bearing is straight out of the American movies they all watch: Tall, friendly, optimistic, self-confident. You could wear a beret, a scarf, and carry what you like to call a 'man purse' and that still wouldn't be enough to hide any of that. No, for us you are a cowboy." Point taken. So, I have resigned myself to my Americanness and all that it entails. It feels more honest.

And, as you can imagine, in Japan the idea of blending in for someone like me is absurd. This is because Japan is one of the most monoethnic countries in the world. Japan allows almost no immigration. As a consequence, roughly 98 percent of Japan's population is ethnically Japanese. This policy has been criticized sharply by globalists who are inclined to interpret it as racist. Foreigners living in Japan say it is almost impossible to assimilate. They may be treated politely but they are always outsiders. Whatever their motivations, the Japanese are a proud people who want to preserve their culture, their language, and their way of life. I admire that. But whether you admire it or not, if you are doing business in Japan you will be forced to respect it.

Japan is a country of law, order, duty, respect, tradition, an extraordinary work ethic, and a strong sense of family and national identity. It soon became clear it is also a remarkable nation populated by remarkable people. What's not to like?

Zachary and I started by exploring on our own. We headed to the busy commercial center of the Shibuya Ward. Tokyo is comprised of twenty-three "special wards," or municipalities, that function as distinct and largely autonomous cities, towns, and villages within Tokyo. With its many electronic billboards and dazzling lights, Shibuya is reminiscent of New York's Times Square or London's Piccadilly Circus. The crosswalk is purported to be the busiest in the world. Every three minutes, some two thousand, five hundred people move in every direction. They are there for the restaurants, to work, to shop in the many fashionable stores, or simply to enjoy time with family and friends. We had lunch, visited with locals, and poked our heads into shops.

From there we went to the nearby Meiji Jingu, a Shinto shrine in the Yoyogi district of Shibuya. Built in 1920, the shrine is dedicated to the memory of Emperor Meiji (1852–1912) who is credited with modernizing Japan. More than a shrine, however, it is a beautiful garden of trees, flowers, and well-kept pathways. Gorgeous cedars line the entrance to this place sacred to the Japanese. The shrine was destroyed by American bombers in 1945 but was rebuilt to reflect the original construction. The shrine attracts not only tourists but locals who want to enjoy the beauty of the heavily forested land. Families strolled through the park while others rendered homage to Emperor Meiji with frequent bowing, washing of hands, and by putting change in the offertory box.

After our independent sightseeing, we booked a tour with a local guide who met us at our hotel. Mei was a pleasant and—according to her own characterization—"a typical Japanese woman." A wife and teacher of middle school English, her husband works for an American tech firm. As a consequence, they have a lot of interaction with Americans. Although she had never been to the United States, her English was, not surprisingly, excellent.

A "typical" Japanese woman is demure in her public demeanor. Where differences between the sexes are being annihilated in the West, Japan remains a traditional society. Women embrace the feminine. The cosmetics industry is huge in Japan, with women spending more on makeup than clothing. And visitors to Japan will appreciate the results. The Japanese are an attractive people. Apparently, US servicemen thought so, too. During the American occupation of Japan, some fifty thousand of them married Japanese women in spite of military policy discouraging it, and deep Japanese resentment of those women who fraternized with the occupier. With the War Brides Act of 1945, soldiers brought these women back to the United States where they faced additional challenges from Americans who learned to hate the Japanese in the aftermath of Pearl Harbor, the Bataan Death March, and the bloodbaths of a dozen previously unknown islands. One thing, however, seems to be universal:

"In Japan," Mei said with complete seriousness, "relatively many families have some problems. One of the main problems is a conflict with the mother-in-law/daughter-in-law relationship. I'm not sure if families in the US have the similar one, though?"

I had to dispel some of Mei's idyllic notions of America.

American influence in Japan is pervasive. "We admire America," said Mei. "America is a model for Japan." She pointed out American influence in pop culture in particular. American movies and music are very popular—as they are all over the world.

Mei then took us to the (Buddhist) Sensō-Ji Temple in the Asakusa district before a quick stop at the vast Tsukiji fish market. Along the way, Mei explained the workings of the Japanese economy, family life, and the strict Japanese sense of duty. Being Japanese sounded stressful. But as in America, attitudes are changing from one generation to another. The current generation of youth feels less bound to tradition than did their predecessors.

Hailing a taxi, we went to the Imperial Palace Gardens. Most of the complex and surrounding gardens are closed to the public since it remains the royal residence of the emperors of Japan. Like New York's Central Park, the sprawling palace grounds, 379 acres in all, are right in the heart of Tokyo's exclusive Chiyoda ward. The land is conservatively estimated to be worth about $12 billion. But real estate in Tokyo, among the most expensive in the world, sells for an average of $9,500 per *square meter*. Remember, Japan is roughly the same size as California, but where California has a population of about forty million, Japan's population is one hundred twenty-five million. Japan has a land problem, and this accounts for the extraordinary price of real estate.

Shortly after our arrival in Japan, Kim Jong-Un began lobbing missiles over the country in a provocative act of aggression meant to capture headlines and demonstrate North Korea's missile capabilities. Sirens sounded at intervals throughout the country, warning people of a possible attack. The tension was palpable because there was no guarantee where one of those things might land. It did not seem it was Kim's intention to hit Japan, but North Korean engineering isn't Japanese engineering, and Kim is, after all, a maniac. Complicating things still further was the fact that with China backing the North Koreans and the United States backing the Japanese, all this might escalate into a world war. Once upon a time, the Japanese, a warrior culture, would have flattened North Korea. But these are different times, and the Japanese are very different people.

In the 1930s, the Empire of Japan was expanding at an extraordinary rate, building—conquering really—what they euphemistically called the Greater East Asia Co-Prosperity Sphere. As we have already noted, Japan has a land problem, and war was deemed to be the solution. The armies of Imperial Japan marched across Manchuria, Korea, China, and the islands of the Pacific. The United States, isolationist and preoccupied with the Great Depression, largely ignored Japanese ambitions.

Until Pearl Harbor.

History has shown all too well how that event awakened the American people. Japanese Admiral Isoroku Yamamoto, planner of the Pearl Harbor attack, famously said afterward: "I fear all we have done is to awaken a sleeping giant and fill him with a terrible resolve."[i] Churchill had a similar, if more positive, assessment. Upon receiving news of the attack, he said he returned to bed and "slept the sleep of the saved and the thankful." With that event, Churchill would later say, he knew the war's eventual outcome was a foregone conclusion.

After some early setbacks, US armed forces, in a bloody island-hopping campaign, systematically pared away territories in Japanese possession until all that remained was Japan proper. M. R. D. Foot,[3] a British intelligence officer and later a much-celebrated historian who was something of a mentor to me, was given the task of estimating Allied casualties were they to undertake a conventional attack on the island. His estimate?

1.5 million men.

Bear in mind, these are just *Allied* casualties. Japanese casualties would likely be infinitely higher. In the three-month battle for Okinawa, US casualties numbered roughly fourteen thousand while Japanese losses were sixty thousand. Both were dwarfed by

---

i   There's some debate about whether or not Yamamoto ever said this. Whether he did or not, it certainly fit with his opinion.

the losses suffered by the indigenous Okinawans—one hundred thirty thousand. If the Japanese would defend such islands tooth and nail—only seven thousand Japanese soldiers surrendered at Okinawa—their defense of the home island would be even more ferocious. These figures made the decision to drop the atomic bombs a no-brainer.

The late historian Stephen Ambrose argued that dropping the atomic bombs on Hiroshima and Nagasaki ultimately *saved* Japanese lives because it gave the Japanese high command the excuse to do what it otherwise could never do: *surrender*. They could justly say to the Japanese people that continued opposition in the face of America's city-destroying wonder weapons was utter madness.

So, on September 2, 1945, Supreme Commander General Douglas MacArthur accepted the Japanese surrender aboard the USS *Missouri*. Writing about this monumental event, Toshikazu Kase, a high-ranking Japanese Foreign Ministry official who was given the difficult task of attending the surrender on behalf of his prostrate nation, wrote this:

Stunned by defeat, [our people] seemed, for a while, to have lost all hopes for the future. But they soon recovered from the initial shock.... I believe, however, that our quick recovery would not have been possible without the generous help accorded by the United States. We were indeed most fortunate that General MacArthur was the Supreme Commander of Allied Powers, for he demonstrated a farsighted vision in shaping the destiny of Japan.

I recall still vividly the short but eloquent speech he delivered at the ceremony. He emphasized repeatedly that he would be guided by "freedom, tolerance and justice" in executing his duties. As I expected the worst humiliation, this was a complete surprise. I was thrilled beyond words, spellbound, thunderstruck. I returned to Tokyo feeling much relieved. I jotted down hurriedly my impression of the ceremony, dwelling upon MacArthur's superb address.

Shigemitsu took this report to the Imperial Palace where the Emperor was anxiously waiting. In my paper, I raised the question whether it would have been possible for us, had we been victorious, to embrace the vanquished with a similar magnanimity. Clearly, it would have been different. The Emperor sighed in agreement.

We must recognize the fact that we were defeated not by dint of superior arms but were defeated by a nobler ideal. The real issue was moral—beyond all the powers of algebra to compute. Hence the precious lesson that a new Japan, spiritually rejuvenated, must be so guided as to enhance the moral behavior to the benefit of humanity.[4]

What a fascinating and honest assessment. Were the situation reversed, the settlement "would have been different." Without doubt. Japan put whole populations to the sword, raping, pillaging, and forcing still millions more into slave labor. It is estimated that in the Rape of Nanking alone the Japanese murdered a quarter of a million Chinese civilians. This is to say nothing of horrors wrought elsewhere in Asia and Oceania, as we shall see. Had the surrender been reversed, and America occupied by the Japanese, the "settlement" would have been like that of every other country conquered by their armed forces. Instead, Kase says he was given a glimpse of a "nobler idea." That nobler idea was, quite consciously, Christian in nature.

In his magnum opus biography of MacArthur, *American Caesar*, historian William Manchester writes that one of the great problems confronting America as it prepared to occupy Japan was the ideological vacuum left by the war. The Japanese people, having been failed by both their Shinto religion and their faith in their emperor, were left with nothing—"[W]hat faiths would support them now?"

Discussing the postwar future of Japan with Secretary of the Navy James Forrestal, MacArthur argued, "the idea of liberty and freedom and the idea of Christianity" would be key to preventing Japan from falling under the influence of communists. "The more missionaries we can bring out here and the more occupation troops we can send home, the better," the Supreme Commander implored.

MacArthur's success was mixed. Although ten million Bibles were imported on his recommendation, the Japanese people did not convert to Christianity *en masse* as he hoped. That said, Japan, a feudalistic, emperor-worshiping, and militaristic society prior to the American occupation in 1945, emerged from the ashes to become not only a great democracy but a great ally. And although they didn't embrace the Christian faith, they did enthusiastically embrace its ideals as set forth in a constitution written by MacArthur and his staff—a constitution thought to be incompatible with Japanese culture. So successful was MacArthur's political metamorphosis of Japan that the country was, in a sense, "spiritually rejuvenated" as Toshikazu Kase hoped. The "moral behavior" of a nation was enhanced "to the benefit of humanity."

Interestingly, what modern Japan is missing is that doctrine central to the Christian faith—*grace*. A culture of shame, Japan has the fourth-highest suicide rate in the world, ranking only behind Hungary, Latvia, and Lithuania. "Japan has no history of Christianity," says Wataru Nishida, a psychologist at Tokyo's Temple University. "So here suicide is not a sin. In fact, some look at it as a way of taking responsibility."[5] Spiritually, America is (now) libertine where Japan is legalistic. Perhaps we would both do well to embrace the whole of the Christian faith rather than part of it.

A three-hour flight from Tokyo took us to the Japanese island of Okinawa. This was a place I wanted to see. On a trip like this, you soon discover that America's influence around the world is Jekyll and Hyde in nature. On the one hand, that influence is often like the good Dr. Jekyll: generous, good-natured, and an exporter and defender of freedom. On the other, America's influence is like the evil Mr. Hyde: exporting the seedier side of our culture.

But not here. This is the place of good America. No, it is the place of *great* America.

The absence of signage made finding it a challenge. It was a steamy hot summer day on Okinawa. When we left the comfortable air conditioning of the taxi, my sunglasses immediately fogged. As a native of the American South, I am used to heat and humidity, but this was something different. Thirty minutes later, Zachary and I were soaked with sweat from walking up a nice, gentle sidewalk leading to what the US Marines who fought here called "Hacksaw Ridge."

Standing on the edge of this escarpment—one of many on Okinawa with similarly bloody histories—Zachary and I tried to imagine it as it was then. That is difficult for several reasons, but complicating things still further was Hacksaw Ridge *now*. Looking out over the peaceful, green slopes below, it bore little resemblance to the black and white photographs of a gray, muddy mass where nothing, not even grass, grew in those violent spring days locals still call "the Typhoon of Steel." On the contrary, in the middle distance, one sees a beautiful coastline populated with hotels, resorts, and industry instead of the battleships and landing craft that filled these waters between April and June of 1945. How could such a place be the site of some of the most brutal, merciless fighting in the history of warfare?

It was more than mere curiosity that brought us here. I came to see this place, indeed, *to feel* the power of it, so I might be reminded of the extraordinary sacrifice made for Americans like me. Yes, Americans like me who have never known the privation and suffering that comes with life under a totalitarian regime. Most Americans have been spared that experience because of men like those who clawed their way, inch by inch, across this island, and dozens of other islands in the Pacific just like it. What sort of mighty men were they who fought and died here? Greatest Generation, indeed.

I have walked many battlefields, from Hastings and Normandy to Marathon and Moscow, but there was something especially savage about the fighting in the Pacific Theater during the Second World War. Read Alabama-born E. B. Sledge's classic memoir *With the Old Breed* and you get a glimpse of one man's personal horror on this and other islands. Only the fighting on the Eastern Front between Germany and the Soviet Union matched it in ferocity. And while Americans quite rightly celebrate Operation Overlord (more popularly known as "D-Day") and the subsequent liberation of Europe, the Battle of Okinawa was similar in scale, longer in duration, and saw far more casualties, but, for some unknown reason, it remains obscure in the American mind.

Consider it statistically. According to historian George Feifer, twenty-two thousand tons of materiel were delivered to Iwo Jima daily during the heat of that battle. That is only 15 percent of the total necessary to sustain soldiers on Okinawa. Moreover, the invasion force consisted of 1,457 ships covering more than thirty square miles of ocean and involved roughly half-a-million men. In contrast to the cross-Channel Overlord invasion, forces for Operation Iceberg, the codename for the Okinawa invasion, were deployed from bases in San Francisco (six thousand, two hundred miles away) and Pearl Harbor (more than four thousand miles away). It was an awesome feat of logistics. By the time the Battle of Okinawa was over, fourteen thousand American boys—and they were mostly boys—made the ultimate sacrifice.

Was it worth it?

Our forefathers thought so. Having made the logical connection between the atrocities to which Imperial Japan was subjecting Asia and Oceania—genocide, rape, slaughter, suicide bombers (i.e., kamikazes), expansionist ambitions—they were resolved to unseat the ideology that gave rise to those evil actions.

And let's be very clear on this point: they were fighting an enemy that was *every bit* as fanatical as ISIS or al-Qaeda. At Okinawa alone, approximately ten Japanese soldiers fought to the death for every one who surrendered. In addition to Hacksaw Ridge, Zachary and I sought out the cliffs from which Okinawan women hurled themselves and their children; the tunnels where Japanese soldiers committed suicide; and the jungles where they rushed headlong into American machine gun emplacements armed with no more than sharpened bamboo sticks. Such was their ideological devotion that the last Japanese soldier did not surrender until 1974.

Even so, the Greatest Generation, with perseverance and determination, fought them, from one bloody Pacific rock to another, until they defeated them and supplanted the evil ideology that produced such fanaticism in the first place. So successful were they that to visit modern Japan is to visit one of the most democratic, peaceful nations on earth. More than that, America is, generally speaking, popular with the Japanese. As Mei told me, "The

Japanese people are envious of America: your way of life and your freedom. America is the standard."

Returning from Hacksaw and the beaches that saw Americans drive a stake through the heart of Japanese fascism, I glanced at my phone and saw this headline: "Muslim Scholar Says Stop Pretending Orthodox Islam and Violence Aren't Linked."[6] What was this, a satirical piece in *The Onion*? Not at all. It was in *Time*. Such a headline is to state the obvious to any rational person only casually acquainted with terrorist acts like 9/11 and Charlie Hebdo. With my heart and mind full of a place that symbolizes America's total commitment to the demolition of an ideology very much like radical Islam, I tried to imagine a similarly idiotic headline in December 1941: "Japanese Scholar Says Attack on Pearl Harbor and Japanese Emperor Worship Are Linked." But it was too much. That was a very different America.

Not unlike America's enemies today, the Empire of Japan judged America to be a spiritually weak nation lacking the will to fight. In this, they were spectacularly wrong. One wonders, however, if now such an assessment of our national character rings with more than a little truth. After all, to that earlier generation of Americans, heroics involved climbing the likes of Hacksaw Ridge to fight a very real enemy; today, progressive heroics means climbing and toppling statues to fight an imaginary one. Americans might do well to remember who we were once..

A short walk from our hotel is the American Village, an American-themed outdoor mall looking out on the bay that has restaurants, bars, ice cream shops, and a small amusement park sporting a Ferris wheel. One evening, Zachary and I had dinner with members of the United States Marine Corps who were stationed near here.

Americans have been here since stepping ashore in 1945, though not without some controversy. At the entrance to the base, one was greeted by a tiny group of protesters shouting such clever slogans as "Yankee go home!"

"What do you make of the protesters?" we asked the Marines.

"They are paid to do it," one said, the others nodding in agreement. "There's never many of them. They don't do much and then, suddenly, local news shows up with cameras, and they start shouting!" They all laughed. "It's a publicity stunt."

This seems accurate. The online footage suggests a much larger anti-American protest, a movement.

"Are Americans popular here?"

One Marine took a swig of his beer and answered on behalf of the others. "It depends. Some like us, some don't. The businesses here would really suffer without American soldiers. Some resent our presence…"

"For the most part," another put in, "I think they like us and accept us. But whenever some knucklehead soldier gets in trouble with locals, it can become an international incident."

For the rest of the evening, we bought them beer, listened to their stories as they listened to ours. They were young men who had been not only here but in the Middle East.

Defending America's global interests is a much bigger operation than most Americans would ever suppose. At present, US military personnel are stationed in roughly 150 countries. Those operations, some just, some not, have met with mixed success. But here?

Japan is unquestionably a postwar miracle and model. One wonders what the Middle East might look like now had our policies in Iraq and Afghanistan been infused with the same resolve, consistency, and principled conviction. At best, those policies have been bipolar; at worst, they have been a betrayal of the people we claimed to liberate.

CHAPTER 5

New Zealand:
Welcome to Seattle

"Not all those who wander are lost."

—J. R. R. Tolkien, *The Fellowship of the Ring*[1]

Distances in Asia are deceptively short on a map. It is 2,902 miles from New York to San Francisco. By contrast, it is 4,445 miles from Tokyo to Brisbane (our flight was routed through there) and an additional 1,422 miles from Brisbane to Auckland. Long-haul flights would become the norm. Once you get used to such distances, the time passes quickly. Sometimes we were so tired we wanted longer flights so we could catch up on sleep.

Japan impressed us. It met most of the measures for national greatness. New Zealand was a change of pace: beautiful, spacious, and, convenient for us, they speak English! Some of the countries on our world tour were nonessential insofar as they were not in the running for our mythical prize. New Zealand, however, had to be included. It has been touted as a land unspoiled by man—a "utopia" in the words of mega-investor and PayPal founder, Peter Thiel—with room to grow.[2] Whether it is, in fact, a utopia, is up for debate, but it is a genuine competitor for the title of the world's greatest country and it certainly has room to grow. Roughly the size of Colorado, New Zealand is a country of only 4.5 million people. Room, indeed.

Those entering New Zealand via Auckland International Airport are greeted by a giant statue of Gimli, a dwarf of *Lord of the Rings* fame. This makes sense when one considers Peter Jackson's movie trilogy has pumped more than $27 million into New Zealand's economy each year—and counting.[3] Hobbit tours and Hobbit souvenirs are everywhere. Look at the top tours on Tripadvisor. Yup, *Lord of the Rings* related. It's even on some of their currency. It reminded me of Scotland in the years immediately following Mel Gibson's *Braveheart.* The image of a long-haired Mel Gibson greeted you at every turn. Did the 6' 7" William Wallace look like Mel Gibson? Hmm. Probably not.

New Zealand is a young country. The first settlers, ancestors of the Māori, arrived in the thirteenth and fourteenth centuries and were probably from Polynesia. The Dutch came in the seventeenth century, and then the English, under Captain James Cook, arrived in 1769. Cook's explorations in this part of the world would prove to be quite important. New Zealand would eventually become a successful crown colony and a dominion. In 1947, it became independent.

A city tour bus is a great way to become acquainted with a city. They stop at regular intervals, you get the lay of the land, and you can get on and off at leisure. But don't stay with the tour groups too long. Get out. Meet people. Buy them a beer and hear what they have to say. Get their opinions on where you should go. Sometimes Zachary and I did these things together, sometimes apart. He was my photographer and I would come to appreciate his perspective on the countries and people we encountered. Bright, hardworking, and with a taste for adventure, New Zealand had much to offer him.

We rented a Land Rover Defender and drove north along both the west and east coasts and directly onto the beaches. New Zealand's landscape merely adds to the utopian impression. A beautiful late winter day—we were now in the southern hemisphere, remember—one immediately understands why so many Americans are moving to New Zealand. The country is, simply put, *breathtaking*. We hiked the cliffs overlooking the Tasman Sea and the South Pacific. And we topped it off with a drive up one of New Zealand's many extinct volcanoes. All are a feast for the eyes. According to the Global Peace Index, New Zealand is also the second safest country in the world, ranking just behind Iceland.[4] Surely, this was Hobbiton and we really were in the Shire.

But, alas, no.

On my second night in Auckland, I finally made good on a longstanding invitation to speak to one of the city's Christian groups. The general impression of these people was like that of Christians throughout the Western world—a people who, feeling their faith besieged on all sides, have adopted a fortress mentality. The result, as one said, is their influence is minimal and diminishing by the moment. There is an obvious reason for this: Christians are no longer a majority in New Zealand. In recent decades, the number of people identifying as Christian has dropped precipitously.[5] Should this matter as we evaluate countries? For some, this is progress. Indeed, driving Christianity from the public square is a goal for them. But as we shall ultimately see, yes, it matters.

Coinciding with our arrival in Auckland was a controversial decision to ban a pro-life student club from the campus of Auckland University.[6] This has ominous implications for religious freedom and free speech for Christians and others in New Zealand. When the emcee for the evening's event announced this bit of news to the crowd of two hundred or so, the audience received it like those who are used to news of defeat. "[Christians] have been bullied from public life, threatened with lawsuits, and generally silenced," one man told me. Sound familiar? Too much so.

Studies like the one at ChristianPost.com referenced earlier suggest somewhere between 10 and 15 percent of New Zealanders attend church, but this hardly seems credible given the degree to which the church has been marginalized. Indeed, it is missing from the culture. After being in the country for a few days, I began to feel something like déjà vu. I was reminded of a line from Bachman–Turner Overdrive's classic road trip song "Roll on Down the Highway": "Look at the map, I think we've been here before."

I think it was about this time I saw the rainbow, a biblical symbol hijacked for a sordid sexual agenda, displayed prominently in Auckland's city center outside a grand stone church built in the Gothic style. Then again, the feeling might have been prompted by the visual of the Sky Tower, Auckland's 1,076-foot Space Needle-like tower that dominates the city's skyline. Or was it the ever-present multicultural emphasis that proclaimed an openness to all things except those that do not conform to approved orthodoxies? I wasn't sure, but I had been here before. Had the plane simply been doing laps in the Pacific only to touch down in Seattle?

And it is for this reason New Zealand is a utopia for Lefties seeking to flee the apocalypse they fear the presidency of Donald Trump will trigger. Yes, according to *Vanity Fair*, Americans are applying for citizenship in New Zealand at a record rate.[7] Conservative news outlets of size don't exist in New Zealand. There is no Fox News, just as there is no longer a Fox News in Britain. Moreover, although America's influence is all-pervasive in this country, it is the wrong America wielding it. It is the America of the Clintons and Obama; of the leftwing social policies of Apple and Starbucks, Google and Facebook, and the Silicon Valley types who are buying land in this country. It was as if they built the Sky

Tower to remind them selves of the land from which they were self-exiled.

A former British colony, New Zealand is heir to strong Christian traditions. The national anthem, "God Defend New Zealand," is essentially a hymn celebrating that heritage. But like so much else in Western civilization—and New Zealand is certainly a part of that culturally if not geographically—it is being spoiled by missionaries of a very different sort than those who were instrumental in the founding of this great nation. And, to be clear, New Zealand is great insofar as it is populated by a generous, friendly, and productive people whose geographic isolation has protected them in time of war and left them largely untouched by the kind of immigration crises currently convulsing Western Europe.

But New Zealand's isolation is rapidly coming to an end, and that, I think, is unfortunate. The country's spiritual decline has been decades in the making and having now naively absorbed the global narrative that Christianity is a religion of bigotry and hate, they are rushing to overthrow it and embrace its alternatives. Given global trends, it is not difficult to imagine what will fill that spiritual vacuum. No, New Zealand is no utopia. Yes, New Zealand is a beautiful country with much to admire, but it is trending, like most of the Western world, toward the suppression of dissenting voices. That it is a land full of volcanoes is perhaps symbolic, because it felt like a cultural Krakatoa in the making.

We loved our visit to New Zealand. Go there. It is safe, the people are friendly, and the scenery is spectacular. And we knew it would rank high on our list because the mechanisms of democracy remain intact, thus making it possible to reverse the negative trends I discussed.

CHAPTER 6

Australia:
A Day with Peter Singer

"The notion that human life is sacred just because it is human life is medieval."[1]

—Princeton bioethicist Peter Singer

After Zachary BASE jumped by wire from the top of New Zealand's Sky Tower, free-falling over one thousand feet, we headed to the airport to catch our next flight.

We watched the University of Alabama's football team steam-roll Florida State while we waited for our flight in the Delta lounge. A seventeen-point victory and four hours later, we were in Brisbane, Australia. Originally, Brisbane was to be no more than a layover of a few hours. But since we had to stop there anyway, why not stay for a couple of days and have a look around? The Great Ocean Road, the Twelve Apostles, the gorgeous scenery of the southern part of the country, we had seen on previous trips. This was an opportunity to see something different.

After religion, geography is the most underrated ingredient of national greatness. We will cover in a later chapter how Britain's geography has been key to its history. Japan's has been a blessing and a curse. Meanwhile, the United States has been blessed with the best geography of any country in the world: spacious, temperate climate, agriculturally fruitful, and easily defended against invaders. Yes, while the Belgians had two world wars forced upon them because bad geography sandwiched them between belligerents, the United States was protected by two marvelous antitank ditches known as the Atlantic and Pacific.

The Australian continent is roughly the same size (a little smaller) as the contiguous United States, and it is largely uninhabitable. The Outback, some 2.5 million square miles and 70 percent of the continent, is home to less than 5 percent of the country's twenty-five million people. Most Australians cling to the coasts. Imagine if 70 percent of the United States was essentially infertile, unusable land. America, God has indeed shed his grace on thee.

Like China, Australia is one of the countries on this tour we visited before. On that prior occasion, I was moderating a debate in Melbourne at the grand Town Hall between Oxford University's Professor John Lennox and Princeton bioethicist Peter Singer on the question "Is there a God?" Lennox is a Christian; Singer is an atheist. The event garnered a lot of attention in Australia. ABC television took interest in it and so did the people of Melbourne who filled the Town Hall.

Before the big event, Singer and I met for lunch. He is one of the most influential philosophers of the last forty years—and is quite possibly the most dangerous. His textbooks on ethics are used in universities all over the world. In 1975, Singer published *Animal Liberation*, thus giving rise to the modern animal rights movement. In his mid-sixties at the time of this, our second meeting, Peter was a lean, bespectacled man with unkempt gray hair and a dour demeanor. In addition to all this, he is a native of Melbourne, Australia.

We met at a sidewalk café in one of the fashionable neighborhoods of his hometown. As we browsed our menus, I listened as he explained his animal rights philosophy. Peter, who is vegetarian for obvious reasons, ordered gnocchi. I ordered kangaroo. I couldn't resist.

Singer is the most philosophically consistent atheist I have ever met. Journalist Kevin Toolis writes of him: "[W]hat is legitimate for Singer is just plain murder for other people." It is Singer's view that man is an animal like any other and he deserves no special status among the various species. That is, he argues, a residual of Christian thought. Worse, he has argued parents should get twenty-eight days with a newborn child to determine if they want to keep it or euthanize it. This is, of course, where atheism, pushed to its natural outcome, takes you.

"Under Singer's worldview," Toolis continues, "if you came across a newborn infant, who had no family, and a mature chimp and could only save one of them, you might actually be under a moral obligation to save the chimp."[2] Very few people—indeed, very few atheists—would say such a thing. But, then again, very few people are atheist ideologues. This is the ugliness of atheism. To say there is no God is not a morally neutral statement. It is to say morality itself is merely an illusion, an artificial human construct with no more validity than the instinctual rules regulating a colony of ants. As Fyodor Dostoevsky so eloquently put it: "If there is no immortality, there can be no virtue and all things are permissible."[3] Ruthless adherence to atheism's logic means exactly that.

And Peter Singer is, unquestionably, ruthless in his application of atheism's logical implications. Like all true ideologues, he places ideas above people because he deems them more important than people. You need not have lunch with the man to figure this out. Read his books. Listen to his lectures. In this, he really thinks he is morally courageous because he subordinates his feeling for what he believes is the greater good. *That's* what ideologues do, and it is why they are so dangerous.

Singer's worldview, never really out of fashion in Australia—on the contrary, he is something of a hero in Melbourne—is gaining momentum. Euthanasia, though technically illegal in much of Australia, is seldom prosecuted. Australians reporting no religion increased noticeably from 19 percent in 2006 to 30 percent in 2016. And, as with global trends everywhere Christianity is in decline, sexual anarchy and confusion are on the rise. Indeed, so confused are things in this respect in Australia, a Christian group's Father's Day commercial celebrating fatherhood was pulled from television because it was deemed "too political."[4] What was in this commercial? Dads with their kids. Outrageous!

The Christian nonprofit in question aired those commercials for years, so why were these sweet, moving spots unacceptable now? Because Australia would soon be voting on gay marriage, and no lobby is more powerful than the present gay lobby. With this in mind, you understand what they object to in this commercial. It isn't the ad per se; it is authentic marriage and the distinctive roles of a man and a woman within that God-ordained institution that offends them. In modern Australia, dads are a political liability and a reminder of a "hierarchical" past many want to leave behind.

Australia is one of the most aggressively secular countries in the world, and like New Zealand, it doesn't really have prominent, substantive conservative voices or media. There is the Left and, well, other versions of the Left. The nonprofit's experience with their tame and socially edifying commercial is typical in this country.

Zachary would not be along for the next four countries. He had other responsibilities and would rejoin me in India. Given some of what lay ahead, this was a good thing.

CHAPTER 7

South Korea:
The Line Between Good and Evil

"Whoever said the pen is mightier than the sword obviously never encountered automatic weapons."[1]

—General Douglas MacArthur

I sat half asleep in the front passenger seat of a Hyundai SUV only vaguely aware of the countryside through which we were passing. The warmth of the car and the bright sunshine belied a colder and grimmer reality. I was jostled from this soporific haze as the car braked heavily. Before us stood two soldiers of the South Korean 25th Infantry Division, each with one hand up ordering us to stop and the other gripping a Daewoo K2 assault rifle. Wearing full combat gear with only their eyes visible behind the black masks they wore to protect them from the bitter wind, one stood behind a maze of concrete and steel barriers while the other approached the Hyundai cautiously. My driver, Don, a former member of the Republic of Korea Army (ROKA), cracked the window and presented a special permit granting us access to this remote portion of the Korean Demilitarized Zone (DMZ). The soldier disappeared into a guardhouse to make a phone call while his companion kept us under close watch.

"We are to wait here while he checks us out," Don said. Don is not his real name. Like many Koreans who interact with Westerners regularly, he has adopted a pseudonym his clients can more easily pronounce than his actual Korean name. The hotel concierge is, say, Jim, and the woman at the check-in desk is Angela—but not really.

After a delay of twenty minutes or so, a Jeep arrived, and another soldier hopped out and strode toward us purposefully. Emerging from the guardhouse, the first soldier returned our permit, told us we were cleared to pass, and fitted a flag to the car door and put a placard on our dashboard. He then informed us this newly arrived soldier would accompany us to make sure we didn't get lost or hurt. Landmines are, after all, strewn all over the DMZ, and those soldiers occupying the 150 guard posts on the northern side of the wire have been known to shoot more than a few people on the southern side. Since the Korean War ended in July 1953, more than a thousand South Koreans, Americans, and other citizens of countries composing the forces of the United Nations have been killed along this dangerous stretch of hotly contested land. But this soldier's real job was, I suspect, to make sure we didn't do some damned silly thing to provoke an international incident.

He got into the back seat and directed us through the barrier and up a mountainside. We parked just below a ROKA guard post manned by soldiers carrying the same K2s slung over their backs as they stood behind mounted machine guns whose barrels pointed menacingly northward.

"No photo," the soldier said as we got out of the car. It seems like an antiquated rule in the age of satellites and drones, but I dutifully obeyed.

The DMZ is a 250-kilometer-long and four-kilometer-wide border cutting the Korean Peninsula in half. On the southern side, squat trees and bushes populate the gray landscape; on the northern side, there is nothing but grass and dirt as all vegetation has been flattened to provide clear sightlines for North Korean machine gunners. On the southern side, a free society flourishes economically, politically, and culturally; on the northern side lies a human and economic wasteland ruled by a hardline communist regime. This place, running roughly along the infamous 38th parallel, has been one of the most dangerous borders in the world and the spot many feared would be the flashpoint for the next world war.

With the use of a pair of field glasses, I could see the guard posts of the North Korean People's Army (KPA) across the wide expanse of this no man's land, and if you were to look very carefully, you could even make out the dark figures of the sentries. Spanning the western and eastern horizons are the barbed wire and earthen walls rolling over distant hills on the South Korean side of the DMZ, machine gun towers perforating the otherwise unbroken line at regular intervals. But that is not all. Roads, bridges, and any potential path KPA troops and tanks might follow southward (as they did in June 1950) are mined with explosive charges that will be detonated in the event of war, thus slowing—one hopes—any advance on Seoul.

It's eerie.

Adding to the eerie quality is the ominous silence. But there was something else and it took me a while to identify it. All of this felt like an anachronism, an embarrassing relic of the Cold War that should have fallen in November 1989 along with the Berlin Wall. Didn't the reunification and freedom fervor that swept Germany three decades ago penetrate these remote regions of Asia? It seems when Berliners were rocking to the music of the

Scorpions, the North Koreans were still goose-stepping to the awkward beat of communist propaganda. Reagan needed to visit here, too:

"Mr. Kim Il-Sung, open this gate! Mr. Kim Il-Sung, tear down this wall!"

North Korea's government and string of wicked, murderous dictators were indeed an anachronism more befitting the time of Lenin or Stalin or Mao than the era of chic celebrity presidents like Macron and Trudeau and Merkel—well, Macron and Trudeau anyway. This is the kind of wall Democrats would have you believe Trump wants to build: a threatening, barbed-wired symbol of tyranny. Nonsense. Unlike Trump's proposed wall, this one is meant to keep people *in* rather than keep them *out*. At least, that is the purpose the North Koreans have in mind. For their part, the South Koreans man their wall defensively. Just as South Koreans are not fighting to cross the wire in a desperate bid to reach the communist utopia of North Korea, the United States' southern frontier problem is not one of Americans crossing the Rio Grande into Mexico so they might take advantage of that country's wonderful social welfare benefits and overturn their electoral process through illegal voting. Trump's wall is defensive in nature and meant to enforce a sensible immigration policy.

Here on the 38th parallel, that is done with guns. And barbed wire. And a wall.

Seoul, a city of some ten million people, is modern and prosperous. While American culture is emulated, Japan, a hated rival, nonetheless wields a great deal of influence, especially in fashion.

"She's Chinese," my guide said, nodding in the direction of a woman on the sidewalk as we sat in the back of a taxi.

"How can you tell?" My question reflected the confusion of a Westerner.

"They aren't pretty," she answered flatly. "And they all look the same." With that, she elbowed me.

"They aren't pretty?" I teased.

"No. They aren't." Again, flat. After a moment, she decided to educate me. "Japanese and Korean women take much more pride in our appearance." She then added an atomic morsel: "We Korean women have thicker skin. That's why we don't wrinkle like white women."

She looked at me. I just raised my eyebrows in genuine surprise.

"You don't agree?" She asked. "White women are ugly when they get old."

I was flummoxed. Was this racist?

"Look there," she pointed. "She's Japanese."

"How can you tell?"

"The way she walks, her style of dress, and she's pretty."

This was an unexpected education in the absence of political correctness. I encountered this all over Asia and Africa. While jarring, it could also be refreshing. All the more so since I was not the target of her offensive remarks.

A lover of coffee, her tour mostly included coffee shops and restaurants she considered chic. She chatted a blue streak of politics, movies, literature, and the latest in women's fashion. There were the occasional surprises:

"I think Korea will be reunited."

"You do? Why?" I asked.

"I think people are people. I think they want it and we do, too."

I took a somber tone. "It is true you both want it. The north, however, wants it on very different terms. North Korea's leadership doesn't want a united, free Korea."

"I don't agree," she said.

Don shook his head. "She is young," he said, nodding at his female colleague. "Her generation does not know what it was like. They only know modern Korea, prosperity, and freedom. They are too ready to trust Kim Jong-Un's empty words."

"I just think we are more open than your [i.e., Don's] generation," she said.

At the end of World War II, Korea was divided in half along the 38th parallel between spheres of communist and American influence. The communists took the north and the Americans controlled the south. From an American perspective, the goal was not an ongoing military occupation but the mopping-up of Japanese forces that ruled Korea for thirty-five years and the establishment of a stable democratic nation. But on June 25, 1950, the communist north invaded the south in a bid to take over the whole country. The KPA drove south, occupied Seoul, and pushed UN forces all the way to Pusan on the southern tip of the Korean Peninsula.

It was a mistake.

The communists of North Korea and China grossly misjudged America's resolve to protect the fledgling democracy then taking shape in South Korea. Actually, they misjudged Truman's resolve, because Congress never declared war. A further miscalculation was the United States' extraordinary logistical ability to put thousands of soldiers' boots and armor on the ground in Korea with great rapidity. Reinforcing the US Eighth Army in what became known as the Pusan Perimeter, General Douglas MacArthur devised Operation Chromite. Chromite proposed a massive amphibious landing of US forces at Inchon on the west coast of Korea near Seoul, the recapture of Seoul, and then a drive straight across the Korean Peninsula cutting the KPA supply lines and their route of escape. In short, the plan called for landing forty thousand troops at Inchon to save one hundred thousand troops surrounded at Pusan.

The Joint Chiefs of Staff thought the plan sheer madness. General Omar Bradley said seaborne landings were obsolete. The Navy and Marine Corps strongly objected. The tides, they argued, were too radical to facilitate such an operation. It would, they said, be an "Asian Dunkirk." General Matthew Ridgway called it "a forty-five-thousand-to-1 shot." Washington deferred to the majority of military opinion which was roughly divided along the lines of MacArthur vs everyone else. Murmurs of MacArthur's arrogance in even suggesting such a plan were rife among those in the know.

But MacArthur, who, along with Robert E. Lee, is probably the greatest military mind America has ever produced, could not be moved. The Joint Chiefs tried to get him to give *somewhere* on *something*. Couldn't he devise a less risky plan? How about landing south of Inchon where the beaches were more secure, and the enemy could not fight from house to house as they could in Seoul, thus slaughtering American boys? For his part, MacArthur argued that such a landing would be pointless because it would not achieve the central goals of recapturing Seoul and cutting KPA supply lines. Besides, if the Joint Chiefs thought the landing impossible, wouldn't the enemy think that, too, and leave the beaches undefended? For him, it was Inchon or nothing.

Wow.

When I consider MacArthur's confidence in his plan, I marvel. A lesser man than MacArthur would have bowed to the pressure. Maybe any man but MacArthur would have bowed to the pressure. Outside his staff, who would attack a tank with screwdrivers had he ordered it, the overwhelming weight of military opinion was against him. And some of those against him, like Omar Bradley and Matthew Ridgway, were men of considerable military reputations of their own. If I'm Douglas MacArthur and I know Omar Bradley—who was, incidentally, the United States Army's last five-star general—thinks my plan is a bloodbath in the making, I think my confidence would be sorely shaken and I would back down. Men generally need the support of others when making risky decisions not only to bolster their flagging confidence in the face of opposition but so blame can be distributed among a variety of people should their plans fail. We all want to be able to say, "Well, so-and-so thought it was a good idea, too."

MacArthur didn't need that. Now, such a man is either an arrogant fool or a man possessed of extraordinary self-confidence for a reason. In MacArthur's case, it was the latter. The man was a genius and he knew it. His track record of success is breathtaking. He took more territory with less loss of life than any general in World War II. He was rightly nominated for *three* Congressional Medals of Honor and awarded one. Along with his staff, he wrote the Japanese constitution which remains, to this day, intact and is, along with the Marshall Plan, quite possibly America's most enduring postwar achievement.

At a conference of military planners, MacArthur confronted his critics. He listened, unmoved, as they laid out all the reasons his plan would be a disaster. Army Chief of Staff General J. Lawton Collins said that even if the landing was successful, which was highly unlikely, MacArthur would be stuck on the beach and he would never be able to retake Seoul. Others concurred.

Chief of Naval Operations Admiral Forrest Sherman summed up the prevailing opinion: "If every possible geographical and naval handicap were listed, Inchon has them all!" Then MacArthur rose to make his case. For forty-five minutes, he held court, addressing each and every criticism of his plan. Rear Admiral James Doyle later recalled MacArthur's presentation: "If MacArthur had become an actor, you never would have heard of John Barrymore." In the end, it wasn't MacArthur who backed down. The Joint Chiefs backed down and reluctantly gave the plan their approval.

MacArthur, however, had no illusions about the risks he was taking and where blame would be placed if the plan failed: "If I fail, everyone will be after my blood.... I alone was responsible for tomorrow, and if I failed, the dreadful results would rest on Judgment Day against my soul."

But MacArthur was imbued with an almost supernatural confidence in himself and in the men he commanded. On the morning of the landing, the fleet was sailing irresistibly toward Inchon when they were attacked. Major General Courtney Whitney recounts what happened next:

> Hurriedly dressing and going to the bridge, I learned that two enemy planes were attempting to bomb the cruiser just ahead of us. The pale lights of dawn had not yet dispersed enough of the darkness for me to follow the course of the action, but an officer reported that both planes were shot down before they could do any damage. I decided, however, that I had better awaken MacArthur because of this danger. When I went into his cabin and gently shook him, he woke, listened while I recounted the incident of the attack, and then turned over to resume his rest. "Wake me up again, Court," he said, "if they attack this ship."

Operation Chromite was a smashing success. Seoul was retaken, the Peninsula cut in half, and hundreds of thousands of KPA troops were encircled, captured, and destroyed. Eisenhower called it a "brilliant example of strategic leadership." Admiral William "Bull" Halsey Jr. said of the victory, "The Inchon landing is the most masterly and audacious strategic stroke in all history."

But the war wasn't over. It was followed by three years of bloody fighting comparable only to America's war with the Empire of Japan. MacArthur wasn't infallible, and he was eventually, and famously, fired by Truman. I have (twice) read both David McCullough's magnum opus biography of Truman—aptly titled *Truman*—and William Manchester's biography of MacArthur, *American Caesar*. Both books are superb. Unsurprisingly, each author takes the side of his hero. McCullough sees MacArthur as an arrogant ass who got what he deserved; Manchester, more even-handed, is aware of MacArthur's flaws but sees Truman as no less prideful and possibly jealous of the general's genius and popularity with the American people.

Whatever the truth of the situation, one thing is certain: men like MacArthur provoke jealousy, especially among other men. Like Napoleon, he consistently disregarded the opinions of other generals and was consistently proved right in doing so. Operation Chromite was just more of the same. Needless to say, many were glad to see him go. MacArthur, like Patton, was never popular with his colleagues, though both were beloved by their respective staffs.

Almost seven decades hence, MacArthur is a name all but forgotten in America. I wager few of America's current generation of college students could tell you much, if anything, about him. I devote so much space to him because the regularity with which his name is mentioned in the Far East took me by surprise. Every tour guide in Japan and South Korea referred to him with reverence.

Was MacArthur arrogant? The question never comes up. They simply don't care and don't question the results. It is the peculiar hobby of Americans to allow questions of personal tastes and politics to override more important considerations. The German high command, for instance, did not believe the American papers when they proclaimed the firing of Patton for slapping a private. Surely it was a ruse! But it wasn't. Had Patton lived in the age of social media, the liberation of Bavaria by Patton's Third Army might never have happened, and that region would likely have been left to suffer a half century of communist rule.

It was to the great good fortune of Japan and Korea that their collective fate fell to a man of MacArthur's extraordinary vision and ability. Manchester was right to call him a Caesar because he certainly had that kind of power, and he wielded it for the good of the people he ruled. America lacks a man of his gifts in the aftermath of operations in Kuwait, Iraq, and Afghanistan.

American boys have given their lives for many a lost cause in far-flung corners of the world. But they have also given their lives for the liberation of oppressed people. Places with names like Kwajalein Atoll, Eniwetok, Peleliu, El Guettar, Pointe du Hoc, Nijmegen, Kapyong, Pork Chop Hill, Ia Drang, Mogadishu, and Wanat, to cite only a handful. Places far from your front door and to which you may have heard some vague reference but are otherwise meaningless to you. Indeed, I wager more people know what Kim Kardashian had for breakfast today than know of the importance of these places.

My father spent four years in Korea. After the war, he was an Imjin Scout, a prestigious designation given only to those who survived twenty or more missions patrolling the dangerous DMZ. When he left it, the Republic of South Korea was a fragile democracy recovering from thirty-five years of Japanese occupation and a devastating war that wrecked the whole of the Korean

Peninsula. I think my father, like so many Korean War veterans, died wondering if all the fighting, the death, the sacrifice, the suffering, and privation was worth it.

As I walked the streets of Seoul, I found myself wishing I had been able to do this before my father passed away. I would have wanted to tell him what I saw. Seven decades since the end of the war that resulted in the deaths of more than three million people, I saw a city as modern as any in America. I saw men and women, fashionable and educated, enjoying a standard of living and a quality of life once unthinkable in this part of the world. I saw businesses and churches flourishing. In short, I saw a strong, vibrant free society.

Standing on a street corner, I paused to take it all in. What would Dad think of this postwar marvel had he lived to see it? At that moment, a group of about twenty happy, healthy, rosy-cheeked elementary school children emerged onto the sidewalk from the subway. Their teachers herded them along as they merrily followed and sang what sounded like a nursery rhyme. In that instant, I knew exactly what my father would have concluded. The scene of those children sealed it. He loved children. Indeed, he would have been moved by the sight of them. That, I can well imagine, would have brought tears to his eyes and a deep satisfaction to his heart. It did mine.

CHAPTER 8

Vietnam:
The War America Lost?
I Don't Think So

"We will lose ten men for every one you lose, but in the end, it is you who will tire."[1]

—Vietnamese Communist leader Ho Chi Minh

I arrived in Vietnam late at night. At the airport, as in so many third world countries, there was aggressive competition to carry my bags, to drive me to a hotel, to shine my shoes—everything. Many travelers are robbed, swindled, or coerced into taxis taking them who knows where before they ever get out of the airport. Beware. I was hot, tired, and ready for a shower and bed.

In addition to his four years in Korea, my father also did two tours here. I did two as well. Of course, mine were under somewhat different circumstances. His tours involved extensive time in the jungle carrying an M16 and trying to avoid being killed by "Charlie." My tour of the jungle was like a trip to an amusement park, albeit a somewhat bizarre amusement park.

Memories of Vietnam haunted a generation of Americans. Those of us who came after them watched Oliver Stone's *Platoon* and Francis Ford Coppola's *Apocalypse Now*, nihilistic films that said more about a particular type of American's worldview than they did about the war. On the other end of the spectrum there were Chuck Norris's Colonel Braddock in *Missing in Action* and Sylvester Stallone's Rambo in *First Blood Part II*, who returned to Vietnam, kicked some communist butt, and restored a bit of dignity to a wounded American ego.[i]

This was the war we lost and the Vietnamese love reminding you of it.

Hopping a speed boat in central Saigon (also known as Ho Chi Minh City), I headed upriver for an hour to the Cu Chi Tunnels. Whenever possible, a boat is the best way to travel in Vietnam. Outside of the upscale parts of the urban areas, the roads are often in poor condition and dusty. By contrast, the speed boats and water taxis move about efficiently. Sitting in the back near the big Mercury outboard motor of this twenty-five-footer, I took in the view of the city, the riverside mansions and bamboo stilt houses, along with the great natural beauty and the trash peppered in our wake as the boat captain skillfully navigated the water hyacinth at high speed.

The Cu Chi Tunnels were one of the many bases of operation for the Viet Cong during "The American War," as they call it. Stretching for miles like capillaries, they are now a national park celebrating Vietnam's great victory over the "American capitalists." Arriving at the park's boat dock, you are greeted with a meal and the beverages Westerners always seem to need. Prior to going into the tunnels, the government requires visitors to watch a twenty-minute film. In the U.S., such a film would be about safety and expected behavior on the tour and, of course, advertisements to capture your tourist dollars. Not here. This was a propaganda film produced in 1967.

---

i   For what it's worth, my father hated—and I mean *hated* with a passion—every Vietnam war movie he ever saw with one exception: *We Were Soldiers*.

78

The film is memorable.[2] In one scene, we are introduced to a beautiful Vietnamese woman named Vo Thi Mo. Although we are supposed to think of her as a typical peasant, her appearance suggests something closer to a model for Jimmy Choo. But don't be fooled by the exterior of this femme fatale. Her first name—or that which the propagandists gave her—means *war*. The female narrator, sounding like Hanoi Hannah, says softly:

"It's Vo Thi Mo, the beautiful and thin girl from Nhuan Duc. She prefers singing to firing, but her determination is huge. "

It continues:

"She follows male soldiers everywhere.... She follows [the] enemy's each and every step. She earned the medal of 'American soldier killer.'"

I lost count of the number of times the narrator used the phrase, "kill Americans" or its variants. I was the only American in the audience and now I knew why. I decided they needed better marketing consultants. No doubt the gift shop at the end of our tour would be full of snow globes, t-shirts, and hats reading, "Kill Americans." This phrase was the Cu Chi Tunnel equivalent of "See Rock City" in my part of the United States. Radical Muslims would love this place.

Departing the amphitheater, the willing were permitted to enter the tunnels unguided. I squeezed through a short passage feeling a bit like the proverbial camel trying to thread the needle. The tunnels are hot and narrow and remarkably extensive. Following the spelunking, a tour guide led us along a veritable path of horrors where she gleefully pointed out concealed traps of every kind— bamboo spears that swing from trees and aim for the face and torso; pits containing iron spikes; landmines; apparently harmless objects rigged with explosives and so on until we arrived at a mannequin symbolizing women like Vo Thi Mo. The mannequin wore lipstick, rouge, and what appeared to be a Burberry scarf. I had no idea the

Viet Cong were at the forefront of fashion. Our guide, jovial and in a voice more appropriate to a tour of a chocolate factory, pointed back to the path we just walked and said:

"Booby trap."

Then, with the perfect timing of a practiced comedienne, she pointed at the mannequin:

"Honey trap!"

The tour group laughed nervously, fearing, perhaps, a trapdoor and impalement or bamboo to the face if they didn't. Regardless, the point was hardly a funny one. Many a good American soldier, taught from youth to be deferential to the opposite sex, found those ingrained behaviors weaponized and used against them by women who lured them to their destruction. Indeed, throughout history, men who have shrewdly avoided death on the battlefield have fallen by the score to a subtler weapon.

"Honey traps aren't just on the battlefield!" one fellow said, eliciting a few chuckles. Hmm.

The tour now over, we stood under a canopy where it was announced that visitors could buy gifts, have a soft drink or beer, relax—*or rent an AK-47*. This is what I love about the third world. No frivolous lawsuits, no Alexander Shunnarah signs. Yup, you could rent a fully automatic assault rifle, the choice of every communist and Islamic terrorist in the world, and shoot at paper targets in the silhouette of a man who is, presumably, representative of an American soldier. I briefly wondered if they had one of Ho Chi Minh or, lacking that, another communist, Bernie Sanders.

But my enthusiasm was not shared by everyone. A general angst possessed our group of mostly Australians and Brits and a handwringing discussion on the morality of using such weapons, even for fun, ensued. I left.

"Hey, Larry, what are you going to do?" someone from Wales asked.

"I'm going to go and empty a couple of magazines into those targets."

I needed to burn off a bit of steam and can you think of a better way to do it?

I was accompanied to the range by a former member of the Viet Cong. A cigarette dangled from his lips carelessly as he handed me a magazine. I fired off my rounds individually, taking my time and getting the most for my money.

The AK-47 is the mousetrap of automatic weapons. Simple and easy to use. AK-47 stands for *Avtomat Kalashnikova*, Russian for automatic Kalashnikov. It is named for its designer Mikhail Kalashnikov, who introduced it in 1947. The United States countered this weapon with the M16, an elegant rifle possessing greater range and accuracy—but also four to five times the per-unit cost. From a Soviet perspective, the beauty of the AK-47 was how easily and inexpensively it could be manufactured, and its user trained to wield it with deadly effect. It is estimated more than one hundred million have been produced, with half of them being made outside of Russia without license. It is the most used assault rifle in the world. I have seen it in Asia, Africa, Eastern Europe, and South America.

My old Viet Cong range marshal flicked his cigarette out and offered me another magazine. But it was time to move on.

This place was like Six Flags—but with ordinance.

What's next? Ring toss with hand grenades?

Vietnam, as I have said, is the war America lost.

Or is it?

I decided to schedule another tour to explore Ho Chi Minh City. I found an individualized tour with transportation included. Perfect.

Local tours are helpful for a variety of reasons, but I like them mostly to get a local perspective. I am, in effect, paying for a conversation with an educated citizen of the country I am visiting. What do they think are the most important features of their city? What are their opinions on the issues of the day? What, if anything, do we have in common?

"I am Anh," my guide said, introducing herself with an extended hand. She appeared to be about fifteen. Surely there was some mistake. But she insisted there was not.

"I am thirty-two." She smiled broadly as she answered my unspoken question. "We [i.e., Asian women] just age better than white women. And we aren't fat like American women." Her smile never dimmed. These shots at white American women were becoming a theme. Disconcerted, I just chalked this up to the typical commentary I heard in Asia: direct and politically incorrect.

"Are you ready?" she asked, and with an exuberance bordering on giddy, she led the way out of the hotel to a street corner where she handed me a helmet while she strapped one on herself.

"Uh, what's this for?" I asked anxiously.

"It's for this," she gestured at a scooter. "That's how we will get around the city today."

I had somehow missed this in the tour information. I looked around for my scooter. There wasn't one. She got on the little two-wheeled deathtrap and sat forward and looked at me expectantly.

"Get on!" she said, revving the chainsaw-sized engine unconvincingly.

Anh couldn't have been more than five feet tall or have weighed more than ninety pounds. I protested.

"Anh, I'm quite a lot bigger than you. Are you sure you can handle having me on the back of this thing?"

"Of course. It is way of life in Vietnam."

This much I knew to be true. Vietnam, a country of roughly ninety-five million people, has no fewer than forty-five million registered motorbikes. Saigon alone has about 7.5 million of them. They are everywhere, weaving in and out of traffic, hopping curbs, on sidewalks—everywhere. You will see as many as five passengers piled onto these small machines. You will even see mothers holding infants on the back while Dad drives.

I played my trump card. Or so I thought. "The helmet doesn't fit."

"That's okay. Today you travel like Vietnamese!"

Unhappily, I got on the back, and my Benjamin-Button-of-a-guide quickly accelerated to about thirty-five miles per hour. Other scooters swarmed around us as we joined the chaos. Scooters and mopeds populate the world's roads in all but America. America is great if only for that reason. But the only other place I saw them driven with this kind of reckless abandon was in Africa and India. Safety simply isn't a chief consideration. Helmetless and uneasy, I was certain this was going to end in an accident similar to the one I suffered a few years ago.

The sight of my large frame on the back of that scooter drew attention. People pointed and laughed. The owner of many motorcycles, I confess I have long regarded scooters as...*unmanly.* To me, they are like manicures, bow ties, and any movie on Lifetime. But riding on the back of one while a tiny woman drives? Well, that's like having to suffer all three at once.

"Ahn," I shouted over the whine of the sewing machine-like sound of the engine, "how 'bout you let me do the driving?" I was sure Phileas Fogg never suffered this indignity.

"Americans cannot drive in this country! It very crazy!"

"I think I can handle it!" I bellowed. "I think you'll feel safe!" This was clearly not true. No one could possibly feel safe on these roads, but I was desperate. If I was going to become yet another American casualty in 'Nam, it would be at my own hand.

Reluctantly, she stopped at a traffic light and we quickly swapped places. When the light turned green, it was like the release of the starting gate at the Kentucky Derby. Motorist acceleration was immediate and their proximity to one another was never at a safe distance. I was in my element.

Leaning forward to my ear, Anh laughingly yelled, "You sure you American and no Vietnamese? You drive like Vietnamese!" For the rest of the day, this was how we saw the city.

On April 25, 1975, a mere five days before the fall of Saigon and the withdrawal of U.S. forces from Vietnam, the chief negotiator for the United States, Colonel Harry Summers, had this famous exchange with his North Vietnamese counterpart, Colonel Tu:

Summers: "You know you never defeated us on the battlefield."

Tu: "That may be so. But it is also irrelevant."

Touring this country some forty-four years later, I am inclined to imagine the conversation differently:

Tu: "You know we drove you out of Vietnam."

Summers: "That may be so. But it is also irrelevant."[3]

Why do I imagine it differently? Simply put, because the communists, at least in this part of the world, have lost. To be sure, the icons and symbols of communism are prominent throughout the city. Communist banners—a yellow hammer and sickle on a field of red—line the road and images of "Uncle Ho" are omnipresent. But it very soon became evident these were meaningless.

The signs of communism's retreat were everywhere: Chanel, Levi's, Tumi, Under Armour, Adidas, Apple, Gucci, Starbucks—there was even a factory outlet mall. Vietnam is following China's model: abandon Marxist economics while pretending not to have done so.

But don't be fooled. Although America's economic triumph is as obvious as the McDonald's Golden Arches we scootered past, total victory is not yet an accomplished fact. Yes, Vietnam has ditched the economics of socialism and has adopted a Western-style free-market economy, but they still maintain the one-party, authoritarian system. This, too, is the Chinese model. Vietnam is not a free society as we understand it in the West, so Westerners should be careful because civil liberties, due process, and the rule of law are lines that move according to the whims of the state.

Even so, America is winning. Capitalism has steadily destroyed the creeping, poisonous weed of Marxism on this continent like Agent Orange. Indeed, American movies, TV shows, music, fashion, products, and retail stores have done what the armies of France did not do, and the armies of the United States were not permitted to do. With a growing free-market economy, who knows? Maybe free speech and free elections will soon catch on, too.

Harley-Davidsons, however, that most American means of manly transportation, well, those haven't yet caught on in Vietnam.

"I really think you a Vietnamese!" Ahn declared with every intention of flattering me.

For my part, I revved the tiny engine of our scooter in what was meant to be a powerful *growl* of acknowledgment. But the *whirrrr!* of the motor just added to the indignity. I might as well have been revving an eggbeater.

With wounded pride, we rode ingloriously into the (formerly) communist night.

CHAPTER 9

Thailand: One Night in Bangkok

"One night in Bangkok makes a hard man humble..."[1]

—Murray Head

As the world tour rolled on, I was feeling tired. We had hit seven countries so far. Travel is exhausting. We became efficient. We were the first to disembark the planes, the first to passport control, the first to baggage claims, and the first to the taxi stands. We had it down to a science.

But I was still tired. It occurred to me I had not taken a single day off thus far. International travel also causes you to lose track of time and, occasionally, even where you are. Is it Saturday? Where am I now? Hong Kong again? You often feel like you need to get your bearings—or get a drink.

After a short flight by the standards I had come to expect in Asia, I arrived in Bangkok and, after locating my hotel, I went out for a walk. On the hotel's recommendation, I headed for the famed Sukhumvit Road. High fashion, expensive hotels, supercars, souvenirs—they can all be found there. But there is an unpleasant side to Bangkok, and I was, unwittingly, going to encounter it.

"Hey there, handsome," a woman—was it a woman?—suddenly reached out to me from my left. Immediately, another grabbed at my right elbow and a third stood, arms crossed, blocking my way, completing the triangulation. Prostitutes all, they appeared from alleyways and were physically aggressive—grabbing, pulling, putting their arms around me. In today's world, this certainly would constitute sexual harassment. To be clear, I wasn't harmed, but I was, how shall I put it? Embarrassed, uncomfortable—horrified.

With more than a little effort, I pulled free and walked on. Such women were everywhere and to notice them, no matter how innocently or momentarily, is to invite them to rush you. I put my earbuds in, turned the music up, and made sure to keep my eyes straight ahead or down. This tactic works with pushy street merchants. Hopefully, it would work with these, well, street merchants of a different sort. Once they see you can't hear them, they tend to move on to the next person coming down the sidewalk. Glancing behind me, I could see the next fellow being assaulted in a similar fashion. He looked bewildered. But the man next to him appeared to be negotiating. I thought of the lyrics of Murray Head's eighties hit "One Night in Bangkok" where the city makes hard men humble as "angels" embrace you with the tenderness of a lover.

Only they aren't angels and it ain't love they are offering. The incident didn't anger me, it filled me with sadness and something more; something like disgust and a wave of nausea swept over me. I can't really describe the feeling adequately, but I thought I might vomit. This feeling was compounded by my embarrassment. With so much worldly experience, so much travel, so many encounters with people at all levels of society, I suddenly felt naïve. It got worse.

Hailing a tuk-tuk, I jumped in and ordered the driver to tour me up and down the Sukhumvit. I just needed a breather until I could decide where I would go next. From the safe distance of this little vehicle, I would see the city.

Tuk-tuks are the automotive equivalent of a rickshaw. Like scooters, they dominate the roadways of the third world. Think of a large motorized tricycle with a roof over the heads of the passengers. The driver, a young man, suddenly wheeled off of Sukhumvit Road. Still shaking from what just happened, I let the wind blow through my sweaty hair and drank deeply from the bottle of water he gave me.

"Where are we going?" I asked.

"You want to see the city, yes?" He gave me a broad smile in the rearview mirror.

"Uh, yeah, but I'll decide where we go. Not you."

"Do you need a suit?" He was still cheery.

"What?"

"Suits are cheap here. Excellent quality. Do you need one?"

"No."

He stopped in front of a suit shop and turned to face me.

"Listen, if you help me, I will help you."

The look of annoyance on my face prompted him to explain.

"I get money for every tourist I bring here. If you go in for just a few minutes, I get paid. I will give you discount."

"I'm a capitalist. I'll do it."

A few minutes later, I returned. He seemed pleased. From there he drove all over Bangkok pointing to this and that landmark. This was more pleasant and I was feeling better. Then he stopped in front of another place.

"It's happy hour," he said, and then, with a sweep of his hand, pointed at what looked like a nightclub.

What? A bar? I thought.

It soon became clear it was a brothel. Women, dozens of them, all scantily clad, milled about and beckoned me. I felt like Odysseus listening to the Sirens' song.

A woman, all smiles, approached.

"They are all 'clean,'" my driver said. "They are checked regularly by doctors. Women on the street? Disease! Not these pretty ladies!"

I recoiled.

"You don't like them?" a man said from the sidewalk. "What do you want?" His question left me with the distinct impression he was prepared to indulge *any* appetite.

"Get me out of here," I said to my driver.

Hearing me say this, the face of the woman who had approached me first, the picture of warmth and affection only moments ago, instantaneously transformed into an expression of startling hatred. Honestly, she was frightening. The transformation was so absolute I halfway expected her to grow fangs and claws before my eyes. I had the urge to run.

We sped away at my insistence, but my driver was sullen, quiet, and probably (rightly) feared his tip was going to suffer. This is a common tactic and I fell for it. I made a rookie mistake. However, this was a new twist on an old ruse. A jewelry store? Yes. An "authentic" Oriental rug outlet? Yes. A souvenir shop? Always. Taxi drivers and guides the world over will try to coerce you to enter these places and spend your money. But a brothel? This was a first for me.

Lonely Planet says of this Bangkok scam: "Expecting your tuk-tuk to take you where you've asked, or your tour bus to drop you back at your hotel? You must be crazy.... This scam becomes a lot more hair-raising at night when the journey to the cool nightclub recommended in your guidebook becomes a tour of dodgy prostitute bars and a refusal to take you home."[2]

After a few minutes, my driver spoke up:

"You aren't a tourist."

"What makes you say that?"

"You don't ask questions and you keep to yourself. It takes a lot to impress you."

"Brothels don't impress me."

I was in Bangkok for only a few hours and was forcefully exposed to the seedy underbelly for which it is famous. The city was living up to its unfortunate reputation. This was the sort of place where the souls of men are sullied and destroyed. I'm sure men (and women) of every sort have been sifted like wheat here. If what happens in Vegas, stays in Vegas, what happens in Bangkok stays with you, seared into your memory.

At this point, my reaction to Bangkok was visceral. I hated it. I wanted to leave. But this is a tale of two cities: that is, one city with two sides. You can't judge a country on a singular experience. If Thailand is known for its sex industry, it is also known as the Land of Smiling Faces, and right now, I felt like I needed to see some smiling faces. Unfortunately, I planned an excursion from Bangkok of an altogether different nature. The very name of where I was headed was depressing: the Thai-Burma Railway, otherwise known as "The Railway of Death." After a good night's sleep, I set out for Kanchanaburi, a town two hours west of Bangkok and the site of the famed Kwai River Bridge.

Many of my readers have, I am sure, seen *The Bridge on the River Kwai* starring Alec Guinness and William Holden. The two play soldiers in a Japanese POW camp. Guinness is the half-crazed Colonel Nicholson, a British Army officer who is determined to assist the Japanese in building a bridge over the Kwai River to demonstrate British engineering and know-how. Holden, the handsome, insubordinate American smart aleck, is determined to stop him. The film won seven Academy Awards and has taken its place alongside other great films based on real history.

Only it isn't real history. Very few films marketed as authentic depictions of historical events—*Bonnie & Clyde*, *Braveheart*, *Titanic*, *A Beautiful Mind*, to name only a few—are authentic depictions of historical events. Most are mutilations of history. In the case of *The Bridge on the River Kwai*, the bridge wasn't destroyed by a team of commandos and it didn't even cross the River Kwai. But this much the film gets right: Japanese brutality in building the Bangkok to Rangoon (now known as Yangon) Railway. It is estimated that some two hundred thousand Asian civilians and sixty thousand Allied POWs were used as slave laborers in the building of the railway, and of these, as many as a third died from starvation, overwork, disease, or at the hands of their Japanese captors.

At Kanchanaburi, I found the bridge spanning a river about the width of the Thames and just as murky. In fact, the prisoners built two bridges, one of wood and one of steel. The former was a temporary structure while the latter is still very much in use. Tourists milled about, snapped selfies, and, a phenomenon common to Asia, women struck sexy poses for the camera of a friend or lover with the split-finger peace sign. This is baffling to me. On a beach or a cruise, I get it. But at a site of such a historic tragedy? No, I don't get that. I have seen this in places of unspeakable horror. I hope it is because they really just don't know better.

Pierre Boulle, whose novel *Bridge on the River Kwai* forms the basis for the film of the same name, never visited this site; the movie was filmed in Sri Lanka. Thus, he got his geography wrong. The bridge crosses the Mae Klong River. But with the movie's success, tourists began flocking to Thailand to see the real bridge. Locals, however, though eager to greet them and accept their money, had only the Bridge on the River Mae Klong to show them. So, in a bit of lateral thinking worthy of admiration, they renamed the Mae Klong. Problem solved! Consequently, today you can see the Bridge on the River Kwai, but locals know it's really just the Bridge on the Mae Klong. But *shhh!* Don't tell anyone.

I boarded the Railway of Death and headed northeast toward the Myanmar (formerly Burma) border. The train was crowded with mostly Thais commuting to and from Kanchanaburi. It's an old train and equipped accordingly, but not uncomfortably. The weather was hot, and the windows were down. That combined with the rhythmic *clickety-clack* of the train had a sedating effect. I looked out the window dreamily as the countryside, beautiful and exotic to the Western eye, rolled past. Paddies spread out across the plain and gumdrop mountains, hills really, perforated the horizon. I was intermittently nudged by someone trying to sell me something: a drink, a postcard, a lottery ticket. I just shook my head and pulled my hat down over my eyes.

At Tham Kra Sae, I got off and poked about, looking at the souvenir kiosks and the wooden trestle bridge before getting lunch along the river. I even rode an elephant. It was all so civilized. Especially the elephant.

In his war memoir *Goodbye, Darkness*, author William Manchester relates how, in the 1970s, he returned to the Pacific Islands where he fought as a U.S. Marine during the Second World War. These were places of torment for him and his fellow soldiers. Upon arrival in New Guinea, however, he was jarred to discover it had become a haven for wealthy vacationers. There were resorts, golf courses, and guided hikes into the jungles that had swallowed so many Americans and Japanese. A ride on the Railway of Death is similarly incongruous if you know anything of what happened in the building of it. There were no resorts or golf courses, but there was that same unreality to it all.

Back at Kanchanaburi, I found the two cemeteries where more than nine thousand Allied dead are interred. The manicured lawns rival those of the American cemetery at Normandy. Looking at graves randomly, I soon lost track of time. These were mostly British, Australian, and Dutch soldiers. They died building the railway. Some nameplates only held the inscription: KNOWN UNTO GOD. I tried to imagine the pain of those parents at home who received the dreaded knock at the door and the impersonal telegram informing them their son was missing in action or had perished in the fighting.

The museum to the fallen, while informative, is in a pathetic state of repair. This is true of so many similar monuments and museums worldwide. My, how the dead are soon forgotten. Pierre Boulle's book, though a novel and therefore not meant to be factually correct, nonetheless achieves something of historical importance: he brought attention to those who, without his book, would almost certainly be utterly forgotten as there would be no museum at all.

Back at the hotel, I sat down and began to write. I thought of the bridge, the railway, and the poor young men who died building them. Involuntarily, a Japanese phrase from the period, a mockery, came to my mind: "Be happy in your work." If you haven't already done so, watch *The Bridge on the River Kwai* and you'll know what that means.

CHAPTER 10

Malaysia: "Muddy Junction"

"Malaysia's status as a model of a moderate Muslim democracy is being called into question by a creeping Islamization ..."[1]

—Sholto Byrnes

Nobody thinks Malaysia is the greatest country in the world. Not even Malaysians. But it is an interesting country and, since I was on this side of the planet, I decided to make a brief stop there. Consider it a replacement for China. Besides, what is happening in this country is, for our purposes, very instructive.

The name of Malaysia's capital, Kuala Lumpur, means "muddy junction" or "muddy confluence" of two rivers, the Gombak and the Klang. That name serves as a nice metaphor for Malaysia as it is a confluence—a clash, really—of cultures. Malay, Chinese, Indian, and European influences are visible throughout the country. According to the 2010 population survey, most of the population of Malaysia practice Islam (61 percent), but Buddhists (19 percent), Christians (9 percent), and Hindus (6 percent) are all present.[2]

Though an ancient people, Malaysia is a young country. A British colony for a century, it suffered Japanese occupation from 1942 to 1945, returned to British rule after the war, and finally gained independence in 1957. Most Westerners, however, know none of that. For them, Kuala Lumpur is probably best known for the 1,483-foot Petronas Twin Towers. From 1998 to 2004, they were the tallest buildings in the world. Whatever notoriety that did not give them, Sean Connery and Catherine Zeta-Jones more than made up for in the 1999 caper *Entrapment*, where Connery and Jones climb all over the towers ninja-style, steal an ancient artifact and leave the Malay police looking like the Keystone Cops.

I negotiated a ride with a Chinese taxi driver named Lim Jie. For two days, we drove all over KL, seeing the major sites: the royal palace of Istana Negara; the KLCC Park and shopping mall; the Batu Caves; the KL Tower; Chinatown; the National Mosque of Malaysia; the Buddhist Temple at Thean Hou; the Golden Triangle; and the Petronas Towers.

Lim Jie proved interesting.

"Are you married?" I asked, making small talk.

He laughed bitterly, telegraphing that the question had an unhappy answer: "No."

"Why not?" He was fortyish, so I assumed he would have a wife and children.

"No money, no honey," he replied.

This is common throughout Asia. I have encountered this very term in China, Hong Kong, Korea, Japan, Singapore, and now here, where women often marry for financial security, not love.

"Asian women will date their not-so-wealthy peers to have fun," he explains. "But they will *never* marry you unless you own something like a nice apartment or you make a lot of money. So I date, yes, but none of those women would marry someone in my financial position."

By global standards, Lim does well for himself. He owns his taxi and he makes enough to lease an apartment in the city, but that is not enough to qualify him for marriage with the kind of woman he wants. So he dates and hopes to make it big someday. Like so many people all over the world, Lim hopes to immigrate to America and, in a stroke, change his fortunes.

"Chinese girls are very high maintenance," he said. "They want money, not love. No money, no honey."

He reflected for a moment and then as if a plan suddenly materialized in his head, he said, "I might marry a Thai woman. Thai women are much less difficult. They think they lucky to get a Chinese taxi driver!"

Since I had just come from Thailand, I suggested he take his taxi north and begin his romantic search—or at least try his chances on eHarmony or some Malaysian equivalent. He appeared to be considering it.

At the Batu Caves, an extraordinary Hindu Temple with a massive 140-foot statue of Lord Murugan, I climbed the seemingly endless steps to the caves while Lim worked on his plan. Tourists milled about taking selfies while others made offerings to the false gods and worshiped. From the top of the steps, I looked once again at Lord Murugan. The Hindu god of war, he is the equivalent of the Assyrian god Ashur, the Greek god Ares, and the Roman god Mars—but much, much bigger. I halfway expected to hear the cracking of stone and see Murugan taking steps forward, crushing tourists under his sandals like Talos in the Ray Harryhausen movie of my childhood. The big statue was creepy in the way all statues of pagan gods are creepy.

Lim's own Chinese folk religion seemed to be pluralistic. He offered his respects to everybody's god(s)—Allah, the tens of thousands (millions?) of Hindu deities, the Buddhist essence, and Jesus. When I tried to explain that Jesus and Allah both demanded exclusivity, he demurred. Lim simply preferred not to know. There was a pragmatism to his broad acceptance of all of these religions. In a country like Malaysia, he couldn't afford to make anyone unhappy.

Public morality in Malaysia is shaped by Islam, a religion no more indigenous to this country than it is to France or Germany. It is an oppressive feeling that makes Calvin's Geneva look like Vegas. The Qibla arrow on the ceiling in my hotel room pointed toward Mecca and a prayer mat hung in the closet. Five times a day, the muezzin calls out over loudspeakers: "Allahu Akbar! Allah is the greatest!"

I beg to differ. When you hear this annoying prayer blaring all over the city in the middle of the night—a sound that is very much like bad yodeling—you are tempted to take matters into your own hands as French actor Jean Dujardin did in one of the most politically incorrect (and hilarious) scenes in cinematic history. Yes, in the French film *OSS 117: Cairo, Nest of Spies*, Dujardin's character, awakened by this noise, beats up the offender. This scene is so politically incorrect I am shocked a French filmmaker would include it.

But I am glad he did.

CHAPTER 11

India: "Tea and Cricket"

"Now India is a place beyond all others where one must not take things too seriously—the midday sun always excepted."[1]

—Rudyard Kipling

India has always fascinated me. Of all the countries we visited on this expedition, India was the one I was looking forward to most. Perhaps this is, in part, due to early in life exposure to stories of the Indian subcontinent. Like other children of my generation, I saw Disney's *The Jungle Book* and eagerly read Kipling's adventure novel, *Kim. Rikki-Tikki-Tavi* was a late discovery for me, but I liked it, too. And since old movies were cool in my childhood home, George Stevens's 1939 buddy flick *Gunga Din* was one of my favorites.

India plays a role in the child's mind in a way Scandinavia, say, just doesn't. India seemed beautiful, vibrant, wild, endlessly diverse, the stuff of adventure, and the land where fortunes were made. Not even Spielberg's *Temple of Doom*, a lousy movie I saw as a teenager, could ruin it for me.

Of course, India is, in a way that only it could be, all of these things and none of them. Moreover, India is emerging as an economic powerhouse. Fortunes are indeed being made. Only America has more billionaires. In a 2007 visit to Oxford University, I attended a lecture by Michael Wood, the celebrated historian and documentary filmmaker, who was promoting his then-new BBC series *The Story of India*. Speaking of modern India, Wood used phrases like "global power" and "great democracy" and characterized the country's future in extraordinarily optimistic terms. I left Wood's presentation wondering if India was, as he seemed to believe, the future source of freedom and civilization. A decade later, I was landing in Delhi to see for myself.

Zachary had rejoined me, and we were supposed to go to Mumbai for a few days before coming to the north of the country. But seasonal monsoon flooding necessitated a change in plans. That meant our stay in Delhi would be longer than initially anticipated, and with such a brutal travel schedule, the opportunity to stay in one place, *in one time zone* for more than a few days was appealing. And this was India, after all, not Syria.

If your Indian point of entry is a major city, your first impressions of the country are strikingly physical in nature. A heat that envelops you. The incessant (and thus pointless) use of car horns. The stench of body odor and old cars coughing-out black fumes, the fragrance of fashionable ladies, and spicy food. The epic vehicular chaos that is of a sort I have only witnessed in Africa and Vietnam. Moving amidst all of it are beautiful, exotic people and the grotesquely disfigured who are ignored by all except those of us who aren't used to seeing them. A man with feet swollen to a size I would not have thought possible wheeled himself along on a wooden cart as a boy with only one foot hopped beside me, hand out. A big, shiny Mercedes purred nearby as if to put an exclamation on this picture of life at the economic extremities.

Welcome to India.

Like much of Asia, India is a collision of Eastern and Western styles, customs, and attitudes. Today that influence is largely American, but Western influence began with the British and predates the founding of the United States. Britain officially ruled India for a century, but unofficially dominated the subcontinent for much longer through the East India Company. No corporation has ever wielded such power—not Google, Amazon, or Apple. As a consequence, although British colonial rule ended in 1947, the influence of that once powerful island in the North Atlantic is everywhere. But not everyone wants to acknowledge the fact.

"Did the British contribute anything positive to India?" I asked an Indian historian over lunch in Delhi.

"Yes," he said with a wry smile. "Tea and cricket."

Of course, as my Indian friend would begrudgingly admit, the British contributed a great deal more to this country and the creation of its modern manifestation—the English language, not Hindi or Urdu or any of the other one thousand languages, remains the lingua franca; much of the architecture is from that period or emulates it; social sensibilities among elements of the upper classes mimic those of the British; and the unity and administration of the country. The British brought with them ideas integral to the Judeo-Christian worldview: equality, freedom, human dignity, and value. As such, they condemned some traditional Indian (mostly Hindu) customs as immoral while instituting others infused with these ideals:

- In 1829, the British outlawed *suttee*, the Hindu practice whereby a widow is burned on the funeral pyre of her deceased husband.

- In 1856, British law allowed widows to remarry.

- In 1870, the Female Infanticide Act was passed to reduce the prevalence of this all-too-common Indian practice.

- In 1872, inter-caste marriages were permitted.

- In 1929, child marriages were banned.

These laws were largely the result of pressure from Christian missionaries who, though unsuccessful in converting this country to their faith, were nonetheless successful in converting many of its laws to reflect the core values of that religion. Like Japan after the Second World War, women were the greatest beneficiaries as the above laws would suggest. They were also given greater access to education.

But the passing of laws and enforcing them are two very different things. India regularly ranks as one of the worst countries in the world for females. This ranking is, in part, because the very practices the British were trying to eliminate are still shockingly common, especially in rural India. Add to this the epidemic of rape, a crime that often goes unreported and unprosecuted in India, and you get a picture of a country that, while endlessly interesting, is great only in the sense of *substantial, large,* or *sizable.*

It was our good fortune to stay at the Imperial Hotel in New Delhi. There are five-star hotels and then there is the Imperial. To step into the Imperial is to step back in time. The hotel is rich in history and just plain rich. Full of artifacts from the British Raj, it is a museum unto itself. Large paintings and prints of battles, landscapes, and colorful figures fill the walls; gifts from the British monarchy are found throughout the property; employees wear the fashion of a bygone era.

In the atrium breakfast room, among all the wicker furniture, one finds a white marble-topped wrought iron table. It seems out of place. But should you drink tea there, you will be informed by one of the many servers that you are honored to sit where India's first Prime Minister, Jawaharlal Nehru (who had a permanent residence within the hotel) regularly drank tea with Mahatma Gandhi and the British Viceroy, Lord Mountbatten. It was there they discussed the terms of the pending partition of India, which created an independent India and a new country, Pakistan, in 1947. Given the fact two of the three men, Gandhi and Mountbatten, would be assassinated, perhaps drinking tea at that table is not good luck.

When staying in dangerous countries or ones wholly unfamiliar to you, spend the extra money and acquire accommodations in a top-notch hotel. Think of it as insurance. Such hotels take your security seriously because their reputations depend on it. You can leave your belongings with confidence, plunge into a busy, dirty, and often unsafe city, and return to a clean room, clean water shower, and food prepared for your much more sensitive constitution. In the case of the Imperial, there are barriers to prevent car bombs, numerous security checkpoints, metal detectors, and people whose job it is to make sure the only people in the hotel are supposed to be there. Also, a good concierge will prevent you from making the mistakes common to Westerners.

"Where are you going today, Mr. Taunton?" the concierge asked.

"I am going to the Jama Mosque and then for a bite to eat."

"Our car will take you. No additional charge. May I recommend a restaurant? And, please, Mr. Taunton, please advise your son not to eat any street food."

This was for our safety, both physical and gastronomical. Zachary and I like Indian food. I grew to like it as a student in London eating on the famed Brick Lane. There, one negotiates the price of his meal as he often does in India. But the truly authentic

Indian food will burn a hole in your stomach—unless you are inured to its effects. Listen to the concierge.

"Yikes!" Zachary said, his eyes watering as he appeared to be choking. We were out at a highly recommended restaurant in Old Delhi.

"That is hot!" he gasped, pointing at a curry.

I am prepared to take many risks, but not when it comes to eating. There's no quicker way to ruin a good trip than Montezuma's Revenge. Stick to bottled water, packaged foods, and reputable restaurants when exploring in the third world.[i]

Zachary and I dispensed with the hotel car, handy though it was, and went our own way. Sometimes we did things together; other times we split-up to cover more ground. This often led to very different experiences. While I was speaking to a group in Auckland, for instance, Zachary was BASE jumping from the Sky Tower.

In one of our crazier adventures, I convinced a rickshaw driver to get in the back and let me pedal him around Old Delhi. This was a harder sell than you might think, since Old Delhi's traffic is insane, and they aren't confident a Westerner is up for the challenge. But I discovered that for ten bucks, a fatalistic Hindu is prepared to let even a Christian drive.[ii]

As I was pedaling furiously through the streets and alleys near the Jama Mosque, my driver sitting in the back laughing or screaming for his life—I never did determine which it was since I dared not turn to look—Zachary was having an adventure of an altogether different sort: a couple of young men, having tried to yank his camera out of his hands, decided to follow and then chase

---

i   I ignored my own rule in Japan and ate barbequed eel. Though hardly a third world country, my stomach was not used to this particular Japanese dish, and I felt sick for a few hours afterward.

ii   To do this well, you must do a lot of shouting. At everyone. Rickshaw drivers are like the cabbies of New York City in this regard.

him through the spice market. The spice market is labyrinthine thus it is an ideal setting for the hunted. Zachary darted into a kiosk and waited them out.

On another occasion, I stepped out of a restaurant on a busy street in Old Delhi (they are all busy) and, no kidding, a cow strolled by, and right behind it stepped a man who opened a basket from which sprang two cobras.

"Touch them, sir! They will not hurt you!" the turbaned charmer pleaded.

I leaped back. "Hell, no!" I shouted. "I'm not touching your snakes!"

The great Jules Verne said, "It may be taken for granted that, rash as the Americans are, when they are prudent there is good reason for it."[2] To this I will add my own advice: when visiting a foreign land, do not touch the snakes of strange men.

Whether it is a journey like ours or a vacation to the beach, you will remember these little incidents fondly and laugh about them for years to come—not the quiet museums or the calm group tours. If your trip is without mishaps, without some element of surprise or mystery, hope for better luck next time because that trip will be quickly forgotten.

Having survived our self-guided tours, we took a train to Agra to see the famed Taj Mahal. The train stations are teeming with people, many of whom are beggars, aggressively touching and grabbing at you much like the prostitutes of Bangkok. Leaving the station, one sees a very different India. But for a few upscale districts, one finds extraordinary poverty and suffering in both the city and the countryside, though it is much worse in the latter.

Entering the Taj Mahal grounds, Zachary headed off to take some photos while I spoke to a local guide. After an hour or so, I began to wonder where Zachary was, so I started looking around. Then I saw him, flanked by two militiamen, appearing distressed and speaking in an impassioned manner. One of the militiamen held his camera.

I do not consider myself a hot-tempered man. But nothing gets me fired-up so quickly as an injustice, especially if it is done to my family. With urgency, I jogged toward them.

"What seems to be the problem here?" I asked.

"Who are you?" the one who was apparently in charge asked.

"I am his father."

"He took my camera and won't give it back," Zachary said, clearly upset. And with good reason. The camera was very expensive.

"He cannot do this," the officer said.

"Do what?" I asked. "Take photos? They inspected the bag before we came in, the camera, too, and said it was fine if we didn't take any videos."

"What is this?" the officer said, handling the microphone on the front of the camera. "Your son says that it is a dead squirrel. You cannot have 'squirrels' in here."

I smiled at the misunderstanding. "That's just a slang term for that kind of mic. That fuzzy cover is to buffer the wind. We call it a 'dead squirrel' because it looks like a dead squirrel."

He laughed. "We just mess with you! You okay! Can we have a picture?"

He returned the camera and we all posed for a photo. They were clearly bored, and this playful harassment broke the tedium.

The Taj Mahal, a mausoleum, is rightly considered one of the so-called "Wonders of the World." Built between 1631 and 1648, it is made of white marble and sits on the south bank of the Yamuna River. Situated as it is on the plains of Agra, it doesn't compete with a city's skyline or mountains that might distract one's gaze, though, beautiful as it is, that seems rather unlikely in any event. Mughal Emperor Shah Jahan ordered its construction to memorialize his much-beloved wife. Like her moods, it is said the mausoleum's marble changes color depending on the time of day and temperature. It was pale when we saw it, which is fitting because she is dead.

After some inspection of the city of Agra, we returned to the Imperial without further incident, noting the countryside from the train. Kipling's observation about the midday sun is spot-on and sometimes the trains are just as bad. Bottled water is sold cheaply on the trains and in the stations, and we drank a lot of it.

Each morning, we enjoyed tea at Gandhi's table—or is it Nehru's or Mountbatten's?—and then explored the city. A hotel car is great when you can get it, but a rickshaw is better. Riding a rickshaw through Old Delhi—for safety reasons, I wouldn't recommend doing it any other way—is an experience not to be forgotten.[iii] Guidebooks will speak of this in charming terms, and, if you're a Westerner, it will seem like the stuff of a Visa commercial. The kaleidoscope of color, the pungent smell of the Khari Baoli spice market, and the utter chaos of it all will captivate you.

But you're looking at it all from a safe distance. In no way does it reflect your life. Look closer. Poke around down the alleyways. Skip the tourist spots where money flows and see what conditions are really like. Rats, mice, open sewage—it's all there. And the countryside is, as I say, worse. This is poverty to a degree and on a scale few Americans have ever seen or even think possible. India is a country of *haves* and *have-nots*, and the *haves* have almost everything. It reminded me of the squalor in which we found our

---

iii   Rickshaws aren't just for tourists. They are a common and effective form of transportation in India (and elsewhere). The traffic in India can be deadly for any pedestrian, tourist or otherwise. A rickshaw keeps you where you need to be, and it enables you to protect your belongings while snapping photos from time to time. Petty theft is a major industry in India, and Westerners offer easy and lucrative targets.

daughter, Sasha, before we adopted her from an orphanage in Odessa, Ukraine.

The memory of my daughter's life in similar conditions was brought powerfully home to me when I was reading on a train. Before we left the station, a metallic rap on my window startled me. I turned to see two Indian boys begging. They gesticulated wildly and, ultimately defeated by the reality that my window did not open, they posed for my camera. With 65 percent of India's population under the age of thirty-five, India is full of such children. Mothers and fathers exploit them, sending them into the streets to beg while cars pause—*or don't*—at traffic lights. India has the highest number of road fatalities in the world. There are many reasons for this—the indifference of Hindus to their personal safety (they walk casually into oncoming traffic); the fact that lines on the roads mean nothing (cars go five-wide on a three-lane as if at Talladega); and the bat-out-of-hell driving (without seatbelts, of course). But it's not hard to imagine that many of these deaths are the children who dart between the cars unseen because their height does not reach window level.

A central premise of our expedition is the idea that human nature is the same the world over. What changes just like time zones are the ideas that form the basic assumptions of a given people or a nation. Once an idea is ingested by a society, its effects play out in the life of that culture. Islam, for instance, produces one type of society while socialism produces another. India is a country that has absorbed *a lot* of bad ideas. Eighty percent of the country is Hindu, and the beliefs of that religion—a belief in fate most of all—have given rise to a caste system that still exists, stultified intellectual and economic growth, and continues to weigh-down India's transition to modernity.

The people? Grand. The history? Fascinating. Should you visit? Absolutely. Even so, in spite of Michael Wood's rosy forecast—and

I should stress I am a great admirer of Wood's work—India is unquestionably a generally backward, undeveloped, third world country. If India is to be the future of freedom and civilization, it is, I fear, in the very distant future.

CHAPTER 12

Russia:
The Mother of All
Socialist Countries

*"Whenever you are unhappy, go to Russia. Anyone who has come to
understand that country will be content to live anywhere else."*

—Marquis de Custine, 1839

The Marquis clearly knew his subject well. Unfortunately, it
was time for us to head to the country the Marquis so loathed.
Russia certainly isn't a contender for the title of the world's greatest
country. Trust me, I have been there many times. Even so, it was
an essential stop on our tour because it is the mother of all socialist
states, and with socialism all the rage in the Democratic Party these
days, review of that philosophy and its origins seems long overdue.

Now, eleven countries into our *Around the World in 80 Days*
journey, we had become a bit numb to the constant long-haul air
travel and hotel rooms. Airline check-in notifications appeared
in my inbox every few days and piled-up unopened. But this one
caught my attention:

Aeroflot: Delhi to Moscow

I have made a lifelong point of avoiding Russia's infamous airline Aeroflot. How did this booking happen? I'd sooner ride the wing of a biplane naked than fly on this old Soviet-era deathtrap.

"What's the difference between a SCUD missile and Aeroflot?" begins a Russian joke.

"I don't know," comes the reply.

"Aeroflot has killed more people."

Such cynical jokes exist for a reason. The Soviet government, which owned the airline, wasn't particularly concerned with the central component of airline profitability: safety. According to the Airline Crashes Record Office, 8,231 passengers have died on Aeroflot flights.[1] Air France, another government-owned airline, is a distant second with 1,783. Of course, the Soviets didn't need to be concerned with safety since Aeroflot was the only airline for the whole of the Soviet Union. If you were an unfortunate citizen of that country who needed to travel from, say, Leningrad to Moscow, none of your options were reassuring.

You could drive, but only an idiot would do that. Soviet-era cars were legendarily bad. Consider this Russian joke:

"How do you double the value of a Russian car?"

"How?"

"Fill-up the tank."

Or this one:

"What do you call a Russian car on a hill?"

"What?"

"A miracle."

This is to say nothing of Russian roads. Given the choice of being beaten with hammers or driving for hours on Russian roads, choose the beating with hammers. You'll have fewer bruises.

You could make the journey by train. This was the safest option, but unless you were one of the Communist Party bosses or a member of one of their families, your conditions were scarcely better than that of illegal immigrants sealed in cargo containers and shipped across the south Texas border midsummer. The railcars often had women whose job, it seemed, was to ensure everyone was miserable. They watched you and barked at you for perceived offenses. And nothing was more offensive than the restrooms on these trains. One look at them and you wanted to yell at her. Trying to hit the toilet from a standing position while the train jerked and swayed—Soviet trains were never smooth—took skill. The urine sloshing on the floor around your shoes was proof few possessed such skill. My advice? Wear wellies. Worse, the toilets, when flushed, emptied directly onto the tracks or right beside them. Imagine the surprise of poor innocents out for a walk discussing the latest food shortage who were suddenly bespattered by sixty-mile-an-hour projectiles.

That left flying, which meant Aeroflot. Hate capitalism's monopolies? Try socialist monopolies. Begin to see the problem?

Twenty-six years after the collapse of the Soviet Union, I still wasn't keen on flying the airline whose planes Nikita Khrushchev called "embarrassing insects" when compared to those used by Dwight Eisenhower. But with neither automobile nor train as realistic options, I was committed. So it was with surprise I read how Aeroflot has become one of the safest airlines[2] in the world. More amazing still was seeing their fleet of sleek, new Airbuses parked neatly in a row. If the old products issued from this part of the world were symbolic of the failure of socialism—and they were—these sparkling planes, non-Russian though they were, gave a strong indication of the New Russia I was about to enter.

After a pleasant six-hour nonfatal flight, Zachary and I collected our luggage and hailed a taxi. The freshly built boulevard between Sheremetyevo International Airport and Moscow was a further indication of change. And our hotel, near Red Square, only reinforced the growing impression that Russia was different. Newly renovated like everything else in central Moscow, the service was good, efficient, and friendly. This alone was enough to make me wonder if Russians had been supplanted by the Japanese. Most un-Russian of all, everything in the hotel room actually *worked*.

Shortly after checking in, I took Zachary for a walk to show him around, explaining bits and pieces of history as we went. I was struck by the extraordinary changes since I was last here a decade ago—Audis, BMWs, Chevys, Fords, Lexuses could all be seen, not just the crap from the Soviet period. More remarkably, drivers seemed to stay in their lanes. The GUM, the famous shopping mall that once hawked bad Soviet products, now has Chanel, Prada, Breitling, Rolex, Louis Vuitton, and similar things I neither can afford, nor want. (Except for a Breitling. Yes, I'd like one of those.) And for the proletarians, there is KFC, Starbucks, Subway and, my personal favorite, Krispy Kreme.

Even Comrade Lenin, whose dead body lies like a medical school cadaver near the Kremlin Wall only a couple of ICBMs away from these bourgeois enterprises, looked less like the roadkill I saw on previous visits. As if to mock his memory still further, Lenin, Marx, and Stalin impersonators worked the tourists nearby. They've been doing it since the nineties. Strictly capitalists, these guys will, if you're a savvy negotiator, pose for photographs for a hundred rubles ($1.75) per shot. While I cannot be certain of it, I thought I saw Lenin turn over in his coffin beneath the glass of the macabre display case that houses him—or what is left of him.

But it is all a Potemkin Village, to use a good Russian term. It's not exactly fraudulent. The changes in Russia are real. Russia is, like China, abandoning socialism and is finally embracing capitalism, and they are doing it in a very big way. But, like the Chinese, they are endeavoring to combine it with totalitarianism. And by every other meaningful measure, the New Russia is a lot like the

Old Russia; they just have better stuff. More alarmingly, there is a growing nostalgia for the iron-fisted days of the Soviet Union.

"What is your opinion of Lenin?" a twenty-six-year-old Muscovite asked me.

"You should be glad he's dead."

He looked annoyed. "Lenin and Stalin did some good things, though, don't you agree?"

I shook my head. "No. No, I don't."

He thought for a moment, a troubled look on his face. "Our current regime is becoming a lot like it was in Soviet times in that you must be careful once again what you say. [Putin] says we have enemies. But freedom isn't everything. Security matters, too." With that conversational flourish, for him, all was right with the world and he was chipper once again. This sort of reasoning is much more typical than you might think.

Russian cities like Moscow and St. Petersburg are a visual feast with the colorful onion domes of St. Basil's and the Church of the Savior on Spilled Blood, the illuminated walls of the Kremlin, the Peter and Paul Fortress, and the sparkling waters of the Moskva and Neva Rivers, but they hide a sinister history. A seventeenth-century traveler to Russia wrote this in his journal: "When you observe the spirit, the mores, the way of life of the Russians, you are bound to number them among the barbarians."[3] As harsh as that is, Russia's history provides little reason to reject his assessment.

Returning to my Moscow hotel one evening, I was jarringly reminded of how little this country has really changed. As I entered the lobby, it soon became clear the place was full of prostitutes hoping to snag Western businessmen. Even if it isn't the oldest profession, it seems to be the oldest, and most prevalent, in Russia. Indeed, I have never stayed in a Russian hotel where this was not the case, be it a hotel of the two-star or five-star variety. It's part of Russia's vast "black economy," that is, those off-the-books activities where everyone profits: the pimps, the security and police who look the other way, and the hotels that lend the women rooms for their transactions.

All this—the despotism, the genocides committed by successive socialist regimes, the suppression of dissenting voices, backwardness, the mind-blowing corruption, and the ongoing exploitation of women—can be attributed to the fact Russia is not now, nor has it ever been, truly Christian. It is that faith that gave birth to the West as we know it. By contrast, Russia's religious experience has been altogether different. Let me explain.

Historians have long regarded 988 as one of the most fateful dates in the history of Eastern Europe. It was in that year Vladimir, Prince of Kievan Rus (think modern Russia), converted to Greek Orthodoxy and Russia with him. The consequences were far-reaching and devastating in effect because it forever separated Russia from the Western world culturally and linguistically. Hence, they never experienced the Renaissance, the Reformation, the Enlightenment, the Scientific Revolution, the Industrial Revolution, or the French man purse craze.

Consequently, Russia has been characterized by perpetual backwardness. Neither fully Western nor fully Eastern, Russia has, throughout its history, been unstable, oscillating between Western liberal reforms and what Marx called "Oriental despotism."

By the twentieth century, Russia lagged behind the West by a good two centuries. The earliest rumblings of the Industrial Revolution could be heard in England in the 1740s. They would not be heard in Russia in earnest until the first of the Five-Year Plans in 1928.

Furthermore, Russians have shown a remarkable tolerance, bordering on indifference, for regimes that are corrupt, deny civil liberties, grant few political freedoms, and make a habit of killing *a lot* of people. In this respect, Putin is just the latest iteration of a longstanding Russian tradition. Like those before him, he has gradually consolidated power, has become Russia's longest-ruling leader since Stalin, and is rapidly building the cult of his personality. Meanwhile, Lenin is still on display and many Russians still show up to venerate him. They'd do better offering their respects to Jack the Ripper or Lizzy Borden. At least they killed several million fewer people.

What were the theological implications of 988? Greek Orthodoxy, as practiced by the Russians, has had a history of xenophobia, a strong strain of anti-Semitism, and otherworldliness in the extreme. It is a religion without grace, of ritual obedience, with little connection to the Bible, and worship of an impersonal god who is unknown and unknowable. In other words, it is typically not very Christian.

The keystone that sits atop the grand archway of authentic Christianity is grace. Without grace, Christianity is reduced to mere religion and is as hollow as the many Orthodox cathedrals and churches that, today, are little more than tourist attractions. The absence of an authentic, robust, vibrant Christianity in Russia made it much more susceptible to the virus of socialism.

I am, of course, well aware of the fact there are many who confuse socialism with Christianity. Such people usually have only a cursory understanding of what one or the other really is. Typically, this is predicated on the erroneous notion that Christianity's chief purpose is in meeting physical needs. This is not so. Christianity's main object is the regeneration and development of the soul. That Christianity and socialism are often confused, however, has not escaped the attention of socialists who have frequently sought to capitalize on the misunderstanding. As for "Christian socialism," it is only a name. One may be a Christian or he may be a socialist, but he can no more be a Christian and a socialist than he can be both a Yankees and a Red Sox fan. At least, he cannot be simultaneously faithful to each party.

Indeed, far from being compatible with Christianity, socialist regimes, Russia's most of all, have historically sought the expulsion of Christianity from public life. Christianity, by its very nature, is subversive insofar as it teaches there is a God whose laws supersede those of man—any man. As I pointed out in the chapter on China, this goes far to explain the antipathy of communist and fascist regimes to Christianity. They well understand Christians do not recognize the power of the state as absolute. Moreover, where temporal law and eternal law are in conflict, the Christian may, in good conscience, violate the former while clinging to the latter.

It is much for the better of us all that many have done so. History is full of examples of courageous Christian men and women who, at the risk of their own lives, sought the destruction of evil laws and regimes. By contrast, socialism exalts the state in the place of God. This stands in opposition to a traditional American view of government, where, as Alexis de Tocqueville observed more than a century ago, "as soon as a man has acquired some education and pecuniary resources…all that he asks of the state is not to be disturbed in his toil." And although the American government has at no time been Christian, it has historically respected the role Christianity has played in public life. Socialism, however, by making the state both the means and the end, violates the very First Commandment: "You shall have no other gods before me." It then proceeds to violate the other nine with wild abandon.

Advocates of socialism always want to point to Scandinavia and dismiss Russia and China and Cuba and a dozen other socialist states as countries that imperfectly applied a perfect system. But such logic won't do. The failure of socialism is not only a wholly unjustified confidence in human government but socialism also begins with an antithetical premise to Christianity; *there is no God.* Fyodor Dostoevsky observed this connection between atheism and socialism long ago: "Socialism is not merely the labor question, it is before all things the atheistic question, the question of the form taken by atheism today, the question of the Tower of Babel built without God, not to mount to Heaven from earth, but to set up Heaven on earth."

In other words, socialism is much more than an economic or political question. It is a spiritual question, if only because it denies the very existence of the spiritual. A former socialist revolutionary, Dostoevsky knew his subject well. Upon his conversion to Christianity, he did more than renounce his atheism; he renounced socialism because it was, in his view, atheism masquerading as political philosophy. In his great novels *Demons* (also known as *The Possessed*) and *The Brothers Karamazov*, Dostoevsky predicted that if Russia's communists (i.e., socialists) ever gained control of the levers of power, it would lead to the expulsion of Christianity from public life, and with it, the annihilation of morality, the rise of totalitarianism, and the proliferation of state-sponsored genocide. He would prove prophetic.

Socialism's whole trajectory hits wide of the intended mark. And how could it do otherwise? In the biblical worldview, the state is a temporal institution meant to serve man, an eternal being. In the socialist model, this is reversed: man, a temporal being, serves the eternal state.

Although modern Russia has largely abandoned socialism, the attitudes, the mechanisms, and the historic propensity to choose totalitarianism over freedom, these things are all quite intact. Worse, Russia is trending away from freedom. Another Russian joke sums this up well:

"How does every Russian joke begin?"

"How?"

"By looking over your shoulder."

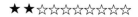

CHAPTER 13

Britain: America Fast-Forwarded

"This blessed plot, this earth, this realm, this England."

—John of Gaunt in William Shakespeare's *Richard II*

London is a relatively short four-hour flight from Moscow, and Zachary and I were looking forward to getting there. Lauri and my daughter, Sasha, were meeting us, and after such a long separation, the reunion would be a happy one. We also love this city. I was a student here as an undergraduate studying history. My work brings me here about twice a year. I love the theaters, the restaurants, and the history. But as much as I love London, I increasingly find it remarkably un-English, un-British, and uncivilized.

Throughout much of its history, the story of England has been one of remarkable good fortune. Indeed, when considering the scope of the tiny island nation's success, one is tempted to conclude there must have been some unseen hand of providence guiding it all. Consider the geography that preserved it time and again from the calamities of the European continent. The gritty independent spirit the Romans could never fully eradicate. The hearty Christian civilization somehow survived the waves of

118

Viking invasions, converted the Vikings, and gave birth to English Common Law, constitutional monarchy, the Reformation, the Scientific and Industrial Revolutions, and numerous reform movements expanding the rights and liberties of its people. Britain also carried a faith that produced a national character and identity propelling the country to extraordinary heights.

And it is a story of faith, specifically, Christian faith. Britain gave us such notables as St. Patrick, St. Ninian, St. Columba, Alfred the Great, William of Ockham, John Wycliffe, William Tyndale, John Knox, Hugh Latimer, Susanna Wesley, John and Charles Wesley, George Whitefield, John Newton, Elizabeth Fry, Florence Nightingale, William Wilberforce, Queen Victoria, William Gladstone, David Livingstone, Charles Spurgeon, Catherine Booth, William Booth, J. R. R. Tolkien, C. S. Lewis, and John Stott.

This is by no means an exhaustive list. These were men and women who shaped the soul and the destiny of a nation, lifting it to greatness. As we have traveled around the world, we have seen its (mostly positive) influence in New Zealand, Australia, Hong Kong, India, and even in Nigeria. Britain was once Christian in a way that France, for example, never was.

But that was then, this is now. Queen Elizabeth II, who has reigned so long and with such dignity, is, perhaps, the last of this breed. Her son, Prince Charles, is typical of the vapid type that has, in successive generations, discarded the Christian legacy bequeathed to them. He will be, he once said, "Defender of faiths," not "Defender of *the* Faith." How appallingly modern. This oh-so-politically-correct statement, meant to reassure the non-Christian population of Britain, is representative of the multicultural mindset. It is an empty statement since religions—especially Islam, the religion that seemed foremost in his mind—say very different things about the character of God, salvation, mankind, government, and freedom. One simply cannot affirm them all as equally valid. On the contrary, Islam undermines the principles of freedom and democracy. But such objections are dismissed in a Western world lacking a core identity.

To visit London is to be jarringly reminded of these things. It's a city of enough statues to keep the anarchist Antifa mobs in America busy toppling them for years. I was powerfully struck by the clash of civilizations—both British—some years ago when I was leading a walking tour of the city. Asked about a statue along the Embankment, I explained it was General Charles Gordon, who was killed and beheaded in Khartoum in 1885 while fighting the radical Muslim forces of Muhammad Ahmad, the Osama bin Laden of the nineteenth century. You see, the violence of Islam is hardly a recent phenomenon as is often alleged. It is as old as the religion. In this particular Gordon statue—there are several in the former colonies—he holds a Bible. How ironic that the nation he once sought to defend from Islam will, by 2035, have more Muslims than Christians.[1]

What happened?

Obsessed with the guilt of the past abuses of imperialism, Britain's atonement took on an extreme form of self-loathing, leading her to abandon her faith and, with it, her strength and identity. Worse, it led her to embrace all she was not—a faith alien to democratic principles, an unequal union at the cost of her sovereignty, and willful blindness to the fact her laws and values are being undermined from within. The Britain of today bears no resemblance to the confident nation that built not only much of what remains of London but much of the world. The nation that stamped out slavery and gave us our legal, literary, and religious heritage is now a country with little sense of its past, much less its future.

I was in a taxi in central London when the driver made an ill-advised turn onto Piccadilly where thousands of demonstrators clogged this main artery in one of the world's great capital cities. At first, the protesters kept to the opposite side of the road, but soon they engulfed the whole width of this fashionable boulevard, bringing traffic to a stop.

They carried signs with such clever slogans as:

"F—k Trump!"

"Feed Your Trump Rage with Enthusiasm!"

"P*ssy Power!"

"Say No to Fascism! Say No to Racism!"

And then there was my favorite:

"Love Trumps Hate!"

The irony of this was too rich with the many expressions of hate emanating from the signage of this mob.

"They need to get jobs," my taxi driver said angrily.

His frustration was understandable. Here he was, trying to earn a living, and protesters were preventing it. But he was wrong on one point. A well-heeled lot, there was little kinship between these people and the poor, hungry masses who populated these same streets in the mid-nineteenth century and about whom Dickens wrote. On the contrary, whether it was from their parents, the lottery, or steady employment, they clearly had some means of income.

"Look at them with their lattes," my driver continued. "Who is oppressing them? Why not protest the Muslims who really are oppressing people? But you won't see them do that. They haven't the balls to do it."

Given that it was largely a parade of women, they certainly didn't. Even so, this man was proving to be Rush Limbaugh with a British accent.

With thousands of people now on every side of this iconic black taxi, I paid Limbaugh-the-cabbie and got out. Bracing myself against the car, I pushed off as if from the side of a pool, squared my shoulders, and moved in the opposite direction of this human onslaught. London hadn't been stormed like this since the Celtic Queen Boadicea sacked and burned the place in 61 AD. Of course, her motley crew wasn't neatly outfitted in Ralph Lauren like these modern pillagers were and she didn't stop to take selfies, either. She also had some justification—her daughters were raped by the Roman occupiers. But the taxi driver was right: who was oppressing these people? And what was their objective?

"Anarchy," said one astute Londoner.

Plowing through the crowd, I cut across Green Park and flagged down another taxi. He got me no farther than the Old Admiralty Building where, once again, I had to abandon the car. Having given up hope of reaching my original destination, I doubled-back toward the city center. The streets were littered with the trash of the people protesting—among a litany of other things—Trump's apparent disregard for the environment.

All of this was oddly misdirected and out of any sense of proportion. Christians are being slaughtered in the third world; the unborn are being slaughtered in the womb and, occasionally, outside of it; and these protesters saw the tampon tax—no kidding—as a sign of oppression and Donald Trump as a would-be Hitler. But it was all so contrived. As C. L. Bryant, radio host and former NAACP leader told me:

"These people want to act as if they are fighting against a racist and sexist regime, but those battles have been waged and won. There are no doors closed to women or to people of color in this generation that were once closed to my generation."

Led by the richest of the rich Hollywood types, they had no idea what real oppression actually looks like. So, they manufactured it, believing if they said it enough, it would be true.

Perhaps they should have been paying closer attention to what was happening 170 miles north of their protest. There, in South Yorkshire, is the city of Rotherham. Prior to 2012, Rotherham was a city unknown to most of the world. Today, the name is associated with scandal, some of the worst (known) mass child abuse in modern history, and a nation's deep shame.

In that year, *The Times* (of London) unearthed one of the dirty secrets of multiculturalism and an indiscriminate immigration policy. Under the explosive headline "Police Files Reveal Vast Child Protection Scandal," *Times* journalist Andrew Norfolk reported:

> Confidential police reports and intelligence files that reveal a hidden truth about the sale and extensive use of English children for sex are exposed today. They show that for more than a decade organised groups of men were able to groom, pimp and traffic girls across the country with virtual impunity. Offenders were identified to police but not prosecuted. A child welfare expert, speaking under condition of anonymity, said that agencies' reluctance to tackle such street grooming networks was "the biggest child protection scandal of our time". The *Times* has published several articles about a pattern of crimes across northern England and the Midlands involving groups of men, largely of Pakistani heritage, and the sexual abuse of white girls aged from 12 to 16.[2]

The "child welfare expert speaking under conditions of anonymity" was Jane Senior, a Rotherham social worker, who detected a pattern in the at-risk adolescent girls with whom her agency dealt. Mostly from broken homes and in state foster care, the files she surreptitiously delivered to Norfolk revealed that since 1997, local authorities knew about, but ignored, the "industrial-scale" rape and trafficking of no less than fourteen hundred white British girls. Traffickers maintained control of these girls with the injection of drugs, physical abuse, and threats, with at least one girl being taken into the countryside where gasoline was dumped on her while her assailant held a match and warned her of the consequences should she tell anyone about her rape. Girls who reported their abuse to local police were ignored, told to stop wasting police time, or, as one was told: "Don't worry—you aren't the first girl to be raped by XX and you won't be the last."[3] As sophisticated as any mafia, Muslim-run restaurants and taxi services facilitated the trafficking of girls, and it soon became clear some Muslim police officers were complicit in these operations.[4]

As Rotherham's police and the city council (who knew very well of these abuses) fell under media scrutiny, excuses for their inaction ranged from fear of charges of Islamophobia to an unwillingness to force British cultural norms on people who do not share those values. Said one police officer: "There was an educational issue. Asian males didn't understand that it was wrong and the girls were not quite there [past puberty]. They were difficult groups to deal with. We can't enforce our way out of the problem."[5]

In other words, reigning political sensitivities led some officers and council members to the conclusion that they must respect the fact the raping of pubescent girls is part of the cultural heritage of the men in question.

The scandal sparked a nationwide debate with many accusing Andrew Norfolk—and, when her identity was revealed, Jane Senior—of racism.[6] Any thought of the girls was overshadowed by progressives who rushed to defend multiculturalism, Islam, and an idiotic immigration policy. This was the failure of political correctness writ large. Perhaps they learned from the experience.

Not at all.

As reports of these abuses were picked up by other media outlets, the criminal gang members were often identified with the broad brush "Asian" men for fear of charges of Islamophobia. But Sikhs, Hindus, and Chinese people peaceably living in the English Midlands quite rightly insisted reports be more specific. These were not random Asians; they were, in every instance, Muslim men, and overwhelmingly men of Pakistani heritage. That media trend has continued to the present. Writing on behalf of the Network of Sikh Organizations in 2018, Hardeep Singh said:

> This cowardly nonspecific description of the perpetrators continues to be used in the British press, to describe men of predominantly Pakistani Muslim heritage convicted in grooming gang cases. We believe this is in part due to the fear of offending Muslims…. The common denominator in such cases is the deliberate targeting of non-Muslim girls, which we believe should be categorised by the police as a hate crime.[7]

"Cowardly" is exactly the right word. Singh, speaking on behalf of a wrongly maligned people, was willing to say what many in media would not say because it did not fit the politically correct narrative. Still, the argument persisted that Islam had nothing whatsoever to do with what happened. Writing under the pseudonym of Ella Hill for *The Independent*, a victim of Rotherham made the connection between religion and rape very clear, saying the rapists told their victims:

> Muslim girls are good and pure because they dress modestly, covering down to their ankles and wrists, and covering their crotch area. They stay virgins until marriage. They are "our" girls. White girls and non-Muslim girls are

bad because you dress like slags. You show the curves of your bodies (showing the gap between your thighs means you're asking for it) and therefore you're immoral. White girls sleep with hundreds of men. You are the "other" girls. You are worthless and you deserve to be gang-raped.

To this, she added, "My main perpetrator quoted scriptures from the Quran to me as he beat me."[8] Cultural elites were right to link this scandal with racism, but not in the manner they intended. The racism charge against critics of Islam is absurd given the fact Islam is a religion, not a race. That said, Islam teaches men that women are lower than themselves, and non-Muslim women are dogs to be used as they see fit. It further teaches them to model their lives after Muhammad, who married Aisha, his favorite wife, when she was six and consummated the marriage when she was nine. Some cultures are superior to others, and a culture that derives its values from a Judeo-Christian worldview is unquestionably superior to anything Islam has to offer.

How did this happen?

According to the 2011 census, Rotherham's population of two hundred fifty-seven thousand saw a significant demographic change from the previous census in 2001. First, those self-identifying as Christian dropped 13.2 percent. Second, the Muslim population increased by 78 percent.[9] As much as by the teachings of Islam, these girls were raped by the failed twin-ideologies of multiculturalism and political correctness championed so foolishly by those who seek a radical societal makeover. But so far, very few seem to recognize this fact. Instead of dealing with the problem at the source, the usual political window dressing has prevailed in the wake of the scandal. Task forces, policies requiring more education for police, and awareness campaigns have all been enacted, and however helpful they might be, they are a Band-Aid on a hemorrhage.

Indeed, in the years following the exposure of the Rotherham scandal, similar Muslim sex gangs have been revealed throughout Britain.[10] As an independent government inquiry concluded, "No one knows the true scale of sexual exploitation in Rotherham over the years."[11] Even so, it is estimated nineteen thousand British children have been exploited by sex gangs *in just the last year*.[12] Yes, while Britain obsessively searches for any hint of discrimination or abuse against Meghan Markle, a woman who has profited handsomely off of her royal associations and her victim status, real discrimination and abuse of the most heinous kind is taking place right under the noses of the British public, but blinded as many are by political correctness, they refuse to see it.[13]

At the 2017 trial of six sex gang defendants, one victim testified of her treatment not only at the hands of these rapists but also at the hands of those who should have protected her: "No one understood. No one wanted to understand. I felt lost, isolated, trapped, ashamed and completely worthless. I was completely owned by these dirty old men who would do with me whatever they wanted, whenever they wanted."[14]

As the defendants were led from the courtroom, unrepentant, they shouted "Allahu Akbar!"—that is, Allah is great.[15]

Here is a worthy cause for #MeToo, a movement determined to root out the oppression of women, be it real or imaginary. Hardly a day goes by when new allegations do not fill the headlines alleging sexual assault or rape by this or that celebrity or CEO. The movement has brought to light authentic abuse but has also ruined careers and lives on the flimsiest of evidence and without due process.[16] Given the overwhelming evidence of abuse perpetrated against one of society's most vulnerable demographics—at-risk minors—in the Rotherham case, one might think these adolescents worthy of #MeToo's considerable cultural clout, right?

Crickets.

The #MeToo elites have been oddly silent, preferring to direct their rage at the likes of a Brett Kavanaugh. One may reasonably conclude this silence is due to the fact Rotherham—to which may be added the names of Bradford, Huddersfield, Rochdale, Aylesbury, Oxford, Newcastle, Bristol, and Telford—does not fit the current progressive narrative that all societal evil may be traced to powerful white men. But as Hardeep Singh pointed out, this would require courage; courage to confront Islam, and courage to admit complicity with a cultural ideology that made such events possible in the first place.

Ironically, London is now the most surveilled city in the world outside of China. At the time of my writing, London has some 627,707 cameras for 9,176,530 people. That translates to 68.40 cameras per one thousand people.[17] And now, according to *The New York Times*, London is employing real-time facial recognition technology, making it the first Western city to do so—all done in the name of safety for the citizens of this island nation in the North Atlantic.[18] For all of its technological sophistication, none of this would have protected the girls of Rotherham. Surveillance cameras, ubiquitous as they are in Britain, cannot make you see what you don't want to see.

Unsurprisingly, London is now more dangerous than New York City. According to *The Telegraph*:

London is now more crime-ridden and dangerous than New York City, with rape, robbery and violent offences far higher on this side of the Atlantic. The latest statistics, published earlier this week, revealed that crime across the UK was up by 13 percent, with a surge in violence in the capital blamed for much of the increase. Seizing on the figures, US President, Donald Trump, claimed the rise

I cool off in Singapore. *(Credit: Zachary Taunton)*

When traveling around the world, much of your time is spent waiting in airports. We would find a comfortable restaurant where we would catch up on news and update family and friends on our progress. *(Credit: Zachary Taunton)*

There are 170,000 Filipinos living in Hong Kong, and 140,000 of them are women working as domestic servants. Here, on this hot and humid Sunday afternoon, they were singing and drinking tea while waiting for their turn to attend church. This one had ten packed services every Sunday.
(Credit: Zachary Taunton)

In Tokyo. *(Credit: Zachary Taunton)*

Zachary on the west coast of New Zealand's North Island.
(Credit: Larry Alex Taunton)

At the Gyeonghoeru Pavilion in Seoul. Built in the 14th century, it is now used for state functions. *(Credit: Larry Alex Taunton)*

With a South Korean soldier who was assigned to lead me along the DMZ. Just over the hill behind us is the barbed wire dividing the Korean Peninsula at the 38th parallel. *(Credit: Larry Alex Taunton)*

Shooting an AK-47 at the Cu Chi Tunnels northwest of Ho Chi Minh City, formerly Saigon. *(Credit: Larry Alex Taunton)*

After I took this photo, I said, "You're a handsome couple." Looking somewhat depressed, the young man pulled down his mask and replied in perfect English: "That's my mom." *(Credit: Larry Alex Taunton)*

I rode this girl through a river in western Thailand. She liked the water. *(Credit: Larry Alex Taunton)*

On the Railway of Death in Thailand with a local guide who was a former Buddhist monk. *(Credit: Larry Alex Taunton)*

The Batu Caves in Gombak, Selangor, Malaysia. The caves are a popular Hindu shrine dedicated to Lord Murugan, the Ray Harryhausen-like figure dominating this photograph. *(Credit: Larry Alex Taunton)*

These militiamen nearly arrested Zachary at the Taj Mahal. After a brief discussion, they asked for a photo. A tense moment became quite amusing and memorable. *(Credit: Zachary Taunton)*

A rickshaw is the best way to get around Old Delhi. Here Zachary rides in the rickshaw ahead of me on our way to the amazing Khari Baoli, the largest spice market in Asia. While there, Zachary would be pursued by thieves. *(Credit: Zachary Taunton)*

Debating the relative merits of our respective systems with Stalin and Lenin impersonators in Red Square. A generation ago, these two would have been sent to Siberia—if not shot. *(Credit: Zachary Taunton)*

Red Square, Moscow. St. Basil's Cathedral is in the background and the Kremlin is the red brick fortress on the right. The Soviets honored three Americans by burying them with other national heroes in the Kremlin Wall Necropolis: socialist and labor leader William "Big Bill" Haywood; founder of the American Communist Party Charles Ruthenberg; and journalist John Reed. *(Credit: Zachary Taunton)*

The Houses of Parliament in London *(Credit: Heather Durham)*

Teaming up with Islamic scholar Dr. Jay Smith to debate Muslims at Speakers' Corner in Hyde Park, London. They gather here every Sunday afternoon by the hundreds to proselytize. Jay's ministry focused on combatting their arguments. *Credit: Heather Durham)*

A typical Nigerian military checkpoint. These are scattered throughout the country and appear more frequently in regions where the Fulani herdsmen militia or Boko Haram are active. But they are no reason to feel safe. Government officials might harass you, demand money, or make arbitrary arrests.
(Credit: Larry Alex Taunton)

The entrance of a hospital in Jos, Nigeria. The sign is an unintentionally hilarious indicator of how Nigerians view firearms. *(Credit: Larry Alex Taunton)*

A cruise ship passes through the Panama Canal's Miraflores Locks. Endlessly fascinating, I could sit here with a cup of coffee all day. *(Credit: Larry Alex Taunton)*

Christopher leaves Oslo Harbor on a Fjord tour. *(Credit: Zachary Taunton)*

The Center for Studies of Holocaust and Religious Minorities in Oslo, Norway is the former home of Norwegian traitor and Nazi Vidkun Quisling who was executed after the war. The walls of the museum are covered with the names of Holocaust victims. *(Credit: Zachary Taunton)*

The corner window of the Åhléns department store in Stockholm, Sweden just after a terrorist drove a beer truck through the window. People covered the plywood with Post-It note messages. *(Credit: Zachary Taunton)*

Christopher enjoys the view from a mountain in Switzerland.
(Credit: Zachary Taunton)

Viktualienmarkt beer garden in central Munich. This couple asked me to
join them. The atmosphere is fun. *(Credit: Larry Alex Taunton)*

Dachau Concentration Camp, Dachau, Germany. A Nazi mockery, the gate reads ***Arbeit Macht Frei***: "Work makes you free." *(Credit: Larry Alex Taunton)*

In a felucca on the Nile at sunset. These captains navigate their vessels with great skill. *(Credit: Larry Alex Taunton)*

The Pyramids of Giza. The pyramid that appears to be the tallest in this photo is Khafre. But the Great Pyramid behind it, Khufu, is, in fact, the tallest of them all. Khafre was built on higher ground and at a steeper angle making it look taller. *(Credit: Larry Alex Taunton)*

Crosses placed alongside a road in the Midi-Pyrénées hamlet of Col de Serrières in memory of local members of the French Resistance. *(Credit: Larry Alex Taunton)*

In no country does one fall prey to the Traveler's Fallacy more than in France.
(Credit: Heather Durham)

could be linked to the "spread of radical Islam," adding that it demonstrated the need to "keep America safe." But critics dismissed his comments as "ignorant" and "divisive," with former Labour leader Ed Miliband calling him an "absolute moron."[19]

However pleasing Miliband's comments might have been to the Trump haters, Trump was right. In my heart, I'm an Anglophile. My heritage is English on my father's side and Scots-Irish on my mother's. Even so, it is difficult to rate the United Kingdom very high when one considers the direction it is trending. There are those in Britain who recognize the damage caused by globalism and the ideology that drives the continental-sized social experiment known as the Open Society. Hoping to reclaim their cultural distinctiveness and sovereignty, they voted for Brexit, thus beginning a populist surge that reverberates throughout the Western world.

In North London is Highgate Cemetery. Among the fifty-three thousand graves are a few notables: Michael Faraday, inventor of the electric motor, and Adam Worth, the real-life basis for Sir Arthur Conan Doyle's evil Moriarty in the Sherlock Holmes stories, are two. Most notable of all is the resting place, a monument really, of Karl Marx. Though Prussian, Marx lived in London for more than half of his life (the last thirty-four years). There he refined his radical secular utopian ideology and produced *Das Kapital*, setting loose upon the world ideas that have wrecked half of it and threaten to wreck the other half.

In South London is West Norwood Cemetery. Among the forty-two thousand graves there, one also finds a few men of renown: Alexander Parkes, inventor of plastic, and Hiram Maxim, inventor of the first portable fully automatic machine gun, are interred here. Perhaps more illustrious than either of these is the grave of Charles Spurgeon. The "Prince of Preachers," Spurgeon was the nineteenth-century's British equivalent of Billy Graham. In 1857, at the request of Queen Victoria, the twenty-three-year-old Spurgeon electrified a crowd of twenty-four thousand at the Crystal Palace with his sermon about the first day of creation.

It is extraordinary to me that both Marx and Spurgeon lived and worked in the same London. While Marx was preaching salvation through bloody revolution, Spurgeon, on the other side of the city at the same time, was preaching salvation through the blood and grace of Jesus Christ. Both were well known in their day, and although there is no indication they ever met, they almost certainly knew about each other and the irreconcilable messages they proclaimed. Both were, in a sense, evangelists competing for the souls of men with their competing visions of humanity.

The war between those two visions reverberates down to our own day, only now Marxism takes residence in radical environmentalism and the language of class warfare frequently employed by the likes of (former) British Labour Party leader Jeremy Corbyn (and Democrats Bernie Sanders and Alexandria Ocasio-Cortez). And it is no longer a contest between merely two visions of mankind. Islam has been thrown into the mix and on any given Sunday, you can find its advocates, in all of their radical glory, spewing their hate of the West, of Jesus Christ, and of those who follow him in Hyde Park. Go there and see for yourself. I do. But wear a stab-proof vest.[i]

The United Kingdom of Great Britain and Northern Ireland is a country that has been retreating from both its heritage and from reason for decades while trending dangerously away from freedom. Freedom of speech no longer has any real meaning in

---

i   I have debated Muslims in Hyde Park a number of times. But a friend of mine was attacked by Muslims after a similar debate and nearly had his throat cut. He has a substantial scar to prove it.

Britain as one simply cannot speak against Islam, homosexuality, or much of anything else—*unless* you want to attack Christianity, then you will be given free rein. (As I write, Franklin Graham's tour of Britain has been canceled in seven cities on the basis he is "homophobic.") It is a chilling warning to America, for we are following the same path to cultural suicide. Britain is America fast-forwarded. Perhaps sanity will once again prevail under the wise guidance of Boris Johnson who has finally led Britain out of the European Union. We shall see.

Before departing this once-great Christian capital of the world for a much different country, I met a man who, upon learning about my project inspired by *Around the World in 80 Days*, got a sly smile on his face.

"There is a place where I must take you," he said.

That place was Fogg's Tavern in Mayfair, named for the intrepid Phileas Fogg of *Around the World in 80 Days* fame. My host's associations with this establishment are now obscure to me. Owner? Friend? Regular patron?—I do not know. Regardless, he led me inside and up the stairs to the exclusive Gin Parlor.

"This," he joked, "is where it all began."

It was time to board our modern equivalent of a hot air balloon—an Airbus A380-800—and journey far, far to the south.

CHAPTER 14

Nigeria:
The Most Dangerous Country
in the World

*"Blessed are those who are persecuted for righteousness sake, for theirs is
the kingdom of heaven."*

—Jesus, the Sermon on the Mount, Matthew 5:10 (NKJV)[1]

"Don't go. I swore I would never go back there," came the voice of my friend Jay Smith on a trans-Atlantic Skype call. "I've been in over sixty countries. I've been all over Africa. I lived there, and I've never felt unsafe the way I did in *that* country. There is something especially terrifying about that place."

"Good to know," I replied. "Alan said that he goes there all the time. He said he even takes his children."

Alan was a British politician who recently attended one of my lectures in London. To hear him tell of it, Nigeria was like Club Med.

"Alan?" Jay was incredulous. "Did Alan also tell you that when he goes, he's traveling with the British government and is accompanied by heavily armed guards in armed caravans?" He

132

laughed cynically. "You? You're going to have an *entirely different* experience."

This was my introduction to Nigeria.

No doubt some of my readers are asking themselves, *Why Nigeria?* It is true Nigeria is not in the running for our hypothetical prize of the world's greatest country. On the contrary, in a discussion with lawmakers, President Trump is alleged to have called it a "sh*thole." But part of our purpose in this book is to acquaint you with what the world is really like, and Africa's most populous and, some say, most dangerous country is nonetheless an important stop.

I was invited there by my friend, Jwan Zhumbes, the Anglican bishop of Bukuru in Plateau State in central Nigeria. He is the shepherd to a diocese that was under siege from the Boko Haram and the Fulani herdsmen militia, both militant Islamic groups, and was, in my estimation, a great man doing great work.

Jwan and I met while doing our doctoral work. He asked me some years ago to come and teach the members of the diocese on issues of faith and culture. In addition to this, I wanted to see firsthand the trials of the persecuted Church and to observe the workings of Islam in the third world as I observed it elsewhere. I decided I would need to do this part of our around the world journey alone. It was simply too dangerous to take Zachary or anyone else.

Before our expedition began, I went to the Nigerian consulate in Atlanta. I wanted to talk to people whose job it was to dispense the kind of advice I needed.

The consulate is an austere, nondescript brick building. Unimpressive by any measure except, perhaps, a Nigerian one.

"Hello," I said, declaring myself to the receptionist who seemed unaware of my presence at her desk.

"May I help you?"

"Yes, I am going to Nigeria and I'd like to get some advice on 'dos and don'ts' for those of us who have never been there."

"You really want to go?" she said with a feigned look of surprise and then, suddenly, she burst out laughing at her own inside joke. She didn't bother explaining it to me. I would get it, she seemed to imply, once I had been to Nigeria.

Regaining her composure, she said what was expected of her: Nigeria is a lovely country, it is very safe, people love it, and so on.

"But what about the US State Department's travel warnings?" I put in.

"Media exaggerations," she replied dismissively. She then presented a box with twenty or so passports in it. "See? Look at all the people who are applying for visas to immigrate to Nigeria!"

Apparently, the French gave the Statue of Liberty to the wrong country. To hear her assessment of things, one might have thought Nigeria was just the victim of bad publicity. Boko Haram? Fulani herdsmen militia? Civil war? Kidnapping, extortion, rape, extreme poverty, famine, child trafficking, corruption, malaria—Bah! Nonsense! Media exaggerations!

Having the sense I would not get the unvarnished answers I came for, I turned to leave. As I did, she stood, looked at me gravely and, with eyes wide, said:

"*Good luck.*"

She said it slowly and with emphasis as if to say, "beware." It was then that I noticed the security camera. Was she saying one thing, that which she was paid to say, while meaning another the whole time? I couldn't know.

In the parking lot, I briefly talked to a man who also worked at the consulate. Perhaps he would give me clarity. He was professional and took my questions seriously. This was the conversation for which I had come. He asked the sort of questions I would expect to be asked:

"Why are you going?" and "Who invited you?" and "Do you know him well?" and "Who is meeting you at the airport?" and "Do you have security?"

My answer to the last question seemed to alarm him: "No, I don't have any security."

He paused. "Are you going alone?"

"Yes."

Was that a look of admiration or did he fear for my life? Spotting his superior driving into the parking lot, he led me over to her. He seemed eager, relieved actually, to hand me off to someone else. But it was no use. I felt like I was talking to the receptionist again.

"You will love Nigeria!" she practically sang. "Nothing to worry about. And the weather is so nice this time of year!"

Then, without any apparent irony, she leaned in and added: "But don't talk to any strangers, go nowhere alone, and if someone wants to fight you, be official."

"Be official"? What did this mean? I didn't know. It was a wasted trip. I left no wiser.

Or did I?

Embassies and consulates are a country's storefront. In them, nations typically endeavor to put their best foot forward because they know these outposts not only represent their country but are quite probably all most will ever see of it. The idea is to impress, to make a statement of national greatness. Tuvalu, for instance, a small island nation in Polynesia, owns a London embassy valued at 11 percent of that country's national debt. That may be taking PR too far, but you get the idea.

So, what is one to think when a nation *doesn't* try to impress you? Well, that tells you something, too. Chiefly, it tells you they don't care. Wherever the Nigerian government was spending its money, it wasn't on marketing. I left the consulate grounds preparing for the worst.

Nigeria is consistently ranked as one of the most dangerous countries in the world, if not *the* most dangerous.[i] Plateau State suffered violent clashes with armed Muslim militia, resulting in multiple instances of rioting and slaughter in 2001, 2008, 2010, and bombings in 2014. Since that time, the bishop told me, Westerners ceased coming.

"Nigeria is like a scarecrow," he said. "You only need to see it from afar to be afraid."

And they are afraid for good reason. Jay Smith, my aforementioned friend, advised me not to go for good reason, too. His opinion on Nigeria was not acquired from Tripadvisor. He went to Nigeria more than once. During a 2008 visit to that country, he spent nine hours hiding in the wheel well of a car while a mob went up and down a blocked highway looking for Westerners to kill or kidnap and hold for ransom. Nigeria was, in his view, unique to the African experience. It wasn't that terrible things didn't happen in other countries; it was the sheer magnitude of them in Nigeria. The bishop told me as much: "Even other Africans are afraid of Nigeria."

At this point, some of my readers are thinking I would be very foolish to go to Nigeria after my friend's warning and the sketchy bipolar advice from consulate personnel. And, were I someone who believed this life is all you get, I would agree with you. Why take the risk? But I am a Christian. As such, some things should supersede safety, Christian missions most of all. Furthermore, I knew Jwan was hoping I would, through my writing, bring attention to the plight of his people.

Some people do risky things because they are ill-informed and unwise. Reading the travel blogs of some world travelers only reinforces this impression:

---

i   This is another dubious stat. In US publications, this statistic is often based on the number of crimes or incidents reported by Americans to the embassies in the country in question. As a result, Central and South American countries score very high because there are a lot of US citizens traveling to these countries.

"Badness exists, sure, but even that's quite rare. By and large, humans are kind. Self-interested sometimes, myopic sometimes, but kind. Generous and wonderful and kind. No greater revelation has come from our journey than this."

These were some of the last words of Jay Austin who, with his girlfriend Lauren Geoghegan, were bicycling around the world. The couple from Washington, D.C. were murdered in Tajikistan in July 2018 by members of ISIS. It was their hope to demonstrate, through the vulnerability of just such a bicycle trip, that people around the world were generally kind and our differences are exaggerated:

"[J]ust trust the universe and the people that inhabit it. And with that vulnerability comes immense generosity: good folks who will recognize your helplessness and recognize that you need assistance in one form or another and offer it in spades."[2]

It is not my purpose to dishonor the memories of these young, well-intentioned Americans when I say this is extraordinarily naïve. Similarly, in 2017 a British woman was murdered in the Amazon while on a forty-day kayaking trip—*alone*.[3] The world victimizes such people daily. Very frequently, they are Westerners who have enjoyed the freedom and moral sensibilities of societies deeply influenced by the Christian ethos. As a consequence, they mistakenly assume the rest of the world is like that, too. It isn't. This same kind of Pollyannaism led Timothy Treadwell to believe he could live among grizzly bears unmolested. He believed the bears would leave him alone if they knew he meant them no harm. But bears kill and eat non-threatening animals every day, and they killed and ate him, too. Man is a bear, or wolf, according to the Latin proverb *homo homini lupus est*: "man is wolf unto man." Indeed, he is. More than "badness," evil exists, and a secular worldview lacks this basic understanding of human nature the way Treadwell lacked a basic understanding of large carnivores.

While visiting some dangerous corners of the globe, I have met those people, students mostly, who seem to have little notion of the perils involved in what they are doing. They are the Steve Irwins of travel, taking extraordinary risks for the sake of an adventure or an Instagram post. That's not bravery; that's stupidity. If we have any self-regard or any regard for the feelings of those who love us, we don't risk our lives frivolously or cause others to do so.

Some risks, however, are worth taking. Christians are called to share in the sufferings of other Christians, especially those who are suffering *because* they are Christians (Hebrews 10:32–34; 12:3–4; 13:3)—and they are suffering and dying at an alarming rate. John L. Allen Jr. of *Spectator Magazine* (UK) writes:

The global war on Christians remains the greatest story never told of the early 21st century.... According to the International Society for Human Rights, a secular obser-vatory based in Frankfurt, Germany, 80 percent of all acts of religious discrimination in the world today are directed at Christians. Statistically speaking, that makes Christians by far the most persecuted religious body on the planet.... According to the Center for the Study of Global Christianity at Gordon-Conwell Theological Seminary in Massachusetts, an average of 100,000 Christians have been killed in what the centre calls a "situation of witness" each year for the past decade. That works out to 11 Christians killed somewhere in the world every hour, seven days a week and 365 days a year, for reasons related to their faith.... In effect, the world is witnessing the rise of an entirely new generation of Chris-tian martyrs. The carnage is occurring on such a vast scale that it represents not only the most dramatic Christian story of our time, but arguably the premier human rights chal-lenge of this era as well.[4]

For most people, this is news and that is because it is, as Allen says, "the greatest story never told." How demoralizing must it be to suffer persecution while your fellow Christians, people who might offer you comfort and encouragement, not only don't visit you but seem little more than vaguely aware of your circumstances.

My wife Lauri's opinion on the matter would weigh heavily with me. If going to Nigeria would deeply distress her, I wouldn't go.

"Do you think I should go?" I asked. "Before you answer, know this: whatever you say is what I'm likely to do here. So, answer *carefully*."

After much thought, she replied. "Does it make me anxious? Yes. Do I want to talk about the 'what ifs'? No. But I guess I think this: if you don't go, who will?"

With that, the wheels were set in motion to include Nigeria as part of our world survey. Bishop Zhumbes sent me this warning:

"Go about this trip confidently. Be friendly, but never betraying that you are a first-timer [to Nigeria]. Do not ask questions that will betray you as someone who has never been here before, though you are indeed a first-timer. And answer only those questions you consider necessary to answer. It shall be well with you."

With that sort of warning echoing in my mind, I boarded my flight bound for Abuja and hoped for the best.

I exited Abuja's Nnamdi Azikiwe International Airport into the African heat. I was startled at the rapidity with which the other people on my flight, many of whom were white businessmen or mining executives, disappeared into an array of armored cars and security details until I stood alone on the curb. Gradually, a Don Williams song crept into my consciousness until I realized the music was emanating from a distant airport speaker, adding a surreal element to it all.

Soon, I saw Jwan, smiling broadly, coming to greet me.

"You are here, my brother!" he said enthusiastically.

We embraced and hurried to a waiting Toyota Sequoia with a prominent decal in the front passenger-side window reading "BISHOP." Jwan's driver, Alex, also an Anglican priest, put my luggage in the back of the car and we sped off.

"You are the proud owner of a record, my friend!" Jwan exclaimed, squeezing my hand.

"What record?" I asked.

"You are the first! You are the first to come!" he said with a chuckle. Then, wistfully, he added, "I was beginning to wonder if I had ever really made any friends in America."

Nigeria was a country of civil war, violence, corruption, child trafficking, kidnapping, and Islamic terrorism long before there was anything worth fighting over. A former British colony, Nigeria was abandoned by the British, never again to return, at the time of the Nigerian Civil War (1967–1970). But now, with a booming oil industry, the problems were exacerbated as factions fought for control of the country and the oil fields. In 2001, 2008, 2010, and 2014, armed Islamic groups attacked Christians throughout the country. Jos, the city where we were going, was a hot spot. According to Jwan, since 2008, even Christian missionaries ceased coming. In terms of Westerners, the country was like Easter Island—signs of them remained, but they were gone.

Alex, weaving his way through the chaotic traffic of shantytown, turned the Toyota north onto the open road and the five-and-a-half-hour drive to Jos. Alex, I would learn, is a quiet, steady support to the bishop. He is a humble man, and I would come to value his presence and friendship. On this occasion as on others, his role was that of the ferryman taking us across the River Styx. That's because the open roads are where the real dangers lie. The Boko Haram, active in the north, were pushed back in the previous year, but the Fulani herdsmen militia remained a serious problem to say nothing of other criminals looking to capitalize on vulnerable travelers.

The nomadic Fulani, recognizing no borders and no private property, drive their cattle all over northwest Africa in search of pastureland. Their cattle can be seen blocking roads, grazing in the medians of public highways, and eating the crops of farmers. The latter has brought them into violent conflict with Nigerian farmers who, understandably, wish to protect their property and produce. The Fulani are regarded as a violent people who are ready to take what is not freely given. Converted to Islam about one thousand years ago, they are often more than ready to use terrorist tactics against any who oppose them. Attacks on the open road are not uncommon, where rocks, nail strips, and burning tires are used to slow drivers and ambush them. One dare not even stop for stranded motorists for fear it is a trap.

To reduce the prevalence of these attacks, the government has established military checkpoints along scattered sections of the highway. Armed with AK-47s, the soldiers manning these forced stops are often of a benign nature, taking a glance into the vehicle before waving traffic though the sandbag barriers or, as is often the case, crude obstacles made of whatever is close at hand—concrete blocks, stones, or logs. Other times, however, the soldiers extort drivers for "dash," that is, a bribe. *The International Business Times*[5] calls Nigeria's roads the most dangerous in the world for a reason. One never really knows who to trust.

Alex had his own method for avoiding the Fulani or any other potential hindrance: move *fast*. With darkness rapidly approaching,

Jwan pressed Alex to pick up the pace. From the back seat, I watched as the Sequoia's RPMs regularly topped six thousand, then plummeted as we braked hard and swerved to avoid rocks or crater-sized potholes before surging to the gauge's red limits once again. Jwan, accustomed to these trips, chatted casually as the car shot across the deserted African plain.

"Next time you come you can teach us on…" Jwan said in his James Earl Jones baritone.

I interrupted. "Did you say, 'next time'?"

He smiled slyly. "Yes. You've cracked the nut now, coming back should be easy. I am picturing it for you."

Jwan is not the bishop for nothing. A man of great faith and courage, he is also a clever man as a bishop in Nigeria must be. His program for his people is broad, encompassing much more than a sermon series or potluck dinners or (bad) basketball leagues. In this part of the world, a minister of the Christian Gospel must minister to the whole person, the whole community. Jwan's vision includes agricultural initiatives, medical clinics, and educational opportunities. The hospitals, once owned and well managed by churches, have been ruined by a government that took them over. Jwan hopes to see them returned to the church for the sake of a suffering people.

"These are areas that have been recently attacked by the Fulani," he said as we passed through a village.

The Fulani often strike in a drive-by fashion. To prevent this, villages create makeshift roadblocks and speed bumps, slowing traffic so villagers can take careful aim at their attackers from positions alongside the road. Not unexpectedly, the area looked like a warzone with burned-out ruins and signs of violent struggle. We would see several villages of this kind as we continued our northward trek.

I was reminded of a line from Joseph Conrad's *Heart of Darkness*:[6]

"Nowhere did we stop long enough to get a particularized impression, but the general sense of vague and oppressive wonder grew upon me. It was like a weary pilgrimage amongst hints for nightmares."

The landscape, sparsely populated, reminded me of west Texas, Arizona, and Nevada. At times, the road stretched to the disappearing point on the far horizon. Villages exhibited homes of every type: little more than sheet metal lean-tos, walled-in mansions for the wealthy, and mud huts with thatched roofs.

After a tense journey, we arrived in Jos. Jwan decided the safest place for me was a compound near the city center. A bored uniformed security guard wielding the ubiquitous AK-47 inspected the car and then signaled for the barrier to be raised. I would be staying alone in a ranch-style house with rebar protecting every window. Architecture can tell you a lot about a place, and this architecture—the walls, the razor wire, the rebar, and sturdy locks—spoke of a past terror.

Thomas, another priest I would come to admire, joined us for a hearty dinner prepared by a housekeeper who came each day. Jwan, ever the gracious host, saw me to my room and checked to see I had everything I needed. When the three of them left, he gave me a key to the house and waited while I locked the door behind them.

The next morning, Jwan and Thomas came to get me. My stay here, only one week, was brief, so the schedule was packed. We attended a wedding for a couple in Jwan's diocese. The reception, held outdoors, was remarkable. Full of singing, dancing, and feasting, it was a joyous occasion of biblical proportions. The groom danced toward the wedding cake as friends and family showered him with money. It's a symbol of prosperity. Before the cutting of the cake, the husband was told he is to provide food for his wife. She was told to prepare it and feed it to him. He then cut the cake and she served it to him. The amount she feeds to him is a sign of things to come: does she feed him well or not so much? From the looks of things, that couple should do all right.

As one finds the world over, the whole ceremony seemed to be organized and run by women. Nigerian women are often quite beautiful. They have fine features, captivating smiles, and dress colorfully from head to toe. The women seemed to be the props and pillars of their families and the local churches. Although a visitor unknown to all, I was immediately given a chair and plate after plate of delicious food.

From there we visited friends and relatives, the hospitalized and the homebound. "You are the pastor today," Jwan said. The people we met were hospitable under the circumstances and pleased to see their bishop. Slowly, a picture began to form in my mind of the vast responsibility Jwan carried as bishop of these people. More than a pastor or even a high church official, he was a community leader. Though slight in stature, he is nonetheless great in the eyes of his people, and for good reason.

Through it all, I reeked of Deep Woods Off! insect repellant. Ninety percent of the world's malarial deaths occur in sub-Saharan Africa, and 50 percent of those occur in Ethiopia, the Democratic Republic of the Congo, Uganda, and Nigeria. In all, some three hundred thousand Nigerians die of malaria each year. Physicians advised me to wear long sleeves and, putting aside social awkward-ness, practically bathe in the smelly substance. But no one seemed to mind my chemical aura. Jwan, ever concerned for my safety, would inspect me each day for mosquito bites. Having lost a son to malaria, Jwan took the possibility of the disease very seriously.

"You have been bitten," he said one morning with grave concern. "That is not good. We must watch that [bump] for the next few days."

Returning to the compound, I bathed—splashed about really—in cold bottled water and, exhausted, went to bed. I drifted off as stray dogs howled. My last semi-conscious thoughts were the opening lines of Toto's "Africa."

My friend, Jay Smith, warned me my whiteness would greatly elevate my exposure to danger, and he was right. This is not a commentary on race. It is, rather, a commentary on economics. Before this trip, Jay related to me how, on a visit to Nigeria more than a decade ago, his hosts hired armed guards to protect him. They did not, however, do the same for Jay's colleague from India. When his Indian friend complained at this apparent oversight, the Nigerian responsible for these decisions replied flatly:

"You aren't white."

His point wasn't that he didn't care about the safety of this fine Indian man; his point was that as an Indian, he was a less lucrative target for would-be kidnappers or terrorists hoping to make headlines. White people in Nigeria are, with few exceptions, oil and mining executives from Western firms that have shown a willingness to pay large ransoms when kidnappers start mailing body parts of captives to their companies and families. Consequently, whites generally live in gated, heavily armed compounds, and move about with security details.

For strategic reasons, I decided to forgo that. I couldn't afford enough security to do anything other than signal criminals I must be important. For a time, I wished I had my Glock 9mm. Then one day we visited a local hospital. At the entrance, a sign read:

"Firearms Not Allowed Beyond This Point (Except Side Arms)."

With that sign, I realized the futility of my wish. This was a country where they didn't even consider a pistol to be a firearm. With everyone carrying AK-47s, I might as well have a slingshot.

Compounding my vulnerability, I had no hope of blending in. In addition to being white, I am much taller than the average Nigerian. Jwan Zhumbes, the bishop of Bukuru, introducing me at a conference, joked, "I will guarantee that Larry is the biggest man in the room!" At every stop while driving through villages or the city, it was only a matter of time until someone noticed me, pointed me out to someone else, and a crowd of onlookers would begin to gather around. No doubt most mean no harm, but in crowds of Muslims, one is conscious of the fact that promises of eternity are a pretty strong incentive to violence. Sometimes these people would press up against me, touching me and asking for money. In such circumstances, it is best to act with confidence and, if need be, to forcefully push people away who get too close to you. As a rule, they will respect it if you do it forcefully enough.

But I was glad to be there. More than that, I was honored to be among the Christians of that country. I admired their courage, their cheerfulness, and their hospitality. They suffered as few Westerners can imagine. The Nigerian Civil War saw more than a million killed. Since the crisis of 2001, where armed Islamic groups attacked Christians and their churches, slaughter has been common.

"If one is out at night walking alone, he cannot be sure he will make it home," Jwan said.

One evening, he took me to meet a man in his diocese named Luke. Luke is an eighty-something-year-old man with a deceptive energy. He and his family greeted us with warm handshakes as we entered the walled compound in which he lives. Such residential compounds are common for Nigerians who are middle class and up. The tops of the walls are covered in broken glass or razor wire and the steel gates are typically operated by a youth. A honk of the horn, the sight of someone peeking through a slit in the wall, and the gate opens.

Luke prepared a feast for us all in a lovely outdoor pavilion. He grew up in the region, received a degree in geology, and was retired from years of service with a British company that once mined tin here.

"We used to have a lot of British people here," he said.

"Where did they go?" I asked.

"They left!" he replied with a burst of laughter. "I really can't imagine why they would want to leave Nigeria," he added sarcastically.

Luke, I would learn, is a thoughtful man who possesses an infectious good humor.

"My father was a pagan. African religion. You must understand that Christianity didn't penetrate this deep into Africa until the early twentieth century," he explained. "I was eight years old when, in the Second World War, I was out in the field with a friend and we saw a British squadron flying in formation. We had never seen an airplane before!" He laughed at his childhood self. "We were certain it must be Jesus returning as the Anglican missionary had told us! We ran and hid!"

But Jesus didn't return that day and Nigerian Christians suffer new challenges from an old religion with a global agenda.

Muslim men in Africa, often having ten or more wives, might have fifty to a hundred children. Their fathers unable and unwilling to support them, these children are shipped off with promises of education and a future. In recent decades, Nigerians like Luke began noticing truckloads of them being dropped off all over the northern and central parts of the country. Few really knew or processed what was going on. These children became a blight. They are at every gas station, begging and rapping on the windows. Unbeknownst to most, these children were radicalized by Muslim clerics while also learning their way around the cities and villages of Nigeria.

When the Boko Haram and the Fulani herdsmen militia were ready to attack Christians, the children became the end of the spear. In exchange for a bit of food and money, they were armed and told to identify where this or that person lived. "Where does the vicar live?" they might be asked. And the children, knowing the city, would lead the terrorists to their targets.

After the first Fulani attacks that led to widespread slaughter throughout Nigeria, Christians began arming themselves, preparing for the next attack. When another attack came, the Fulani suffered great losses. Embittered, they concluded Luke, a reasonably wealthy man by Nigerian standards, had armed Christians in this part of the country. He did. With help, they identified his house and attacked.

"I was watching television and heard gunfire," he explained casually. "At first, I thought it was some distance off, but then I realized it was within the compound. They were over my wall." He then pointed to where they breached his security.

Machine gun fire sprayed the side of his house, shattering windows. A sly fox, Luke had a preplanned escape route. He and his family exited the back of the house and through a hidden gap in the wall. They all lay in a field and watched the house burn. From there, he called another member of the church, Patience, and asked her to come and get his family.

It was my honor to meet her, too. A lawyer of graceful bearing, she had driven out into the countryside to help.

"I was terrified," she told me. "I was shaking. Literally shaking, as I drove past burning houses and fighting. I was certain I would be killed."

But she nonetheless went. Let me underscore that point. *She went.* This is courage defined. I was humbled by the courage and faith of these people. To me, Luke and Patience were like Christian superheroes. Were such people given the means and help they currently lack, they would change the world. American Christians, by contrast, have allowed their culture to be hijacked by evil elements hell-bent on the annihilation of the unborn, freedom of speech, religious liberty, and the family as we know it. This is happening is because Christians have preferred silence to what I will call a soft persecution—a lost scholarship or promotion, perhaps, or being ostracized socially.

There is much we could learn from Nigerian Christians. The United States Congress named Nigeria the most dangerous country in the world for Christians. Even so, those I have met here are joyous, optimistic, and prepared to defend themselves while also proclaiming the love and hope of Jesus Christ in one of the most spiritually dark places on earth.

A few days later, I spoke to a gathering of priests and their wives, addressing questions of Islam and American culture. From there, Jwan took me to meet his brother-in-law, Emmanuel Dalung, who is the Secretary of All Farmers Plateau Society. It is his job to train the pastors to farm so that they can, in turn, train their congregations.

As we walked through Emmanuel's garden, he pointed out different plants he was growing and testing, and he explained his agricultural philosophy as we went.

"A pastor must undertake physical transformation," he said. "Once people are transformed spiritually, their physical transformation is easier."

There is a measure of profundity in this. A man cannot be expected to do something he neither understands nor values.

"In America, less than 2 percent of your people farm. Yet they feed the world. In Nigeria, it is reversed. Almost 80 percent of the people farm and they cannot even feed themselves. Africa has perpetually been its own destroyer."

The conversation turned to America and Donald Trump. Used to such conversations with Europeans, I braced for the worst.

"We are nervous about America. We need America to be powerful and confident, not an America full of self-doubt and apologies. Your people seem to have lost their way."

"What do you think of Donald Trump?" I asked.

"We like Trump!" he replied. "He has helped us against the Muslims. We think he is right about America, too. Not only do we think he should make America first, but we think America should be in charge of the world. Someone must counter the power of the Russians, the Chinese, the Saudis, and the Iranians. If not, we Nigerians are lost."

Returning me to the compound, Jwan squeezed my hand and said, "My people would put you on their shoulders and carry you as a champion. I am serious, my friend. Because you have put yourself at great risk for them." But the man and the people he shepherds are the real champions.

"Now that you have come," he added, "Perhaps others will see that it is safe and start coming again, too."

He expressed this hope often. He wants major American investment in his country. I always remained silent, not wanting to disappoint him. But I knew I could not leave him with false hope. I looked out of the window at the barren landscape and thought hard for the right words.

"It won't happen, Jwan," I began. "They aren't coming. I'm an anomaly, I'm afraid."

I then explained how Western churches are fighting their own battles and how this, combined with the instability and terrifying nature of Nigeria, made Western investment unlikely anytime soon. Nigerians must redeem Nigeria and not hope for salvation from the West. It's a hard truth, and it broke my heart to say it.

The bishop took this news as well as anyone could.

There is a sense in which Nigerian Christians feel forsaken by God. It is the end of the earth. When a shooting takes place in America, it makes international headlines. Unfortunately, violence of this nature, often targeting Christians, occurs in this part of the world with great regularity and usually goes unreported in Western media. It is as if these people don't matter. Recently a freelance videographer working for BBC told me he offered them footage of Nigerian churches being burned to the ground by the Fulani. BBC refused it. They simply weren't interested.

Even so, the country isn't forsaken by God. As I discovered, a cheery Christian community flourishes there. For me, Jwan Zhumbes and the Christian people of Nigeria, are a living example of a great theological truth of which the Apostle John wrote in the first chapter of his Gospel:

"The light shines in the darkness, and the darkness has not overcome it."

It was time to leave. While I was packing up, Jwan appeared at my door. He appeared to be upset.

"What is wrong?" I asked.

"It took the housekeeper a long time to answer the door," he began. "For a moment, I feared something had happened to my friend during the night."

"I am fine," I said. "I slept well."

Jwan, ever pastoral, inspected the mosquito bite on my upper arm. "It does not look good. You are taking your malaria medication?"

"Yes."

This interaction is a neat summary of the dangers of Nigeria—they come from both man and nature. To quote one Nigerian writer, "Unfortunately, much like traveling on our roads, life and living in Nigeria is becoming alarmingly cheap, brutal, and unpredictable."[7]

The journey from Abuja to Jos was harrowing. Now it was time to do it again but in reverse. A long, perilous drive, it is not for the faint of heart. Each year, there are roughly 615 fatalities in Nigeria for every one hundred thousand vehicles. Compare that astonishing figure to the United States: twelve. That's before you factor in terrorism and the constant threat of roadside ambushes. Nigeria is leading the world in all the wrong categories.

I had said goodbye to Alex, Thomas, and many others at the cathedral the previous day, and Jwan and a new driver, Moses, were here to take me back to the airport. If you imagine a western where the protagonist rides through Apache territory from one outpost to another, a trail of dust behind him and an arrow through his hat, you'll have the right mental picture. Sketchy people are not unique to Nigeria. But Nigeria's sketchy types tend to be heavily armed and that makes things a bit dicey.

Moses, our driver for this real-life version of *The Fast and the Furious*, is a sturdy, quiet fellow in his mid-twenties. Being a bit prone to car sickness on these brutal Nigerian roads, I opted to drive or sit in the front passenger seat during much of my visit. But when we were about an hour out of Jos and at the front end of this long, lonely highway, Jwan ordered Moses to pull over.

"We must now move you to the back seat," he explained to me. "We know not what evil lurks for you in the bush."

This sentence, spoken as it was in an older, more sonorous British English that is extinct in all but former British colonies, had an ominous quality to it. I moved to the back where the windows were tinted. Jwan reclined my seat slightly to conceal me further. He then gave Moses a uniform like that of a traffic cop and told him to put it on.

"He will look official," Jwan explained. "The checkpoint guards are less likely to give us trouble."

With that, Moses, who clearly liked wearing the uniform, pulled the Toyota Sequoia back onto the highway and took aim at the far horizon. The engine roared as he pushed the RPMs into the gauge's red limits as Alex did when we traveled this road a week before. I have never seen a vehicle endure such punishment and I have punished *a lot* of vehicles. It wasn't merely that we were going fast, it was the duration of it, the pounding of the road, the constant hard braking and reacceleration. Five and a half hours is a long time to push a vehicle, any vehicle, so hard. I feared the engine might blow or—

—"What happens if we blow out a tire?" I asked, already sensing the grim answer.

Jwan's reply was typical of the man's penchant for the eloquent understatement: "It would be a very bad day for us all."

What these Christians accept as normal is, for the typical Westerner, extraordinary. Some accept it because they don't know anything different. Others accept it because they must. Intelligent Travel, an independent group providing risk assessment to travelers, rates Nigeria a 97 percent travel risk.[8] "Safe" is a word that has no application to Nigeria unless it's used in a sentence like "It's a safe bet you'll be kidnapped in Nigeria" or "It's a safe assumption your trip to Nigeria will be *eventful*." Nothing about Nigeria is safe.

Not the political situation or the economy; not the medical care or the availability of it; not the religious context or the roadways. Life expectancy in Nigeria is fifty-three. Not safe. Yet God's grace was evident in how the Christians there managed it. They didn't worry about those things they could not control. They simply did the best they could and left the rest to God's sovereign mercy.

Moses, whose name seemed perfectly suited to his task on this day, led us at high speed through the African desert where evil often lurks.

"Get me to the Promised Land, Moses," I joked. The young man smiled and, having connected his smartphone to the car stereo, he started his personal playlist that began with something unexpected.

"You like Rascal Flatts, Moses?" I asked. He nodded enthusiastically in the rearview mirror. I just shook my head, wondering if the band ever imagined a scenario like this when they—or whoever—wrote this piece of music. I cannot now recall the song, but it surely must have been "Bless the Broken Road."

"Now that you have been with us, my friend," Jwan began, "how does the reality of our country compare to your expectations?"

"A South African friend of mine told me Nigerians were a huge people," I said. "He has never been to Nigeria, but he told me Nigerians were like the actor Michael Clarke Duncan, the big guy in *The Green Mile*. Huge. So, I expected to feel like a grasshopper in their sight."

At this, Jwan and Moses laughed uproariously. Moses convulsed with laughter.

"Instead you discovered that it is *you* who are of the tribe of Anak!" Jwan joked, referring to the biblical tribe of giants. "We are more like Asians in size. You saw how you were bigger than almost everyone you met in this country! But that myth is part of the reputation of Nigeria in Africa. Nigeria and Nigerians are feared. Even by other Africans."

I will say it again: Nigerian Christians are remarkable. Tough, charismatic, and possessed of an irrepressible joy, no one could ever conquer a people of such spirit. Not the Boko Haram, not the Fulani herdsmen militia, not a corrupt government, and not the liberal policies the West has tried to force upon them. The unrelenting pressure of violence, corruption, and pestilence have combined to produce a diamond of a people.

But the West has failed them—abandoned them, really. Deep into the country, away from the operations of oil companies with their heavy security and guarded compounds, Westerners were nowhere to be found. Nowhere.

And yet, remarkably, the anti-Western narrative of colonialism was not reflected among the Nigerians I met. Quite the opposite. I don't mean to suggest Nigerians think British colonialism was all peaches and cream. But these are a sophisticated, educated people who recognize the British, particularly the Anglican Church, brought many good things to Nigeria—education, hospitals, infrastructure, and, most importantly, Jesus.

Speaking at a conference in London some years ago, Peter Akinola, the Archbishop of the Anglican Church in Nigeria, boldly chastised the West:

> You came to my country and told us there is only one God through whom we could be saved, Jesus Christ, and we believed you, and followed Him. You told us there is only one true book to know him, the Bible, and we believed you, and read it. Now you tell us Allah of Islam is also god, and that we can use the Qur'an to learn about God. You invited the Muslims here as guests, and they have now become your hosts. So now I come to your country to remind you of what you have forgotten.

Wow. A friend of mine who was present on this occasion said it was one of the most powerful talks he has ever heard. You see, to Nigerian Christians, there are two manifestations of the West:

The good one that brings freedom, education, healthcare, and the eternal hope of Jesus Christ; and the bad one that uses every coercive power it possesses to bully the third world into implementing permissive policies on abortion and homosexuality. Regarding the first, they want to know where that West went. Why did the Western church start something and not finish it? Regarding the second, to say they deeply resent it is a gross understatement.

Prior to President Obama's 2015 visit to Kenya, his administration attempted, unsuccessfully, to force that country (and other African countries) to change their laws on homosexuality and "gay rights." For many Africans, this was both arrogant and unwanted—and it was. For them, this is America at its worst. More than once, I was asked if American churches were all gay.

"What's wrong with the American church?" One man asked me. "On television, we see so many people in church"—they all get TBN and DayStar on satellite—"but then we read they are all liberal [his word], approving of gay marriage. Don't they believe in the Bible anymore?"

Watching CNN International and BBC as their news sources, it is no wonder they think this. But they have a point. I could do little more than shrug and hold my palms up in resignation because the question is all too valid. And yet, despite us, these Nigerians were a people who felt affection for America.

Approaching a military checkpoint, Moses slowed the Toyota. The guard, spotting the uniform Moses was wearing, saluted and waved us on. Moses, loving every second of the respect the uniform garnered for him, smiled to the point of laughter.

"Moses," I warned, "You've got to act like you get saluted every day. To them, this must appear old hat for you. If you look like you're enjoying it too much, they might get suspicious."

He tried to suppress his smile, but it was no use. Much to my amusement, the salute, the second one of the day, thrilled him. Punching the accelerator, we were once again blazing a dusty path across the African plain.

A few hours later, we reached the international airport in Abuja. I thanked Moses for his driving and I thanked God for Toyota. My heavens, did that Sequoia take a beating, and so did I. My multitude of formerly broken bones ached from the journey.

Jwan walked with me into the terminal until airport security permitted him to go no farther. We embraced as friends and brothers in Christ. Watching him leave, I thought of the task before him. Turning to make my way to the Lufthansa check-in counter, I realized Phil Collins's "Take Me Home" was playing over airport speakers. Fitting. I took one more fleeting glimpse at the figure of Nigeria's great Christian bishop in the distance.

Minutes later, I was going through passport control.

"Will you come back to Nigeria?" the woman inspecting my passport and ticket asked.

Taking the question at face value, I said I wasn't sure, it depended on circumstances, our finances, and so forth. She interrupted.

"Will you come back to Nigeria?"

Again, I said I wasn't sure and again she interrupted.

"Will you come back to Nigeria?"

"Yes," I said, realizing no other answer would be acceptable.

"Good," she said, handing back my passport. "I am glad you enjoyed your visit to our country."

Before boarding the plane, another woman checked my boarding pass.

"Your ticket, please."

I handed it over. Raising her eyebrows, she said, "Double-oh-seven?" She then examined me dramatically from head to toe and added flatly, "Yes, I think so."

Having no idea what she was talking about, I looked at my ticket for clues:

"Seat Assignment: 007."

I gave a wan smile and joined the enthusiastic rush that always accompanies boarding a plane. Elsewhere, such enthusiasm baffles me, but here it made sense. Since the crisis, not even Lufthansa remains in the country a moment longer than is necessary. The planes land, unload their passengers, refuel, reload, and leave in just over an hour with the same crew.

I was seated next to a Nigerian woman from Lagos who now lives in Atlanta who asked me where I had been.

"Jos."

"In the north?" she exclaimed. "Did you drive that road?!"

"Yes."

"From Abuja to Jos and back again?"

"Yes."

"You had armed escorts, I suppose."

"No."

She looked at me wide-eyed over her reading glasses. "No?! I would never do it! Lagos is, hmm, okay, but the north? Even I, a Nigerian, would never go there! What company lets you do that?! I've not heard of it being done!"

As we waited for departure, I received a text from Jwan:

"You are an awesome and a wonderfully daring figure, my friend. You have proved to me that you are a beloved brother and a friend indeed.... May the Lord be with you. Anticipating the news of your safe arrival."

As the plane lifted off, I thought about my courageous Nigerian friends and the extraordinary work God is doing through them and all we, in the West, could learn from them. Reclining my seat, minutes later I was sleeping more deeply than I had in a very long time.

(People rating: ★★★★★★★★★★)

CHAPTER 15

South Africa:
The Power of One

"I saw that virtually all of the achievements of Africans seemed to have come about through the missionary work of the Church."[1]

—Nelson Mandela

I returned to London where Zachary rejoined me, and together we flew to Johannesburg, South Africa, an eleven-hour flight right over the heart of Africa. South Africa is a country also regarded as one of the most dangerous in the world. Our taxi driver from the O. R. Tambo International Airport to our hotel provided some perspective on how we might think of his country when compared to Nigeria.

"Is this your first time in Africa?" he asked.

"No," I replied.

"Where else have you been?"

"I was recently in Nigeria."

He shivered. "Very dangerous," he said. "Big people." At that, I smiled.

While South Africa isn't Nigeria, make no mistake, it is a dangerous place. Let's consider the murder rate per one hundred thousand people in the countries we have visited so far:

USA	5
Singapore	0
Hong Kong	0
Japan	0
New Zealand	1
Australia	1
South Korea	1
Vietnam	2
Malaysia	2
Thailand	3
India	3
Russia	9
Britain (UK)	1
South Africa?	36

No doubt some of these figures are less trustworthy than Enron's account ledgers, but still, they give us some basis for comparison. This is what is reported, so the real figure may be much higher. (Nigeria did not contribute to this study completed by the World Bank).[2] Regardless, South Africa's murder rate is comparable to that of a warzone. For instance, in Somalia, where the government is fighting al-Shabab militants, the number is thirty-eight per one hundred thousand people. Afghanistan's is forty per one hundred thousand. This is not a statistical category where the high score wins.

In terms of safety, the difference between these countries and South Africa is where one is at risk, to a greater or lesser degree, throughout all of them, South Africa's danger spots are well known. Practically speaking, I wouldn't advise just anyone to travel to Nigeria or Afghanistan. (If you do, make sure your affairs are in order as you might not be coming back.) One can, however, enjoy a lovely vacation in South Africa if you know where to go—*and where not to go.*[i]

That said, the hotel was nervous about our movements. "When walking, we recommend that you stay within the area where the roads have been closed by our security."

This simply would not do. We had a mission to fulfill. Still, to placate them, one night we had dinner at a hotel-recommended African restaurant where we were served crocodile and fried earthworms. According to BBC, every year crocodiles kill about one thousand people, with most of those fatalities coming on this continent. It seemed fitting to eat one of them instead. (And, no, crocodile doesn't taste like chicken.) Earthworms? Even if they do eat us all in the end, I simply couldn't do it.

Beyond murder rates and crocodiles, South Africa is dangerous in other ways that would surprise—or, in our case, delight—Americans. Take, for example, the almost complete absence of enforced tort law. Just watch some of the sketches of South African comedian Leon Schuster online and you'll know what I mean. Outrageous and outrageously funny, Schuster does things a comedian in the United States simply wouldn't dare do for fear of a lawsuit. My eldest son Michael, a lawyer, says, "South Africa takes a draconian view of contributory negligence." A South African friend of mine, Roland Bernard, has a simpler phrase for it: "We call it 'sh*t you can get away with in Africa.'"

This would all become quite evident when, with Roland's strong encouragement, we decided to go on a safari. Ian, a guide of

---

i   Be careful taking the advice of military personnel. I have had a number of them tell me how much they enjoyed some of the dangerous countries we are discussing here. But unless you are planning to take along one hundred thousand of your heavily armed buddies, your experience is in no way comparable.

English extraction, picked us up at our Johannesburg hotel in his Land Rover Defender and drove us the two hours to Pilanesberg National Park. Located northwest of Praetoria, the park, though no Yellowstone, is large, covering some 212 square miles.[ii] With a clickety-clack of the Defender over the cattle grid, we knew our safari had begun.

"Keep the windows up anytime we are stopped or just rolling along slowly," Ian advised. Neither Zachary nor I had any intention of lowering them.

On safari, you are looking for the "Big Five": lions, leopards, elephants, rhinoceroses, and Cape buffalo. Pilanesberg has them all. How do you find them? Just look for a traffic jam with people leaning out of windows and poking from sunroofs to get photos. That was always a clue a member of the Big Five was nearby. I mean, who leans out of a window to get a photo of a golden-breasted bunting or a red-billed oxpecker? Human nature being what it is, people want selfies with the Big Five.

Cars rolled through the park as they would through Yellowstone looking for these magnificent creatures. But unlike America where one occasionally sees bears, here deadly animals abound. (I haven't even mentioned the terrifying black mamba.) What is it in human nature that makes people think a photo snapped from a little closer to the cliff's edge or with the window down while a maneater is only feet away will be so much better? Park rangers appeared randomly and barked at these stupid people over loudspeakers but to little avail.

"Look at these fools." Ian was annoyed.

"Do people ever get killed on safari?" Zachary asked.

"Yes," our guide said casually. "One of my colleagues was killed. He was with an American woman who rolled down the window on the passenger side to get a picture of a lion. But they didn't

---

ii   Yellowstone covers about thirty-four hundred square miles.

see the big lioness circle behind the car. She came up along the passenger side and reached in before either of them saw her. It tore the woman from here—" He pointed to a spot just below his chin. "—to here—" two fingers on his stomach. "She bled to death."

"And your friend?" I asked.

"No, the lioness did not get him. He had a heart attack on the spot and died."

One can only imagine the lawsuits following an incident like that. Ambulance chasers would sue the park, the tour company, Land Rover—anyone with so much as a rand in their pocket. But this is Africa, and the thinking is much less litigious and, frankly, sensible: *Don't want to be killed by a lion? Keep your window up.*

Driving past a half-eaten rhino, Ian knew we were onto something.

"That kill is fresh. Lions are nearby."

Shortly thereafter, they appeared, along with cheetahs.

If I could wish it into being, every child would go on safari like this. The animals are simply breathtaking. For a half hour or so, we followed cheetahs as they stalked a wildebeest. As they passed directly in front of our vehicle, I was surprised at the size of the cheetahs. They were quite tall. But I was also equally surprised at the savvy wildebeest that always stayed about a quarter-mile distant. This was, an African said to me, "proper Africa."

For many Americans, their understanding of South Africa is limited to the 1989 hit *Lethal Weapon 2.* After that movie, South Africa, largely unknown to me beyond vague recollections of the Boer War and old episodes of *Wild Kingdom*, took on a very sinister quality. The baddies in that movie are blue-eyed, blond-haired men who are essentially Nazis who somehow escaped the Allies' notice in World War II. They are white supremacists and proud of it. Who better to beat up, shoot, drown, and chuck these guys off buildings than the white-and-black buddy team of Mel Gibson and Danny Glover?

Apparently, I wasn't the only one who thought white South Africans were all racists. I recall Roland telling me about his first visit to America in December 1994 when he was thirteen years old. An Afrikaner, he arrived at JFK with his parents and sister. It was with excitement the family piled into a taxi and headed for Manhattan. The cabbie, a black man, detected their accents and asked where they were from. When Roland, good-natured and naïve, replied that they were South Africans, the driver stopped the taxi abruptly and demanded the whole family get out. Bewildered, they were left standing on Robert F. Kennedy Bridge with their luggage stacked at their feet.

Of course, the reality of South Africa and assigning guilt for that country's past and present struggles is not so, well, black and white. Bryce Courtenay's 1989 novel *The Power of One*, offers a glimpse into the national, ethnic, religious, tribal, and historical complexity of South Africa and, as the title suggests, hints at the astonishing impact a single individual can make on the course of history. And South Africa has a fascinating—and bloody—history.

In 1652, Jan van Riebeeck and ninety employees of the Dutch East India Company arrived in South Africa. Their job was to establish a station that would provide fresh provisions of food and water for Dutch ships making their way past the Cape of Good Hope. Within a decade, Dutch ambitions expanded to include the colonization of the tip of the African continent.

Due to the new colony's success, more laborers were needed. Soon, other settlers began arriving from Germany and Holland, bringing with them slaves from India and Mozambique. From the start, slavery was integral to this society. Dutch farmers, known as Boers, began moving inland, encroaching upon lands claimed by the Khoekhoe and Sans tribes. Conflict was inevitable, and the Boers, possessing superior arms, devastated their rivals. Over time, the Boers developed a culture different from the Netherlands and the Dutch settlers living on the Cape. They called themselves Afrikaners and their language, a variation of Dutch, was Afrikaans. In 1795, they established their own republic.

In that same year, however, a new tribe landed on the Cape: the British. Just as the Afrikaners displaced the Khoekhoes and Sans, the English displaced Afrikaners and indigenous tribes alike as they fought for control of a territory that had become extremely valuable to the British as a supply point for their ships on the Indian trade route. In 1806, the British took possession of the land by treaty and English settlers began arriving by the thousands, alarming Afrikaners.

Worse for the Afrikaners, the British were then engaged in a struggle to end the slave trade. In 1807, Parliament outlawed the practice in the colonies, and in 1833, they outlawed it altogether. Deeply resentful of their British masters and their understanding of Christian morality, the Afrikaners, driven out of the land and determined to hold on to their customs and their slaves, began the Great Trek to find new land to settle.

Driving northward, the Afrikaners encountered tribes facing a problem, not unlike their own. Another nonindigenous people were sweeping southward with great military efficiency, conquering, killing, and driving all before them: the Zulu. Less powerful tribes were crushed between the advancing Afrikaner and Zulu armies. Eventually, after a series of setbacks, the Afrikaners defeated the Zulus and established the Republic of Natalia. The British, partially under the pretext of ending the slave trade, invaded and annexed Natalia, making it the British Colony of

Natal. Thus, the Afrikaners once again packed up and trekked northward and proclaimed two new republics, the Orange Free State and the South African Republic (later the Transvaal).

Are you seeing the pattern here?

The British, determined to secure their borders and end the slave trade, found additional motivation to bring the Afrikaners under British rule with the discovery of diamonds and gold in these regions. By 1898, the British subdued the last of African tribal independence and in 1902, they concluded a victorious (but bloody) war with the Boers.

But if the Afrikaners lost the war, they eventually won the political settlement. Outnumbering their British rulers, they gained ascendancy in the government and an Afrikaner nationalist party would increasingly set aside British notions of racial equality for the older Afrikaner ways. By 1948, apartheid, a radical system of racial segregation, was in place. It required a rigid separation of the races: whites, "coloreds" (people of white and black parentage), blacks, and Asians (primarily Indians) all had to carry racial identity cards, but only whites had any political or legal standing. Racial purity was enforced, outlawing sex and marriage between the races. And only whites could vote.

This system remained in place until one extraordinary man walked onto history's stage:

Nelson Mandela.

If ever men are born to fulfill a specific mission—Martin Luther, Lincoln, Churchill—surely Nelson Mandela was one of them. He set himself to the destruction of apartheid. Through a life of hardship, almost constant conflict, and twenty-seven years of imprisonment, it is remarkable Mandela never lost sight of this objective. Mandela was a man of singular vision. In 1964, while standing in the dock and having just been given a sentence of life imprisonment, Mandela addressed the injustices of this sentence and apartheid:

"I have cherished the ideal of a democratic and free society in which all persons live together in harmony and with equal opportunities. It is an ideal which I hope to live for and to achieve. But if needs be, it is an ideal for which I am prepared to die."[3]

Most remarkable, however, is the fact that once he achieved his goal and gained political power with his election as president of South Africa in 1994, he did not embark on a path of revenge. He might well have done so, following the examples set by other political prisoners of the twentieth century—Lenin, Stalin, Hitler, and Castro. What made Mandela different? Was it merely a matter of temperament or was there something else at work in this man who exhibited such rare restraint?

According to Mandela, it was his father, a minor chieftain and believer in pagan African religion, who gave him his stubborn, rebellious nature. But it was his mother, a devout Christian, who molded his character. She had her son baptized a Methodist and educated at a Methodist school. It is generally accepted Mandela was a Christian, but apart from the eternal residence of his soul, whether or not he was, is for our purposes anyway, irrelevant. Why? Because it is quite clear, Christian or not, Mandela's moral outlook was unquestionably shaped by that religion. Throughout his life, he would both attend and teach Sunday school—even while imprisoned. But it was as a child Mandela recognized the power of the Christian creed.

In his autobiography, *The Long Walk to Freedom*, Mandela writes: "The Church was as concerned with this world as the next: I saw that virtually all of the achievements of Africans seemed to have come about through the missionary work of the Church."

Hardly a politically correct statement then, and even less so now, it is nonetheless true. Mandela—who had every opportunity to become a dictator in the mold of Zimbabwe's Robert Mugabe—promised to serve only one term. A promise he fulfilled. Urged by members of his political party to take revenge on their former white oppressors, Mandela flatly refused, and instead insisted on forgiveness and reconciliation. Those are core Christian principles. Such things are conveniently forgotten in the narratives of other great reformers: William Wilberforce, Abraham Lincoln, Martin Luther King Jr., and even Gandhi, who, though Hindu, based his program of nonviolent resistance on the life and teachings of Jesus of Nazareth.

Zachary and I visited Mandela's home, now a museum, in the shantytown of Soweto. A brick house, it is a humble dwelling, though much nicer than most of what one finds in Soweto where people are crowded in metal shacks. But Soweto is a great step up from Alexandra, where conditions are much worse. Tourism has improved Soweto. Not so for Alexandra. It is a very dangerous place; tour groups don't go there.

"Do not go there," a hotel employee advised me. He was direct. "You are a white man. You cannot hope to go unseen. Even I, a black South African, would never go there."

That settled it. Having had enough of the Fulani in Nigeria, I was not looking for any unnecessary adrenaline rushes.

We instead took a taxi to the Apartheid Museum. A world-class museum, it chronicles the history of South Africa's racial tensions. It is a powerful presentation of a nation's struggle and of its attempts to overcome. Mandela figured prominently into the narrative.

But what of Mandela's influence today?

Let us return to New York City and the Robert Kennedy Bridge. What the cabbie didn't know about the thirteen-year-old boy he unceremoniously kicked to the curb on that cold December day in 1994 is that this boy would twice be given the honor of meeting

Nelson Mandela as a national champion rugby player and team captain. Recollecting these meetings, Roland Bernard told me:

> Mandela was one of those figures who enters the room and you feel it. He had an amazing presence. That strange aura he carried.... Humility and compassion emanated from him. It may sound like a Hollywood, Disney-like characterization, but anyone who ever had the privilege of meeting this amazing man will tell you it is true. His impact is still felt [in South Africa].

Today, because the successors of Mandela have little respect for his vision of national unity based on forgiveness, reconciliation, and the common good, South Africa has slipped back into tribalism, violence, and human degradation. For instance, the nation's leading political party, the African National Congress (ANC), has endorsed government seizures of farms owned by whites and giving them to black farmers. This is, they say, to right the wrongs of colonialism, but it's nothing more than racism and revenge disguised as government aid and has led to the massacre of many white farmers.

Nevertheless, Mandela's vision lives on in people like Roland. Those brief encounters with Mandela profoundly affected the young rugby star who, by lineage, should have been Mandela's enemy. Instead, Roland, who now lives in comfortable retirement in Cape Town after a successful professional career, became a convert to Christianity. As with Mandela, he feels strongly the tenets of that faith require him to make a difference in this world before moving on to the next.

This is the Power of One.

CHAPTER 16

Argentina:
Like Whitney Houston
and Bobby Brown

"On March 24, Argentina commemorates the 40th anniversary of a military coup that 'disappeared' thousands of people, a deep trauma in Argentina's national psyche."[1]

—Uki Goñi in *The New York Times*, March 21, 2016

The next stop on our world tour was Argentina. Direct flights were not an option on our RTW ticket, so we booked a flight from Johannesburg to São Paulo, Brazil, and from there to Buenos Aires. As we drove through the streets of this capital city, it looked like almost any other socialist city in the world.

A country's poverty can be attributed to many things: work ethic, poor geography, a lack of natural resources, war, and so on. More often than not, however, corruption is a major contributor. This takes on a physical manifestation. A quick survey of Transparency International's annual Corruption Index[2] indicates there is a direct correlation between a country's wealth and the degree to which it is a hotbed of corruption. This is because businesses simply do not want to invest in countries where there is a lack of political stability and a high degree of dishonesty.[i] Hence, the poverty of India and Nigeria isn't an accident of history, nor is the postwar wealth of Japan and South Korea, countries where honesty in trade and obedience to the government are socially reinforced doctrines.

Zachary and I explored Buenos Aires entirely on our own. There is much to be seen and enjoyed: the architecture, the pleasant plazas and gardens, the beauty of the coastline, lovely coffee shops, museums, and a friendly populace. But all of it, even the friendliness of the people, is eclipsed by the often-gloomy outlook of the citizens of this country, if not for their futures, then for Argentina's. One finds this throughout most of Latin America, where an astonishing one in five people report being offered a bribe in exchange for their vote and more than half of those surveyed believe corruption is getting worse in their country.[3]

One morning, Zachary and I decided to take the ferry across the Rio de la Plata to Colonia del Sacramento, Uruguay. (We aren't including Uruguay in our survey. Consider it a freebie.) A quaint village, the cobblestone streets, old walls, and churches date from when it was a Portuguese colony. Today it is mostly a tourist destination for photographers.

"You're from the United States," a woman said to me on the ferry. It was a statement, not a question.

"Guilty."

"I thought so. You look like it. But I also heard you talking to him." She pointed to Zachary.

We chatted briefly, and she admitted that she had been to the United States to visit family a few times and like so many people we met in every country on this tour, she hoped to move there.

---

i   Some businesses, such as the oil and diamond industries, are so lucrative that Western investors are prepared to suffer what may come. Corruption is simply calculated into their bottom lines.

"Why not stay here?" I asked.

She let her shoulders sag demonstratively. "It is very hard to get ahead in this country. The government likes to say that everything is free, but nothing is free. My relatives there have it made. If you work hard in your country, you can have a lot of success."

She was, of course, referring to corruption. To be fair, Argentina is not the most corrupt country we have visited thus far on our global tour. Nor is it more corrupt than some of the countries remaining on our itinerary. It is just another country eviscerated by socialism, fascism, socialism again, stillborn attempts to modernize, and one corrupt government after another. And Argentina, like other countries we have seen on this trip, has a dark history that casts a long shadow over its future.

In early 1944, with the Third Reich crumbling, Heinrich Himmler, head of the Nazi SS, sent agents to Buenos Aires, Argentina. Their task was to establish an escape route for high-ranking Nazis should Germany lose the war. When that outcome became a reality in May 1945, Nazis flowed into Argentina (and throughout South America) where they were welcomed by the government of military dictator Juan Perón.

Why?

That South America was colonized by the Spanish and Portuguese is not news to most. What is less known, is the degree to which Germans, Austrians, and Italians emigrated to South America long before the world wars. Supermodel Gisele Bündchen,[4] for example, is the descendant of such immigrants. She is a sixth-generation German-Brazilian and is ethnically German. Bündchen is not unique in this. Many Europeans were not fleeing Europe but coming for business opportunities. Hence, they often brought with them a love of the home country and strong anti-Semitism.[ii]

So, when World War II ended and the Allies were combing Europe for war criminals like Adolf Eichmann, Josef Mengele, and Klaus Barbie, many German, Austrian, and Italian South Americans happily funded Perón's efforts to facilitate their escape to Argentina and establish them with new identities and new lives. Argentina's military dictators—they had many—admired the Nazis and their methods. So much so, Argentina (and Chile) sought their advice on government policy and even created German-style concentration camps. Under Perón and others like him, tens of thousands were murdered, tortured, imprisoned, or simply vanished.

Those scars don't heal in one generation, nor even in two. And, sadly, those practices become ingrained governmental habits all too readily accepted by hopeless populations that have become used to them. The relationship some countries have with dictatorship is a bit like the Hollywood romances of Burton and Taylor, Desi and Lucy, Tina and Ike, or Whitney and Bobby. You know, one of those love-hate relationships everyone knows is destructive, even the participants, but for reasons defying all understanding, they just can't stay away from each other.

That's Argentina.

It is a country with a history of governmental brutality, systemic corruption, continual human rights violations, and a fatal attraction to dictatorship. Yes, just when things are looking up and you think Whitney is finally going to leave Bobby, the two reunite. Juan Perón is the best example of this, but hardly the last iteration of it. Take, for example, Argentina's former president—and current vice president—Cristina Kirchner. Although she was not

---

ii   To be clear, I am in no way suggesting that Ms. Bündchen is an anti-Semite.

a dictator as we generally imagine it, her presidency nonetheless bore remarkable similarities with past practices.

If you like Hillary, you'd *love* Cristina. Kirchner was the first lady of her country. She was politically ambitious and longed to be her country's first female president. She ran for president, but unlike Clinton, she won. For a time, she enjoyed great popularity within her party and with much of the country. Unfortunately, also like Clinton, the stench of scandal follows Kirchner everywhere—even in her post-presidential life.

The most spectacular of these scandals involves the bombing of a Jewish community center in Buenos Aires in 1994 where eighty-seven people were killed and more than a hundred injured. Evidence strongly suggests it was approved and orchestrated by the Iranian government. Special prosecutor Alberto Nisman publicly accused the Argentine government, Cristina Kirchner in particular, of a cover-up to secure favorable trade deals with Iran. In the early morning hours of January 18, 2015, the day Nisman was to testify before the Argentinian congress and reveal evidence against Kirchner and the Iranian government, Nisman was found dead in his apartment with a single gunshot wound to the head. The government quickly ruled it a suicide. To date, no one has been prosecuted in the attack on the Jewish community center.

That's Argentina.

And this is to say nothing of other traits common to South America—widespread poverty, a society of haves and have-nots, a Catholic Church that has probably seen more conversions to Marxism than Bible-believing Christianity, and the frequent disappearance or murder of journalists who try to expose these evils. Argentina is trying to face its past and seems to be trending upward. But the historian in me is a cynic because all too often these countries have no future. Not really. There is only the past repeating itself.

Those countries that managed to break bad historical cycles are transformed at a fundamental level. More to the point, they are transformed spiritually. I have great long-term hope for China, for instance, not because the present government is democratic, but because the Chinese are converting to Christianity in huge numbers. That has everything to do with the Christian reformers who are at work there. Argentina shows no signs of that kind of change; rather, it shows signs of American material influence, and that is a mixed bag.

CHAPTER 17

Brazil: Apocalypto

"I decided to defy the demon. He had never helped me. Maybe Jesus would."

—Brazilian who converted from Brazilian cult to Christianity

In his introduction to *The Screwtape Letters*, C. S. Lewis, who very much believed in an unseen spirit world, writes:

> There are two equal and opposite errors into which our race can fall about the devils. One is to disbelieve in their existence. The other is to believe, and to feel an excessive and unhealthy interest in them. They themselves are equally pleased by both errors and hail a materialist or a magician with the same delight.[1]

Yes, the Devil is happy to produce in man a smug atheism or a belief in the occult—anything so long as it is not belief in Jesus Christ. Traveling around the world, one gets the distinct impression the strategy is working. In Europe, which is all but dead to Christian belief, socialism—atheism's political manifestation—is the fashion. That worldview, such as it is, is gaining ground in America.

But don't be fooled. Belief in the occult is very much alive. If you spend any meaningful time in Africa, you are sure to encounter it there. Indeed, one day I was sitting in the office of Jwan Zhumbes, the Anglican bishop of Bukuru, Nigeria, looking over the vows the church requires of its priests. This stood out:

"I swear that I am not a member of any secret societies..."

"Jwan, what is this vow all about?" I then read it to him. "Is this a reference to Freemasonry?"

He laughed heartily at my naiveté. "No, my friend," he corrected me. "It is referring to ancient African religion, secret societies that involve the eating of human flesh and drinking of human blood. This is very prevalent here and exists at all levels of society."

Yikes.

Fast-forward and we encountered the occult again in Rio de Janeiro where I encountered the occult again a Brazilian convert to Christianity. His name was Alex. He owns a taxi service. The conversation was not scheduled or planned; he just happened to be driving us to our hotel when I started asking him questions.

"Are you a religious man?" I asked.

"I am," he said.

I bored down into that a bit and discovered he is an evangelical Christian. He went on to tell me that prior to his conversion, he was raised to believe the teachings of Candomblé, a secretive Brazilian cult.

As he started to explain what practitioners of this cult believe, it sounded very much like my conversation with the bishop—ritual sacrifices, dark forces, possession, Linda Blair-like projectile vomiting—okay, I made that last bit up. But you get the picture.

"Was this religion imported from Africa?" Zachary asked.

"Yes. With the slaves who were brought to South America."

"Did your whole family believe this stuff?"

"Yes," he said. "My father was a leader in the cult. My parents, sisters, aunts and uncles, and our friends were part of it. Cults like it are very popular in Brazil."

At this point, I was wondering how many Brazilians held these beliefs, but such statistics are useless because secret societies are, by definition, *secretive*. Alex estimated three out of ten Brazilians were members of such groups. Who knows?

Alex then told us it was his father's conversion to Christianity that changed everything. Once his father converted, one by one, the family left Candomblé and converted, too. Even family friends became Christians. Alex said his father is now a pastor in a local church. This seemed rather amazing. I asked to meet his father and a dinner meeting was hastily arranged.

Alex's father, who I will call Célio, kindly accepted our invitation. Sitting across from Zachary and me, he told us his story in Portuguese as Alex translated. What he had to say is different from the conversion stories you hear in your typical American Sunday school class. I will paraphrase what he said:

> I came from a family that believed in Candomblé. I was taught it by my mother and grandmother. I talked to a spirit just like I am talking to you. I could see it. It could appear anytime, anywhere. Through it, I could talk to my dead relatives. When my grandmother died, I could talk to her. Or thought I could. It was just the demon assuming her voice. I was unhappy. Oppressed. I tried to commit suicide at ten. The demon always demanded sacrifices: an animal, my money, my food or possessions, a relationship. Something. In return, it promised me many things, but never gave them. I wanted to know why it didn't help me! I asked and would be told of something else I had to do.

At this point, I interrupted and asked if the demons ever demanded human sacrifice.

Not in my particular branch, but in some, yes, they sometimes demand that people be killed. When I was married and Alex was sixteen, I was at a club dancing. For reasons I cannot explain, I started crying uncontrollably. A Christian who had probably strayed from the faith—he shouldn't have been in this kind of place—saw me and told me about Jesus. I went to church. The demon appeared to me and told me that if I went again, he would kill Alex.

Alex looked startled, stopped his translation, and talked with his father animatedly in Portuguese. Alex then turned to us and said, "I did not know this!" To which Célio replied, "I didn't want to frighten you." Célio then continued his narrative.

I decided to defy the demon. He had never helped me. Maybe Jesus would. I started going to the church to explore Christianity, but the demonic oppression got worse. I developed sickness. Then one day I made the decision to receive Christ as my savior and Lord. I felt I had to tell others in the cult that I was no longer one of them. So, I went to the Candomblé temple to tell them and my demon that I had become a Christian. When I left, I fell unconscious in the street. My brother called an ambulance. I was declared dead on the scene, but I was having an out-of-body experience. I could see my body in the street, my brother, and medical personnel all around me. I suddenly woke up. It was like I had died to that cult. From that moment, my life changed. I never saw the demon again. For the first time, I had peace. My friends and family could see that something in my life had changed and they wanted the peace I had. Some, still in the cult, started following me to see where I was going and what I was doing. [He laughed at the recollection.] Soon they became Christians, too. That was twenty years ago. Fifteen years ago, I became a pastor in the church.

That is his story. You can choose to believe it or dismiss it as a bad acid trip. Either way, I offer this: *Célio believed it.* And he struck me as a perfectly rational man. Furthermore, such conversion stories are common in Africa and South America.

The next day, Zachary and I took a tour of the Brazilian rainforest with a local naturalist. Again, I steered the conversation toward the spiritual.

"Do you have any religious beliefs?" I asked.

He shrugged. "I believe in dinosaurs," he said with a chuckle, deflecting the question.

"So, you don't believe in God?"

"Sometimes. Whenever I am in trouble!"

In the space of twenty-four hours, I had, in C. S. Lewis's terminology, met a materialist and a (former) magician.

G. K. Chesterton is credited with saying, "When a man stops believing in God, he doesn't then believe in nothing, he believes anything." Regardless of who said it—no one has ever been able to definitively source the quotation—the statement is true.

In developed countries, atheism has not produced a belief in nothing. On the contrary, it has produced a belief in anything: socialism, multiculturalism, environmentalism, New Age—you name it. Romans 1:18–32 warns that when man suppresses belief in the One True God, which gives order and understanding to his world and serves to anchor him in rationality, this is what inevitably happens. In the Apostle Paul's words, "Claiming to be wise, they became fools." Such foolishness is manifest in the developed world's growing inability to distinguish between man and animal, man and woman, and right and wrong.

We have mistaken our sophisticated use of technology with a sophisticated understanding of life and its meaning. The combined intelligence of Microsoft, Google, and Apple, while able to create self-driving cars and put the power of a supercomputer at our fingertips, cannot give us purpose or answer life's basic question: Is there a God and, if so, what does he want from me?

By contrast, the third world is much more spiritually sophisticated than is the first world. They generally need no convincing the spiritual realm is real, but the pendulum often swings to the opposite extreme. There we find people who believe in every kind of spirit, every kind of God. These are the magicians of whom Lewis spoke. Such a belief has an irrationality all its own. Talking with Célio and Alex and noting the prevalence of occult practices in South America, one gets the sense that without the many Christian missionaries who penetrated these countries long ago, we might be looking at Apocalypto on a continental scale.

The Apostle Paul's words in Romans 1:19–20, a chilling warning, are nevertheless a gracious call to recalibrate our spiritual bearings:

> For what can be known about God is plain to them, because God has shown it to them. For his invisible attributes, namely, his eternal power and divine nature, have been clearly perceived, ever since the creation of the world, in the things that have been made. So they are without excuse.[2]

Brazil, like most of Central and South America, suffers from systemic corruption. According to Transparency International, it is even more corrupt than Argentina. Going to South America? Watch your wallet. The 2016 Rio Olympics brought this clearly into view for all the world to see. Raw sewage polluted reservoirs designated for water sports; facilities were unfinished or inadequate; monies were wasted or simply disappeared, and promises went unfulfilled. Writing for the *National Post*, Scott Stinson says:

> Not following up on plans is one thing, but the context here is that many of these projects were cited as reasons for why Rio, a troubled city in a troubled country, should want to host such a costly spectacle as the Olympics. Schools, subways, parks, housing, clean water: all of these long-term gains would flow from the short-term spending that the Games would spark. Unless they didn't. So far, they didn't even spark the simpler things.[3]

And yet, there is so much to like about Brazil. In 2010, I was invited to speak at Mackenzie Presbyterian University in São Paulo by then-university chancellor Augustus Nicodemus Lopes. One of the oldest universities in Brazil, Mackenzie has about forty-five thousand students. Lauri accompanied me and we thoroughly enjoyed our time with the faculty and students we met there. As a gift, they sent us on an all-expenses-paid weekend at Iguazu Falls. An extraordinary natural wonder on the border with Argentina, it is ten times the size of Niagara Falls.[i]

---

i   If you've seen the film *The Mission*, this is where the scene with Robert De Niro climbing the falls was filmed.

Even if you just take a walk on Copacabana Beach, journey into the rainforest (with a guide), or visit one of its many wonderful museums, you will be very impressed with much of what you see. Zachary and I did all these things and treasure the experiences. We highly recommend them. But again, this is the Traveler's Fallacy. This is not the same as living in Rocinha, Rio de Janeiro's famed favela perched on a hillside right behind our hotel, as more than one hundred thousand people do. These slums (Rocinha is just one of many) are scarcely better than Soweto or Alexandra and they are home to roughly 6 percent of Brazil's population. Prostitutes are scattered along the streets, in alleyways, and near hotel entrances, even in the fashionable districts. And theft, drugs, murder, and human trafficking are common.

So bad is crime in the favelas the police have adopted a brutal means of dealing with it: snipers. Police snipers, literally licensed to kill, are positioned and authorized to shoot suspected criminals. This is being done regularly. No arrest. No trial. No prison. Shot dead from 250 meters away, locals left to clean up the mess.[4]

On our last day in Rio, Zachary and I hiked up to the colossal Christ the Redeemer Art Deco statue atop Corcovado. Completed in 1931, the statue stands ninety-eight-feet tall and is ninety-two-feet wide from outstretched fingertip to outstretched fingertip. The figure of a compassionate Christ looking down on Rio de Janeiro is visible from anywhere in the city. Brazil's problems feel so insurmountable for a country that has never been able to climb out of the third-world quagmire. But there is reason to harbor a tentative hope for Brazil where one simply cannot for its southern neighbor, Argentina. Authentic Christian belief is growing in Brazil in a way it is not in Argentina. What does the future hold? It's difficult to say, but this much is sure: they will need all the help Jesus Christ can give them.

CHAPTER 18

Chile:
South America's Most Stable
Democracy?

"History teaches you that dictators never end up well."[1]

—Augusto Pinochet, dictator of Chile (1973–1990)

Remember the days when everyone flying dressed as if going to church? Not anymore. No, flying, once luxurious, is now, in the words of the late Christopher Hitchens, "a humiliating experience." I attribute this to a variety of factors but none more than 9/11. Since that fateful September day in 2001, airline travel has taken on an often-miserable quality.

You hurry up to wait.

Your luggage is weighed and if it is even slightly over the limit, you might be forced to repack on the spot, your underwear and socks spilling onto the floor for all to see.

Then, the TSA (or their global equivalents) regularly abuse their power, making snarky remarks or unreasonable demands just to let you know they can.

You disrobe to pass through security and, if you are part of the random selection, you're felt up by a guy in rubber gloves, again, for all the world to see.

Throughout all this, you try to keep an eye on your carry-on as it travels down a conveyor belt. In it, among other things, is packed your laptop, phone, a host of chargers, and the little snow globe you bought your daughter or grandson.

Somewhere on the same conveyor belt is a plastic bowl containing your watch—though not a Rolex, it's one you deem valuable enough—wallet, passport, boarding pass, sunglasses, and pocket change.

On the other end, as the TSA-types tell you to get your things and get out of the way, you frantically put your belt and jacket back on as you hop along wearing one shoe while holding the other, your passport and boarding pass clenched in your teeth, your shirt partially untucked, and your carry-on, in disarray, trailing behind.

This is to be expected if you fly. Making things worse at this point in our journey was the fact our flight itinerary in South America was a source of continual frustration and stress. The problem was not the flight, but the bookings, all made through an incompetent travel agency that directed us to wrong terminals, failed to purchase flights, and consistently put us in undesirable circumstances.[i] In his circumnavigation of the earth, Magellan fought scurvy and (unsuccessfully) Filipino warriors; Zachary and I fought corruption and the inconveniences associated with modern conveniences. On the whole, I think Magellan had it worse.

Arriving at our hotel, Zachary and I misjudged the square footage of the hotel elevator and stepped into a huddle of women speaking in an easy Spanish. Apparently returning from an

---

i   Check your itineraries carefully. The travel or airline agent often gives little thought to what they are requiring you to do, scheduling a 3 a.m. flight or two stops when flying direct was an option.

afternoon of shopping, their hands were full of the day's spoils. Holding my arms up and turning awkwardly to face the door, I was met with an oversized bag from Banana Republic. I smirked at the irony. A derogatory term for Latin American governments, to this group of affluent women it was territory to be conquered, plundered. To me, it was a fitting metaphor.

Or was it?

All over South America, you see it. Ostentatious displays of American commercial enterprise dominate the fashionable parts of cities like São Paulo, Rio de Janeiro, and even Buenos Aires. Nike, Starbucks, Calvin Klein, Apple—they are all there, and to own their products is to be hip and cool. American businesses have accomplished worldwide what the CIA, the United States armed forces, diplomacy, and trillions in US tax dollars could not in fifty years: advance the American way of life. Nowhere in South America is this more evident than in Santiago, Chile.

Over the last three decades, democracy in South America has flourished. Writing for the Brookings Institute, Daniel Zovatto describes South America's democracies:

> Latin America is a paradox: it is the only region in the world that combines democratic regimes in almost all countries with large sectors of their populations living below the poverty line (27.9 percent for 2013, according to ECLAC), the most uneven economic distribution in the world, high levels of corruption and the highest homicide rate in the world. Nowhere else in the world is democracy shaped by such an unusual combination of factors. It is a fact that our democracies exhibit important deficits and symptoms of fragility. The main unresolved issues are institutional problems that affect governability and the rule of law, independence and interconnection between state

powers, hyper-presidentialism and reelection, corruption, constraints to freedom of expression, poor performance of electoral and political systems, lack of gender equality, and citizen insecurity, all factors that undermine its functioning.[2]

That statement is true of South America generally, but Chile is an outlier to the rest of this troubled continent. It isn't a banana republic.

The geography of some countries makes them virtually ungovernable. Authorities in Brazil cannot, for example, effectively control what happens in the mysterious Amazon rainforest, an area roughly the same size as the forty-eight contiguous United States.[ii] Russia's enormity, covering eleven time zones, has been a historic problem. Malaysia, consisting of 878 islands, and Indonesia, 17,508 islands, make for unwieldy governance. And Ukraine's lack of natural barriers has made them a doormat for invading armies since time immemorial.

As nations go, Chile's geography, though beautiful and interesting, is awful. 2,653 miles long while only an average of 110 miles wide, the country is chiefly uninhabitable mountains. Worse, it is actively volcanic and thus prone to epic earthquake disasters. Yes, geographically speaking, if Chile were a square on a Monopoly board, it would be the slums of Baltic Avenue and the United States would inhabit the exclusive districts of Boardwalk and Park Place.

Mitigating this potentially insurmountable obstacle to national greatness is the fact that Santiago, in central Chile, is home to one-third of Chile's eighteen million people. That makes governance as well as social and economic development possible for

---

ii   Roughly 60 percent of the Amazon rainforest lies within the borders of Brazil.

such an elongated state. Remarkably, Chile has largely managed to overcome these difficulties and they have become Latin America's most stable democracy.

The secret to Chile's success is found in a free-market economy relying on the development of industry where most of Latin America has remained agricultural. This has generated not only wealth but also stability. When Stalin complained that American Communist Party leader Jay Lovestone failed to convert working-class Americans to communism, Lovestone gave a compelling reason for that failure: "The American poor didn't seethe with class resentment and turn to revolutionary ideologies because upward mobility gave them the chance to rise." Supposedly, Stalin shot back that Lovestone needed to end "this heresy of American exceptionalism."[3]

Chile's growing prosperity has likewise given birth to a thriving middle class. Furthermore, since the brutal dictatorship of Augusto Pinochet ended in 1990, successive Chilean presidents have shown a willingness to devolve federal powers in favor of the local governments, expand civil liberties, and demonstrate greater transparency.

What about faith? Chile, like the rest of Latin America, is overwhelmingly Catholic. But only 13 percent of Chilean Catholics attend mass regularly. Evangelical Christianity, however, has grown rapidly in recent decades. It is estimated that evangelicals now number 15 percent of Chile's population. Growth among the poor has been spectacular. Writing for Reuters, Lisa Yulkowski says:

> One change that could spark even greater growth among evangelicals is the fact that the movement has gained acceptance among Chile's middle class. "It used to be looked down upon for a middle- or upper-class person to say they were evangelical," said Francisco Ruiz, a 60-year-old

former Catholic priest. "It's no longer embarrassing, and businesspeople are starting to take notice and hire evangelicals because of their reliability." Ruiz, who is still a practicing Catholic, said he didn't think the more traditional Catholic Church was prepared for how this could reshape the religious landscape in Chile.[4]

But if the Protestant ethic gave rise to capitalism and prosperity as Max Weber famously observed, prosperity often gives rise to a fatally irreligious spirit, and that, too, is at work in Chile. Socialists, socialists, and anarchists are finding universities fertile for their ideologies. Sound familiar? Homegrown terror groups are burning churches, destroying infrastructure, and attacking opponents. So great are these problems that some suggest Chile's image of stability is only a veneer.[5] But with a rapidly growing church, there is much reason for optimism in the face of these threats.

Zachary spent a day with a local family he met through some friends. That day, those conversations, became a highlight of his trip. He returned to the hotel chipper and, as usual, thinking about food.

"Hey, Daddio, guess what I just saw?"

I had no idea. "I dunno. A sniper on a rooftop aiming at me through the hotel window?"

"Funny. No. I saw a P. F. Chang's. Let's go eat there."

So far on this trip, we had eaten (or were offered) barbeque eel, cow's tongue, squid, shark fin, kangaroo, earthworms, crocodile, some kind of snake, and other things I could not identify. P. F. Chang's, whatever its pretensions to the contrary, is about as American as it gets. I was all in.

How does one assess Chile, this peculiar country once dominated by the Incas, this place the Spanish subdued and colonized, where Sir Francis Drake bombarded and pillaged, this long, narrow, mountainous country of active volcanoes that gained its independence in 1840, suffered the military dictatorship of Augusto Pinochet, and is now a tentative model for other South American democracies?

Chile defies simple categories. Its history is remarkably similar to that of its neighbor, Argentina—a former colony, civil war, military dictatorship, a penchant for governmental corruption and brutality, Milton Friedman economic reforms, and an ambition to join the great democracies of the world. But where Argentina remains trapped by the gravitational force of its history, Chile seems to have reached escape velocity, leaving the dark atmospheric pressure of the past while maintaining a trajectory for better things.

I was tired, and it was time for some tasty P. F. Chang's potstickers.

Peru:
"The Strangest, Saddest City
Thou Can'st See"

"I cannot say I enjoyed the very little I saw of Peru: in summer, however, it is said that the climate is much pleasanter."

—Charles Darwin, *Voyages of the Adventure and Beagle, Vol. III*

The flight from Santiago to Lima is a tolerable four hours, following the spine of the Andes northward. Running some four thousand, three hundred miles, the Andes are the longest continuous mountain range in the world. Looking out on the endless snowcapped peaks, I was reminded of Piers Paul Read's horrifying and triumphant book, *Alive*. It is the story of the Uruguayan rugby team whose plane crashed somewhere in these mountains in 1972. It is South America's version of the Donner Party. Don't read it with a full stomach.

Zachary, along with my wife Lauri, had been in Peru before, traveling high into the mountainous interior as part of a medical mission team. The photos of that trip were of beautiful snow-capped peaks, misty green valleys, bright sunshine casting long shadows and sparkling on the clear waters, and unique, often attractive, architecture.

Lima, however, is something altogether different. Herman Melville, a travel writer of sorts, was not impressed with Lima. In his classic *Moby Dick*, he writes:

> Nor is it, altogether, the remembrance of her cathedral-toppling earthquakes; nor the stampedoes of her frantic seas: nor the tearlessness of arid skies that never rain; nor the sight of her wide field of leaning spires, wrenched copestones, and crosses all adroop (like canted yards of anchored fleets); and her suburban avenues of house-walls lying over upon each other, as a tossed pack of cards; it is not these things alone which make tearless Lima, the strangest, saddest city thou can'st see. For Lima has taken the white veil; and there is a higher horror in this whiteness of her woe. Old as Pizarro, this whiteness keeps her ruins forever new; admits not the cheerful greenness of complete decay; spreads over her broken ramparts the rigid pallor of an apoplexy that fixes its own distortions.[1]

This assessment seems a bit harsh, but Melville must be forgiven. He was, after all, manic depressive. Even so, he had a point. Lima is depressing. *La garúa*, the almost perpetual haze hanging over the city, the largely grassless landscape, the absence of color, the unattractive dirt cliffs, and the fact it almost never rains, thus leaving everything covered in a moist brown film, makes for an unpleasant ambiance. No wonder Peru is one of the world's top cocaine producers. People are looking for something, *anything*, to feel better. Some things drive people to drink. In Peru, it seems, they are driven to snort a few lines—or drink them.

On their previously mentioned trip to Peru, Zachary and Lauri suffered from altitude sickness, a very common side effect for those who are unaccustomed to sixteen thousand feet. Their hosts gave them tea, telling them it would help. It did! They *immediately* felt better! Turned out, the tea was made from a coca plant, the source of cocaine. Though containing much smaller quantities of the illegal substance and perfectly legal in Peru, it is nonetheless illegal in the United States. Indeed, many Americans consuming this tea have, much to their surprise, failed subsequent drug tests.

There's not much to celebrate about Peru. From the early 1980s to 2000, Peru suffered a gruesome civil war fought between government forces and the Maoist (i.e., communist) terrorist group Shining Path. There were really no good guys here. Tens of thousands were kidnapped, tortured, and murdered indiscriminately. In 2012, William Neuman offered this assessment for *The New York Times*:

> Peru has seen impressive, although uneven, economic growth in recent years, but many of the inequities that helped set off the guerrilla conflict remain, including crushing poverty in urban slums and villages and marginalization of indigenous populations.[2]

Unfortunately, this remains true today. In March 2017, Shining Path, determined to protect its coca fields, attacked a police convoy. Cocaine is a highly lucrative business to Shining Path and the dense Peruvian jungles offer the terrorist group an effective hiding place. And although their strength and numbers are diminished, such an attack is evidence they remain a threat to Peruvian stability.

The horrors of a civil war in Peru's not-so-distant past, horrors committed by a (mostly) defeated enemy as well as the government that continues to exercise power, is an unsettling truth that cannot be easily dismissed as Peru seeks to enhance its global image as an emerging democracy.

This is a very gloomy assessment of Peru, and it must be admitted that I, like Darwin, saw very little of this country. Perhaps were I to see more of the country away from the coast, to experience more of its people, I would feel differently. Until then, I am with Darwin to this extent: "I cannot say I enjoyed the very little I saw of Peru."

Looking for a romantic getaway in Latin America? I suggest scratching Lima off your list of potential destinations.

CHAPTER 20

Panama:
Where America Did the Impossible

"I took the Canal Zone, and let congress debate, and while the debate goes on, the Canal does also!"[1]

—Theodore Roosevelt

We are now in Panama City—the capital of the Central American country, not the capital of spring break destinations in the Florida panhandle.

Superficially, Panama City looks like almost any other Central or South American city: cheap, dirty, prefabricated concrete housing developments that look too much like the Khrushchev era crap you see all over Russia and Eastern Europe; signs of long since abandoned infrastructure projects; trash and extreme poverty; and the blight of so much of the world, graffiti.

Driving into the city, we passed a traffic barrier upon which someone had painted "F**K THEM." Who was "them"? Socialists? Capitalists? Democrats? I didn't know. This was, I suppose, postmodern graffiti, permitting you to fill in the blank and direct the insult to anyone of your choosing. I went with Democrats.

In spite of all this, I felt immediately encouraged by our arrival in Panama. Lima's landscape, the perpetual haze, and the lack of color were, as I have said, depressing to me. By contrast, Panama was sunny, green, and warm. Like almost all Central and South America, the country still suffers from government corruption. But there are indications this country is making a strong bid to redefine itself.

Panama is best known to most Americans for its namesake hat, Roberto Durán, Manuel Noriega, and a canal. The connection between our two countries, however, runs much deeper.

For ninety-six years, the United States owned a ten-mile-wide and forty-eight-mile-long strip of land that is, along with places like Djibouti and the British territory of Gibraltar, among the most militarily strategic in the world. Known as the Canal Zone, the United States administered and controlled this strip as a vital piece of American foreign policy and economic viability.[i]

Even the New York Yankees deemed Panama to be of strategic importance. In 1946–1947, they traveled to Panama to play an eleven-game series against the Panamanian national team and U.S. armed forces teams. Indeed, my father, then an eighteen-year-old member of the Navy's lineup, played Joe DiMaggio and the Yankees in the Canal Zone at Balboa Stadium, one of the most memorable events of a life filled with memorable events.[ii] In

---

i.   Technically, the United States maintained sole ownership of the Canal Zone from 1903–1979. As part of the Torrijos-Carter Treaties, the Canal Zone was abolished in 1979, and for the next twenty years it was jointly administered by the United States and Panama until the US relinquished complete control to Panama in 1999.Pudae andebit quas aut latemo et doluptis magnatur

ii.   Before my father joined the US Army's 82nd Airborne in 1949 and, from there, the US Army Rangers in 1950, he briefly served in the United States Navy. When his officers discovered the boy who lied about his age to enlist was, in fact, a tremendous athlete and baseball player—he later played for one of the St. Louis Cardinals' minor league teams—he was reassigned to the Canal Zone and the Navy's baseball team. He never forgot the Yankees' and Dodgers' visits to the zone. The Yankees even pulled a player or two off those armed forces teams. My father was not one of them. It was not meant to be. It seems his unique talents were required elsewhere.

attendance as spectators for these games were a young Panamanian named Héctor López—"that's when I really started thinking about playing professionally"—and the President of Panama, Enrique Adolfo Jiménez.

The Brooklyn Dodgers' Jackie Robinson played here in 1947, too, against, incidentally, DiMaggio's Yankees. The two players and their respective teams met again later that year in the World Series. In 1955, Pat Scantlebury, who was born in the Canal Zone, became the first Panamanian player of many to make the Major Leagues. Hall of Famers Rod Carew and Mariano Rivera are Panama's greatest contributions to Major League Baseball.

But it all started with the Canal.

The dream of a canal across the isthmus of Panama (or Darién, as it was also called) dates back to the Spanish Conquistadors who made the perilous journey across it in 1513. For the next 350 years, there would be numerous adventurers who would make proposals for a canal, most being fanciful with promises of fortune for investors. Many would-be explorers and surveyors died of disease, starvation, or at the hands of hostile tribesmen, while others simply disappeared. The jungles of the isthmus quickly earned a reputation as one of the most dangerous places on earth.

Visions of a canal took on new energy with the California Gold Rush of the 1850s. Theoretically, ships traveling between New York and San Francisco would save seven thousand, eight hundred miles in the journey, which meant a savings of five months and a fortune in costs. But the American Civil War and Reconstruction turned America's focus inward.

Into this void stepped French impresario Ferdinand de Lesseps, the impossible figure behind the successful building of the Suez Canal. Through sheer force of personality, de Lesseps, a man who was as daring in his exploits as he was charming with the ladies of Paris, convinced the French government and French investors to back another canal venture. And why not? He did it before and with the proposed new canal being a mere fifty miles in length instead of the 120 miles necessary for the Suez, it seemed a much easier undertaking. Whoever was first to build it was sure to find the rainbow's end.

But de Lesseps and his backers never reckoned on the challenges awaiting them in the isthmus. The climate, mountains, swamps, rain, heat, and humidity were nothing like the conditions of the Suez, to say nothing of pestilence. French work on the canal began in 1881 and obstacles were numerous from the outset: machines rusted with alarming rapidity, mudslides and flooding plagued the project, the overall plan lacked specificity and clarity, and more than twenty-two thousand laborers died from malaria and yellow fever.

In 1889, the canal project ground to a halt as de Lesseps's company declared bankruptcy and accusations of graft and inhumane work conditions flew. After an official inquiry, he and his son were convicted and sentenced to jail. The verdict was later overturned, but the old man, now eighty-four, was broken and ruined. The French effort to build the Panama Canal, like so many grand projects before it and since, began full of hope, fanfare, and promise, only to end in shame and failure. The inventor of Murphy's Law wasn't born in Panama for nothing.

But Ferdinand de Lesseps nonetheless—and rightly, I think—remained a hero to the French and many Europeans. The failure of his Panama Canal venture notwithstanding, de Lesseps was a man of extraordinary vision, energy, and determination. And he showed the way to an American of similar mettle who would finish what he started.

Enter Theodore Roosevelt.

The America over which TR presided was a very different one from that of today. Populated by a confident, industrious, and increasingly prosperous people who were deeply proud of their country, even in the aftermath of a bloody civil war, Roosevelt's America was looking for opportunities to flex its collective muscle and establish its place among the great powers. Therefore, the prospect of completing a project that defeated the French people and ranks with the Great Wall and the Pyramids as one of the engineering wonders of the world had tremendous appeal. In 1898, the United States vanquished Old World Spain in a decisive three-month war, amputating her colonies from her and announcing America's presence on the international stage. Now America would symbolically vanquish France and give teeth to the Monroe Doctrine: the Western Hemisphere was for America.

Political considerations were the first to be overcome. What is now Panama was then a Colombian province. After the Colombian government refused to let the United States build a canal, the Roosevelt administration, not to be deterred by such trifling details, backed Colombian rebels in the isthmus and, in 1903, the Republic of Panama was born. American work on the canal started in 1904, and it was soon beset by the same problems that plagued the French—chiefly, malaria and yellow fever. Like the Colombians, however, these obstacles were soon conquered through the efforts of US Army surgeon William Gorgas, who rightly identified mosquitoes as the carriers of disease and introduced measures to control the insect. In 1914, the Panama Canal was completed.

We went to the Canal and watched the ships passing through the Miraflores Locks. In all, ships are raised eighty-five feet to meet the level of Gatun Lake, and then they are dropped by a series of locks on the other side. It is a marvel of engineering. Standing on the beach in Panama City you can see the ships lined up waiting for their turn.

Taxi drivers often make for the best—and most interesting— tour guides. They know a city as few do. And with taxis so cheap in South America, we used a lot of them. One driver, a bit of a nut, told us Panama was full of Russian and American spies and he knew things the CIA didn't know about Russian activities in Panama. Another talked about his family in Pittsburgh and how Panamanians hated Noriega. And still another told us of how he abandoned the priesthood to become an Uber driver.

"I just couldn't accept the idea of God. Too many rules."

"What you're describing is law," I put in. "Didn't they introduce you to the doctrine of grace in your priestly order?"

"Not in mine. You weren't allowed to ask questions. Just obey."

For the next hour, we drove back and forth across the Bridge of the Americas, which links Central and South America, discussing his dilemma until we had him take us to Casco Viejo.

Casco Viejo—Old Town—is an upscale restaurant, hotel, and shopping district where tourists and Panamanians alike window shop and socialize. Tours of the beautiful islands set out from the bay. At night, the string lights of rooftop bars glitter as pulsating music fills the air. Panamanians like to party. But this still felt (mostly) family friendly. On the other side of the city, prostitution, legal and regulated in Panama, and casinos flourish. This delineation of the city between safe and seedy is stark but it makes it easy to avoid the unpleasant aspects of life here.

To the southeast lies the infamous Darién Gap, an impenetrable jungle populated by antigovernment Colombian revolutionaries, drug runners, sex traffickers, and other dubious types. Looking to drive the Pan-American highway from Prudhoe Bay, Alaska to Ushuaia, Argentina on the tip of South America? You'll have to take a boat here because no roads pass through the Darién Gap. The Gap sits like a cork on top of South America, and that is essentially the purpose it serves. It is a barrier between Panama and Colombia and other less stable regimes of South America. President Trump could not hope for a better bulwark than what nature provided Panama in this jungle.

Even so, immigrants hoping to make it to the magic kingdom of America attempt to traverse this jungle. Some think it the most dangerous stretch of real estate in the world. It is a green, dark, frightening Hotel California of sorts, with many going in and very few coming out. I could find no guide to take us there, not even to the outskirts of it. Go figure.

Panama isn't a serious competitor for our mythical prize, but it is an interesting country and one to which I would like to return. If Lima isn't (in my opinion) a good vacation destination, Panama is. The islands and beaches are beautiful; the history fascinating; and the hotels and tours inexpensive. Furthermore, you are a short flight from the U.S. (four hours from Atlanta and Houston, three hours from Miami) and you will suffer no jet lag. Just embrace the Traveler's Fallacy and you'll be fine.

Go there. You will find a country striving to overcome the corruption endemic to Central and South America. If you get bored, Cartagena, Colombia, another interesting city, is merely an hour-and-a-half by air away. Or you can take your chances in the Darién Gap—but I wouldn't recommend it.

On to the real competitors in our world survey.

Oh, I almost forgot. The famous Panama hat? It isn't even made in Panama. It is made in Ecuador, and the Ecuadorians are more than a little peeved about this situation.

CHAPTER 21

Norway:
The Best Country in the World?

"Bernie Sanders wants the U.S. to be more like Norway. Is that even possible?"[1]

—Headline for *The Week*

Zachary and I headed to Norway. Joining us for this part of the trip was my twenty-four-year-old middle son, Christopher. Graduate school prevented him from participating in the entire expedition. Even so, Christopher is a well-seasoned traveler. He has been in Eastern and Western Europe and Asia before, and together with his little brother he was ready to do a deep dive into Scandinavia.

We started our survey of Norway by exploring the explorers: a tour of the impressive Fram Museum, which houses ships, planes, tools, and other artifacts of Arctic exploration. Since a third of Norway falls within the Arctic Circle and we were just below that imaginary line, who needed a dogsled to get there? On a clear day, we might just as easily have Uber'd it, albeit an Uber with four-wheel drive and a differential lock feature.[i]

---

i   I am, of course, being a bit sarcastic here. The Fram Museum isn't simply a record of expeditions just inside the Arctic Circle. It is a museum of expeditions to the North Pole.

With or without a four-wheel drive, we were on the home stretch and with several countries to go, we saved what are allegedly the best countries in the world for last. It is here, in Europe, that competition for the title of the world's greatest country comes down to something like semifinals. Let's take a moment to recall what this project is all about.

As this trip has rolled along, we have visited and evaluated countries in Oceania, Asia, Africa, and South America—nineteen in all, on our way to a total of twenty-six. As we have said (and seen), there are not twenty-six potential rivals to America for this elusive championship. That list is no more than ten, and probably closer to five. Even so, we have included countries at the extremities of wealth, power, population, and global influence to provide us all with a measure of perspective.

Now, we turn our attention to Europe. The America-haters on the American Left generally love the soft "socialist democracies" of Europe, and those in Scandinavia most of all. Let's once again look at *Condé Nast Traveler*'s "Best Countries to Live in" list:

1. Norway

2. Australia/Switzerland (tie)

3. (Due to the tie for number 2, there is no number 3)

4. Germany

5. Denmark/Singapore (tie)

6. (No number 6)

7. The Netherlands

8. Ireland

9. Iceland

10. Canada/The United States (tie)

AROUND THE WORLD IN (MORE THAN) 80 DAYS

As you can see, no countries from South America and Africa made the list. Singapore was the only country from Asia, and North America *just barely* made the top ten. Predictably, this list is dominated by countries in Europe.

With this in mind, when we were planning this trip, we deliberately bookended it with those countries considered to be models for what the Left thinks America should be: New Zealand, Australia, and Singapore on one end and a handful of European democracies on the other. A trip like this requires some judicious choices since it wasn't possible for us to visit every country in the world nor even every country in Europe. Scandinavia, however, was a must-stop.

It was with great anticipation that we landed in Oslo. Yet another study listed Norway as the "World's Happiest Country."[2] What would the greatest country in the world be like? Should we send a message home and tell family and friends to pack up and join us in the *new* Old World where we could colonize and start over? Surely the Norwegians perfected the broken human condition that has given the world broken, bad government. After millennia of civilization, the Norwegians got it right, providing a model, a path of light leading humanity to personal bliss and national utopia.

First, let's immediately discard a longstanding fallacy regarding Scandinavia, one championed by American socialists like Bernie Sanders and Alexandria Ocasio-Cortez, namely, that Scandinavian countries are examples of successful socialism.

They aren't.

These countries do enjoy a great deal of economic success. The standard of living is high. So is life expectancy and the average wage. But Scandinavians are not operating on the same economic model that ruined Russia, China, Venezuela, Cuba, North Korea, Vietnam, and a dozen more countries.

Strictly speaking, in a socialist country the means of production are owned by the government. That is (or was) true of the aforementioned socialist states. It is not true of Scandinavian states. These countries embrace a free market, recognize no minimum wage, and generally take a hands-off approach to business. Also lost on progressives is the fact Norway is oil rich—crude oil and natural gas account for 40 percent of Norway's exports[3]—and just plain rich, consistently ranking as one of the world's wealthiest countries.[4]

So, in what way, then, are they socialist?

They aren't. The myth of Scandinavian socialism is exactly that—a myth. In an address at Harvard's Kennedy School of Government, Danish Prime Minister Lars Løkke Rasmussen said as much:

"I know that some people in the US associate the Nordic model with some sort of socialism. Therefore, I would like to make one thing clear: Denmark is far from a socialist planned economy. Denmark is a market economy."[5]

Forbes offers some clarity:

To the extent that the left wants to point to an example of successful socialism, not just generous welfare states, the Nordic countries are actually a poor case to cite. Regardless of the perception, in reality the Nordic countries practice mostly free market economics paired with high taxes exchanged for generous government entitlement programs.[6]

In other words, Scandinavian countries, while aggressively free market and pro-business, have developed strong social welfare programs within the framework of their capitalist economies, and therein lies the confusion. Where this was once the work of the church through benevolence ministry outreach in local communities in Britain and America, in Scandinavia this has been secularized, and the tithe has been replaced by heavy taxation to provide these social services.

And the taxes *are* high.

My first impression of Norway (and later, Sweden) was one of cost. It is not for nothing that *The Telegraph* named Norway one of the most expensive countries in the world.[7] Everything—be it a mediocre hotel, a taxi, a hamburger, clothing, or an "I ♥ Norway!" T-shirt—will put a dent in your wallet.

From the moment we arrived, we suffered something of a monetary hemorrhage. At the rate we were going, we would have to forgo the remaining countries on our tour and see if we could find a spot in steerage on a freighter headed for America.

This illustrates an important and frustrating point lost on advocates of socialism. I cannot recall the number of times people supporting this government and economic model have told me how everything is "free," be it education or healthcare or even unemployment. Neither the Norwegians nor anyone else have ever figured out how to give the masses free stuff without somebody paying for it. Just because you didn't write a check for a copay for your semiannual dental visit doesn't mean it was free. It means you paid for it—probably grossly *over*paid for it—by other means. But to the unwary, it does *seem* free. Don't be fooled. Norway is absurdly expensive. Unsurprisingly, their tax rate consistently ranks among the highest in the world.

High taxes, however, annoying as they are, aren't usually a sign of societal disintegration. Certainly not in Scandinavia. But we soon discovered Scandinavia is infected with the pro-Islam, anti-Christianity propaganda that grips so much of the Western world. Consider a conversation I had with an African immigrant to Norway.

"Are you a religious man?" I asked, deep into our conversation.

He looked trapped, nervous. After a moment's hesitation, I decided to go first, so to speak, and reveal my own position.

"I didn't mean to upset you," I said. "I am just curious. For what it is worth, I am a Christian."

He looked relieved: "Well, I am an Ethiopian, so you know that I am a Christian."

"Why the reluctance to tell me?"

"Because in this country, you can be an atheist and you can be a Muslim, but you cannot be a practicing Christian. I came to this country years ago to escape Muslim persecution of my people. Now it is here, only it is with the law. If you're a Muslim, you can blow people up and the Norwegian government will reluctantly punish you. There will be no meaningful consequences. But if you are a Christian and you say the wrong thing, you can lose everything."

This theme was repeated.

As I chatted with a woman who noted my American accent, I saw she was wearing a cross necklace.

"What is the significance of your necklace?"

She told me about a friend who travels and buys jewelry and brought back a selection. She briefly considered a pair of earrings, but then said, "No, I'm going to take this" as if summoning her courage. She added: "It reminds me of my grandmother, who didn't [just] read the Bible, she studied it."

"Sounds like you have a good grandmother."

"I do. I really admire her."

"She seems to be a good role model."

Her fingers went to the cross. She twisted it. "She is. It can be dangerous to wear this here, but I do it. I should be able to do it. What is happening in Europe is wrong."

"I agree," I said. "That cross is a powerful Christian symbol. It is this country's heritage. It is Europe's heritage."

Such conversations are not unique to Norway or Sweden. They are characteristic of much of Europe. They always leave you with the feeling you have been talking in code with a member of some underground resistance. Being an American, however, who is used to being open about what he believes, I never fully appreciate their difficulty. I can't. Freedom of speech in the United States, while in mortal peril, remains viable in a way it no longer does in Europe.

But even if Norway doesn't appear to be returning to Christianity anytime soon, they did, briefly, seem to be learning from the open-door immigration policies adopted by much of Western Europe. Sylvi Listhaug, Norway's plainspoken immigration minister, made no bones about the immigration policy she was pursuing. In an interview with *The Spectator* she said:

> The Norwegian model is very different and very clear. If you are an economic migrant, you are declined in Norway. We send people back to Afghanistan if they are not in need of protection; we send them back to Somalia if they are not in need of protection. Police are also sent out to areas where illegal immigrants are suspected of living and working. If we find them, we send them out. That has also decreased crime in Norway, that's very good.

Listhaug has sharply criticized the immigration policies of Germany, France, and Sweden most of all, causing outrage in Berlin, Paris, and Stockholm. Her response:

"I don't give a damn."[8]

Because Norway is not a member of the EU, she had every reason to ignore their protests. However, Listhaug was forced to step down as progressives in her own country successfully smeared her as a racist. Such is the tactic employed against all critics of mass immigration and the Islamization of Europe.

The boys and I paid a visit to the Norwegian Center for Holocaust Studies. This excellent exhibit is housed in the former home of Vidkun Quisling, the Norwegian Nazi who betrayed his county and declared himself head of the government after the German invasion in April 1940. From there, we went to Norway's Resistance Museum in Akershus Fortress.

At the Resistance Museum, I picked up a copy of David Howarth's excellent book (now a movie) *We Die Alone*. It is the epic tale of Jan Baalsrud who, after Norway's occupation, fled the country only to be sent back as a commando to carry out the demolition of Nazi targets. The mission was betrayed by a Norwegian collaborator, resulting in the deaths of every member of Baalsrud's team. Baalsrud was forced to make his way to Sweden with the Germans in hot pursuit. It is not only Baalsrud's story, it is the story of those Norwegians who fought to restore their country's freedom.

Norway has much to commend it. We found the people friendly in a way they simply aren't in some other parts of Europe.

As I stepped into a not-so-Korean restaurant—it appeared to be Norwegian the way P. F. Chang's is American—to use their bathroom, a server pointed me to a spiral staircase leading to a basement. Since my accident, I sometimes walk with a slight limp, my left foot drooping just a bit. Starting down the stairs, my left foot caught the edge of a step and I tumbled to the bottom gracelessly. A room full of diners, alarmed, turned. Embarrassed, I tried to compose myself and act like nothing happened, but it was no use; the steps, made of a rough-hewn slate, sliced my rapidly swelling shin and I was bleeding profusely. I feared I had broken the same leg *again*.

Diners and servers alike sprang into action. Soon my wounds were being dressed from a restaurant emergency kit by a crowd of people. All the while, the boys, outside in the rain, were thinking, "Man, Dad must've really had to go to the bathroom."

I am grateful to these fine Norwegians whose lovely dinner was interrupted by an American crashing into what was meant to be a quiet evening out. Everyone we met—on the streets, on tours, in restaurants—was simply delightful.

Norway is the opposite of anywhere in Africa—safe, clean, quiet, and law abiding. The fjords are beautiful. The infrastructure is well maintained. And yet, there is something a little depressing about this country. Perhaps it is just the country's extreme northerliness—Oslo is roughly the same latitude as Anchorage, Alaska—thus a great deal less sunshine than what I am accustomed to.[ii] But I think it is something more than all this.

Neither Norway nor any Scandinavian country is the socialist utopia American progressives think it is—or would have us think it is. Economically speaking, it is quite the opposite. Worse, from a progressive point of view, Norway is a big proponent of school vouchers. But Norway is increasingly a potential model for progressives in just about every other way—social policy, an alarming decline in free speech and religious liberty, immigration policy, and willful blindness to the dangers of Islam.

Norway is not a great country. It might have been. It still might be. It is the northern latitudes' equivalent of New Zealand, and like New Zealand, it is being destroyed by the same progressive policies destroying most of the Western world; policies that have these countries trending away from freedom, not toward it. Norway is repeating Quisling's error, only this time they are betraying their own heritage. *Foreign Policy* put it rather succinctly: "The refugee crisis has forced Europeans to choose between the moral universalism they profess and the ancient identities they have inherited."[9]

---

ii   Oslo gets an average of 1,668 hours of sunshine a year. Birmingham, Alabama, my home, averages one thousand hours more than this.

But isn't Norway the world's happiest country? Nonsense. Norway's designation as the world's happiest country is based on yet another dubious United Nations report.[10] You might think this ranking comes from simple "yes" or "no" responses to the question, "Are you happy?" It doesn't. That is essentially what Gallup[11] did and guess who dominated the top ten? Paraguay and Latin America. Neither Iceland nor a single Scandinavian country appeared in Gallup's top ten.

So how did the guys at the UN produce entirely different results? After spending an afternoon reading the UN report, that is still unclear to me. This is because their study is 184 pages of abstruse data and reads like this:

"The U.S. corruption index rose by 0.10 between 2006/7 and 2015/6. With a coefficient –0.53 in the happiness regression, the negative effect on U.S. happiness is 0.054. Reversing the rise in perceived corruption would therefore raise happiness by 0.054…"

Digging a bit deeper, we find that this report, as with any UN report I've ever read, has a very definite political agenda. It concludes:

> To escape this social quagmire, America's happiness agenda should center on…an expanded social safety net, wealth taxes, and greater public financing of health and education…. [A]cknowledge and move past the fear created by 9/11…Trump's ban on travel to the United States from certain Muslim-majority countries is a continuing manifestation of the exaggerated and irrational fears that grip the nation.

So, from a haze of data on global happiness, the authors of this report make the illogical leap to America, Donald Trump, and the lack of "a social safety net"—i.e., lack of socialism—as the sources of unhappiness? They could have saved themselves time, money, and the clever use of dubious statistics and just interviewed Bernie Sanders.

And while we are on the topic of national happiness as an indicator of socialism's ability to deliver earthly bliss, let's look at Gallup's *least* happy nation: Ukraine. I've spent a lot of time in that country. I've written a book about it, and I can tell you Ukraine has been economically, intellectually, and spiritually assassinated by socialism.[iii] Five more socialist (or formerly socialist) countries appear in Gallup's bottom ten. As the twentieth century demonstrated all too well, socialism has the opposite of the Midas touch—whatever it touches turns to crap.

Besides, one need only see Norwegian Expressionist artist Edvard Munch's composition *The Scream* to know this country isn't party central. (Beyond this, Munch was also known for such cheery observations as: "Disease, insanity, and death were the angels that attended my cradle, and since then have followed me throughout my life.") As I strolled through the National Gallery in Oslo, upon seeing the painting, I found it fit the mood of a people who live so much of their lives in darkness.

Don't believe me?

According to the Norwegian Institute of Public Health, an astonishing one in seven people in Oslo will test positive for cocaine.[12] To put this in some perspective, only 0.8 percent of Americans are current users of that drug. Furthermore, Norwegians and their Scandinavian neighbors take more antidepressants than any other country in the world.[13] It seems they rank high in happiness only because they are, well, high.

---

iii   The book is titled *The Grace Effect*. Please buy it, preferably in bulk.

CHAPTER 22

Sweden:
Where No One Is Special

"The Winner Takes It All." [1]

—ABBA

We took a train from Oslo to Stockholm, just like the Nazis used to do it. Now we were in Sweden, or Stepford as the boys would call it.

Visiting a city and want a bit of local flavor? Take a guided tour. Although there is no substitute for exploring on your own, meeting people, and research, a good guided tour—and sometimes even a bad one—will tell you a lot about what the locals think is important in their city, how they see themselves, and how they want *you* to see them. They want to impress you.

In search of just this kind of experience, the boys and I took a tour by boat. The city of Stockholm is built on fourteen islands connected by bridges spanning a network of canals, so a boat tour is a relaxing way to see the major sites.

Officially, we took the Stockholm River and Harbor Cruise, but it might have more accurately been called the "Sweden Is Awesome (or Used to Be) Boat Tour." Given that globalism is so fashionable in Europe, the headset commentary on this tour was surprisingly—*jarringly*—nationalistic. "We conquered this" and "we dominated that" and "we defeated them." In short, "we are awesome—or we used to be."

I loved the poetic, strident nature of my male and female lecturers as we floated along. They might as well have said, "If you aren't Swedish, you're *gödsel*." I'll let you guess what that means. Globalism may be the fashion, but not so much that one can't assert their superiority over other nations. It was as if my guides knew why I was there and were making a case for Sweden as the world's greatest country. They went on to enumerate Sweden's contributions to civilization:

America? We discovered that.

Skype? We invented it.

Spotify? Rock on.

The flat-screen? You're welcome.

GPS? We found it.

Pacemaker? *Thump, thump.*

Barcode? *Beep!*

IKEA? You guessed it.

The Girl with the Dragon Tattoo? Damn right she's a Swede.

It was also a Swede, Alfred Nobel, who invented dynamite. That alone makes Sweden awesome. Nobel made his fortune manufacturing cannon and other armaments and in a great twist of irony, his name was given to a peace prize. It's a bit like naming it the Smith & Wesson or Kalashnikov Peace Prize. Regardless, each year the Nobel Peace Prize committee awards recipients in— *Oslo, Norway.* Go figure.

Of course, the commentary wasn't void of politically correct elements. On the contrary, nationalism soon gave way to a knee-slapping revision of Swedish history. You might think history is simply what it is, that you cannot revise what has already happened. It's over and done, right? But you'd be naïve for thinking that. In a culture war, history is rewritten and weaponized to give justification to modern agendas.

In this case, Vikings, we were told, were a gender equality society, with men raising children at home and women going off to war. Somehow, I missed this theme in Beowulf (yes, he was a Swede) and in studying the real historic exploits of Vikings with cool names like Eric Bloodaxe, Ivar the Boneless, Gunnar the Hero, Björn Ironside, Sweyn Forkbeard, and, my favorite, Harald Bluetooth.

But Viking men were much more than stay-at-home dads. They were also primitive socialists. Yup, that's what the lady said. This was deduced from the fact Vikings drank beer from a vessel called a *das horn*. Since you can't put a horn down because it has no flat surface, you had to pass it. That, said the narrator, was meant to teach sharing and responsibility to the whole community: "'Lagom' as we say in Swedish, meaning 'just enough.'"

Nonsense, I say. The Vikings never had enough. It sounded more like a Viking drinking game than a lesson in collectivization. Vikings as socialists? There's revisionism for you. The Vikings didn't share stuff, they stole it—

—On second thought, perhaps they were socialists after all.

Moving on to modern history, we were told of the virtue of Swedish neutrality. Neutral since the 1880s, mandatory military service was abolished in 2010. Sweden doesn't do world wars. In fact, the Swedes haven't fought a war for well over a century. Yet, as the guide freely acknowledged, the Swedes collaborated with the Nazis *and* the Allies, letting the former use their railroads and the latter use their airfields. Of this, the guides did not seem especially ashamed. Quite the opposite. Smugly, our narrators spoke of Swedish cleverness in navigating neutrality both profitably and painlessly. Hearing all this, I had the urge to call for one of those

DNA ancestry tests. There must be some mistake about these current occupants of Sweden being descended from Vikings. The progeny of Eric Bloodaxe? Surely not.

What about religion?

"Sweden," the guide began, "is a secular society, which means we celebrate equally both the Christian and pagan traditions...we don't go to church much." The last bit was superfluous. An afternoon in Sweden and you know people don't go to church much.

As we motored through one of the river locks, our guides emphasized collective achievement while frowning upon individual achievement.

Advertising alcohol on television is against the law as it's deemed to promote a bad lifestyle. Homosexuality? No problem.

Alcohol is strictly controlled by politicians, which explains a lot. It seems the expression "drinks are on the house" was extended to healthcare, education, and big government, only the house was yours, not theirs, and the bar tab the politicians ran up became rather hefty and your children and grandchildren are saddled with paying it. Meanwhile, the bureaucrats keep shouting for another round. (On you, of course.)

Sweden is markedly different from Norway. Perhaps it is due to the fact its greater proximity to Russia has influenced its development to a much greater degree.

"In Sweden, no one is special," the guide proudly proclaimed.

Upon reflection, I had to admit that in this, Sweden has succeeded marvelously. Indeed, I can't think of a single special Swede since ABBA released "Dancing Queen"—which has new meaning for me now that I know Sweden was at the forefront of the gay revolution. Zachary, who liked Norway quite a lot, had a negative reaction to Sweden, calling it "creepy." Christopher agreed. I knew what he meant. They celebrate sameness to such a degree the country can feel creepy in the manner of a Stepford. IKEA makes sense in this context. The furniture, the décor, it's all the same. You can walk into someone's house and immediately identify where they bought everything from the couch to the spatula. No one, nothing, stands out, and this is deemed virtuous.

I was reminded of a Russian proverb that says, "The tallest blade of grass is the first to be cut by the scythe." Sweden's proximity to Russia is more than geographic. The socialist mindset has crossed the border in a big way.

One immediately understands why the American cultural Left aspires to remake America in the image of a country like Sweden.

But that isn't a good idea.

Norway's (former) immigration minister Sylvi Listhaug believes Sweden has a major immigration problem. In an interview with *The Spectator* while she still held that post, the immigration minister didn't mince words:

"We have a lot of people from Sweden coming to Norway; we are neighbors and have a good relationship. But of course, we are a little bit concerned about the immigration policies they have. We see that they have big problems in some of the cities."[2]

For their part, Sweden's government, greatly angered by these statements, vociferously denied that Ms. Listhaug's assertion had any validity. This, however, does not alter the fact she was right. Sweden has opened its doors to more immigrants per capita than any other EU country. Once a homogenous society, some 13 percent of Sweden's population is now foreign born, with most coming from Islamic countries.[3] An alien culture, they are not integrating, and Swedish society is undergoing radical change:

Gang-related gun murders, now mainly a phenomenon among men with immigrant backgrounds in the
country's parallel societies, increased from 4 per year in the
early 1990s to around 40 last year. Because of this, Sweden
has gone from being a low-crime country to having
homicide rates significantly above the Western European
average. Social unrest, with car torchings, attacks on first
responders and even riots, is a recurring phenomenon.
Shootings in the country have become so common that
they don't make top headlines anymore, unless they are
spectacular or lead to fatalities. News of attacks are quickly
replaced with headlines about sports events and celebrities,
as readers have become desensitized to the violence.[4]

In opening their borders to Muslim extremists, European
countries, Sweden most of all, have effectively let the Orcs into the
Shire. What is worse, they still don't seem to recognize the fact—
or they are afraid to say it. "Merely to ask whether Sweden could
integrate Afghans today as it had Bosnians two decades before was
to risk accusations of racism."[5] All this—the stupid immigration
policy, the resistance of Muslim immigrants to integrate or even
respect the values of their European hosts, Islamic extremism, and
an unwillingness to acknowledge it as such when it occurs—were
all evident in the aftermath of the April 7, 2017, terrorist attack
here in Stockholm.

On that day, Rakhmat Akilov, a Muslim immigrant and
asylum seeker, stole a beer truck in the heart of the city's shopping district and careened down a fashionable pedestrian lane.
Before the rampage ended, five people were dead, and fourteen
others injured.

One morning, the boys and I walked from our hotel to the
street in question. Sitting at a sidewalk café, I tried to imagine the

scene unfolding before me. With such heavy foot traffic, it wasn't difficult to picture the terror at the too-late realization the truck bearing down on pedestrians had no intention of stopping. Even so, there was little to signal an unknowing visitor to this place that anything out of the ordinary ever happened here.

My coffee finished, I walked the length of the street, from where the carnage began to the corner window of the Åhléns department store where it ended. Plywood took the place of glass and people covered it with Post-It note messages, turning it into an extemporized memorial. Some of the notes were nonsensical. Others spoke vaguely of love conquering or love winning. What that meant in the context of a terrorist attack is not clear. Still others, however, identified the source of the problem: "Leave Islam," declared just such a note.

But they mostly don't get it.

Reversing course, I headed back up the street and went to several businesses along the terrorist's bloody route, asking shop owners and their employees what, if anything, they saw of the attack on that awful day. One said he was on vacation. Another told me he was in a back office and saw nothing. One woman just shrugged uncomfortably.

Then I met Lily.

Lily is a twentysomething who works the counter at a cosmetics boutique. At the time I walked in, we were the only two people in the store. Her blond hair framed a striking Nordic face and pale blue eyes. She might have been a poster for a Swedish vacation or a member of ABBA.

Then I asked about the attack.

The customer service veneer immediately evaporated and was replaced by a deep pathos. Such a look, indescribable really, seemed incongruous with such a lovely face and on one so young. In impeccable English, she described the horror of that day.

Lily was upstairs with a customer when she heard tumult from the street below. Turning to look out of the window, she saw the truck driving down the lane at high speed. Some people were running; others were motionless. As the truck passed only feet from where she stood, behind it, she saw the broken form of a boy lying in the street. A woman was kneeling over the child when a man sprinted in, swept up the boy in his arms, and disappeared into a side alley. A father? A bystander? Lily didn't know.

The women hurried downstairs. A young intern who worked on the ground floor was hysterical. "She had seen a lot more than I had. Crushed bodies and blood. It was unimaginable." The four of them locked themselves in a tiny bathroom behind the counter. They called the police and waited fearfully, listening, hoping for salvation. Two and a half hours later, there was a knock on the storefront glass. The women cracked the bathroom door just enough to see a man in a black uniform, black body armor, and carrying an automatic weapon.

They closed the door abruptly and locked it again. Was he one of the good guys or a terrorist? They didn't know and chose to stay put. Calling the police again they described the intimidating figure and were told to let him in. Cautiously they abandoned their refuge.

"We didn't trust him," Lily said.

"Why?" I asked.

"He looked pale, terrified," she said. "He was very young. I had no confidence that he could protect us."

But that day's terror was over. She thinks about it a lot. "People can be so evil," she observed thoughtfully. "The man [who did it] was married and had children, yet he targeted women and children. Why would he do that?"

The answer seemed obvious to me. It was well known that Rakhmat Akilov was Muslim and declared his allegiance to ISIS and his desire to kill Swedes on their behalf.[6] I offered Lily a clue:

"Do you think religion had anything to do with the attack, Lily?"

To this point, she spoke freely, passionately, articulately. But not now. Now, her response seemed like a statement prepared by the European Union committee on immigration and diversity: "Not for me," she said somewhat nervously. "I don't think religion is like that. For him maybe, but not for me."

Were I to ask any educated person what inspired kamikazes, the suicide bombers of the previous century, to fly their planes into American ships during the Second World War, they would undoubtedly say emperor worship and imperial Japanese policy—and they would be right. So why the inability to make the connection between terrorism committed by Muslims and their religion? Political correctness. It has rendered the progressive mind incapable of the sound reasoning our fathers and grandfathers exercised in saving the free world from fascism and communism.

In her answer, Lily—so bright, so wounded and victimized by the events of the April 7, 2017, Muslim terrorist attack—revealed that whatever she has learned about human nature and its capacity for evil, she had not learned the most obvious lesson of all: some religions and some philosophies exacerbate that evil and give justification to it.

In this, however, Lily is not alone. Europe hasn't learned anything either. And whether they choose to acknowledge it or not, Sweden, Scandinavia, and the whole of Europe is engaged in a struggle, an undeclared war of civilizations.

The stakes?

In the words of ABBA, "The Winner Takes It All."

CHAPTER 23

Switzerland:
A Great Country for Swiss

"In Italy, for thirty years under the Borgias, they had warfare, terror,
murder, bloodshed—they produced Michelangelo, Leonardo da Vinci,
and the Renaissance. In Switzerland, they had brotherly love, five
hundred years of democracy, and peace—what did that produce?
The cuckoo clock."[1]

—Orson Welles in *The Third Man*

Christopher, Zachary, and I flew from Stockholm, Sweden to Zürich, Switzerland. From there we took a train to Lucerne. At first glance, apart from the mountains, a traveler from Sweden would notice very little difference between the two countries— modern, clean, efficient, and expensive. We simply exchanged one neutral country for another.

But, oh, the mountains! Whatever Switzerland's "greatness" status, it is most certainly one of the world's most beautiful countries. While I had been here before, the boys had not, and I enjoyed watching their facial expressions as they looked out the train's window at the spectacular landscape. They spent plenty of time skiing and traveling in the Pyrenees, but beautiful as the

Pyrenees are, these were the Alps. Castle ruins, lovely villages, and chalets dotted the landscape.

About 1.5 times the size of the Dallas-Fort Worth metroplex with a population of only 8.5 million people, Switzerland is not a large country. But according to the measures employed by most using the statistical approach to determining national greatness, if Norway is number 1.a., Switzerland is 1.b. In yet another (and most recent) ranking of best countries, *US News & World Report* named Switzerland the best country in the world for the fourth straight year. As we have demonstrated with similar rankings, precisely how they arrive at these conclusions is a less-than-transparent process. But one didn't have to dig too deeply to find this:

> Nearly 4 out of 5 respondents agreed that LGBTQ individuals should be entitled to the same rights as non-LGBTQ individuals, with women (82 percent) agreeing more than men (76 percent), and 18- to 24-year-olds registering the highest share of sentiment that strongly agrees with that view (37.4 percent).[2]

As we have said, a given ranking will be determined by the criteria you used, and those criteria say everything about what is important to you. This specific measure seems to be employed ruthlessly by just about every major ranking we have seen. Not only is it shallow and reflective of a perverse agenda, but it is also a very small special interest group. Far more people are concerned about issues affecting faith, security, and the economy, but these seldom factor into the calculations.

I was in Switzerland as a college student backpacking through Europe in 1991. A couple of bad experiences left me hating the country. Making things worse, when I left Switzerland I traveled east to Innsbruck, Austria, where I stayed at a bed and breakfast recommended by my guidebook. It was a mistake. The bed and breakfast, I soon discovered, was owned by an old lady who was a Nazi—that is, actually a World War II-era member of the Nazi Party. That was miserable. But that is a story for the next country on our tour.

Now, my circumstances were markedly different. So were the impressions. And I was determined not to fall prey to the Traveler's Fallacy. But there were hints of that earlier foray into this country. On that occasion, I found many of the Swiss to be rude, unhelpful, and arrogant. Perhaps this was an experience unique to me.

Nope.

According to *Culture Trip*, Switzerland is the most unfriendly country in the world.[3] This is, of course, strictly subjective. But I have even heard numerous French complain about how rude their neighbors to the east are. And when a Frenchman, especially a Parisian, tells you that you are rude, it is time for an intervention. I am with the French on this one. The Swiss are frequently an unpleasant people.

However, this much must be said in their defense: the Swiss don't seem to think so. This apparent contradiction is no contradiction at all. In other words, yes, the Swiss have a well-earned reputation for being ill-mannered to visitors to their country, but the Swiss see themselves as quite civil, and that is a recipe for national success. I mean, if a family must be rude, let marital and sibling bliss prevail within the household and their unkindness be directed elsewhere. The Swiss have no obligation to be nice to travelers to their country any more than those travelers have an obligation to go there. Indeed, the Swiss would prefer they didn't. For this, they have been characterized as xenophobic.

Writer Mark Hay says:

In the popular imagination, Switzerland is a land of fancy cheese and chocolates, alpine idylls, and chalets galore. A nation with a robust direct democracy, strong universal healthcare, and an uncannily potent economy, it's a political model for many casual observers—there are literally posts on question forums like Quora asking whether Switzerland should be considered a functional utopia. Offering up a little nature, a little culture and a lot of comfort, it's no wonder Switzerland's a tourist darling, steadily siphoning off more American travellers every year. Yet below Switzerland's shiny veneer, there's an undercurrent of xenophobia that might make it a less than comfortable destination for at least one group of people: observant Muslims. Swiss Islamophobia predates the antimigrant panic sweeping Europe today, and runs far deeper. And you're probably equally likely to feel it as a Swiss Muslim or a just visitor. [sic][4]

I disagree sharply with this assessment. Hay writes for *Vice*. For the uninitiated, that is, to put it mildly, a leftist publication. And although he is voicing an opinion popular with many of his ideological stripe, it is a leap in logic to assume a people who like their country as it is are, as he says, "bigots" because they don't want to allow the mass resettlement of a people from an alien culture within their borders. And the Swiss, like an increasing number of other Europeans, do recognize it as a culture alien to Europe. According to the Swiss Broadcasting Channel, a poll of Swiss residents found the following:

Asked whether Islam should be granted the same official status as Christianity and Judaism, 61 percent of 15,617 respondents said "no" or "probably no".... Of those who were open to a third official religion, 19 percent said "yes" and 20 percent "probably yes." Almost two-thirds (62 percent) said there was no place in Switzerland for Islam. In addition, 80 percent thought Christian values were part of the Swiss identity.[5]

This is significant, and it goes far to explain the Swiss attitude on immigration policy. We have seen the effects of Islam on our global tour and I have more than hinted at the problems associated with that religion. But to understand what is happening in so many of the countries we have visited, to understand what is happening in Europe, we need to look at the religion a bit more.

As a Christian, I believe the words of Jeremiah 17:9: "The heart is deceitful above all things, and desperately wicked; who can know it?" We all, each of us, have evil tendencies. Some religions and philosophies restrain our darker impulses while others exacerbate them. Being a Christian does not make me morally perfect. Clearly not. But it does make me less evil than I might otherwise be. When Evelyn Waugh was rebuked by a woman for his rudeness to her, the famous English novelist replied: "You have no idea how much nastier I would be if I was not a Catholic. Without supernatural aid I would hardly be a human being."[6] This is because the Christian faith encourages us to repent of our evil, to confess it to our God, to seek his forgiveness and restoration, and to fear his wrath if we do not.

By contrast, atheism, for example, exacerbates our evil tendencies. We have seen the global effects of that philosophy, too, in atheism's political manifestation: communism (i.e., socialism). Stalin, Hitler, and Mao all killed millions of their own citizens because they did not fear judgment in the next life for their actions in this one. Indeed, secular regimes killed more than one hundred million people in the twentieth century alone. That's more than all religious wars from all previous centuries *combined*. The point isn't that all atheists are genocidal maniacs; it is, rather, that atheism offers no compelling reason not to do whatever one wants to do. The aforementioned mass murderers understood that.

Like atheism, Islam unquestionably exacerbates man's innate evil. And I do mean *man*, because Islam is a religion that gives religious justification to the carnal appetites of men: sex, violence, misogyny, theft, deceit, destruction, tyranny—you name it, so long as it advances the cause of Allah. Historian Andrew Hussey says Islam resembles "a ruthlessly efficient war-machine rather than a religion." In this way, the Quran and the Hadith are consulted like Clausewitz or Sun Tzu. This doesn't mean all Muslims are terrorists or would-be terrorists. Certainly not. But those Muslims who model their lives on the life of Muhammad, as all Muslims are commanded to do, are cause for more than a little concern. Where Jesus said, "For all who take the sword will die by the sword" (Matthew 26:52) and modeled a life of peace. Muhammad said, "I will cast terror into the hearts of those who disbelieve. Therefore, strike off their heads and strike off every fingertip of them" (Quran 8:12) and modeled a life of violence. In 627 alone, he ordered the beheading of between six hundred and eight hundred Jews of the Banu Qurayza tribe.[7] The Quran makes this very clear: non-Muslims must convert, pay a tax, or die.

At this point, some readers will maintain there is no appreciable difference between Christianity and Islam on the question of violence. This is what is called the fallacy of false equivalence. Consider the January 2015 Charlie Hebdo terrorist attacks in Paris. That the magazine was bombed everyone knows. What few know, however, is between 2005 and 2015, the magazine devoted thirty-eight covers to obscene and offensive depictions of religion or religious figures.[8] Of those, twenty-one were aimed at Christianity, while only seven targeted Islam. Yet those seven covers netted two terrorist attacks and sixteen people dead. Were Christians truly as violent as Muslims, there would have been no less than six Christian attacks on Charlie Hebdo.

There have been none.

There are many other examples of the very different responses Christians and Muslims have had to unflattering depictions of their religion: Martin Scorsese (director of *The Last Temptation of Christ*) is still alive while Theo Van Gogh (director of *Submission*) is dead, shot eight times in a street in Amsterdam and a butcher knife left in his chest. Richard Dawkins has made a fortune attacking Christianity and lives handsomely in Oxford while Raif Badawi, a Saudi blogger who was publicly lashed fifty times for his criticisms of Islam, is in jail awaiting 950 *more* lashes. And Salman Rushdie lives under the perpetual threat of assassination for his depictions of Islam while Rushdie's friend and fellow writer Christopher Hitchens enjoyed celebrity status among the Christians he denigrated.

Christianity and Islam are not comparable. I am aware of no Christian suicide bombers, neither the Methodists nor the Baptists carry out public lashings for apostasy, and it wasn't the Amish who flew those planes into the Twin Towers. Islam is a religion defined by law. Nowhere in the Quran does it call for Muslims to be at peace with non-Muslims. Christianity, by contrast, is a religion defined by *grace*. Its founder, Jesus Christ, modeled it. Thus, to kill in his name, as he predicted some would do, is inconsistent with his teaching. (John 16:2–3)

Some will object that a relatively small percentage of Muslims commit atrocities, but that is beside the point. There are relatively few Ultimate Fighters, but they have a lot of fans. Consider a BBC poll conducted in 2015. The network announced its results triumphantly,[9] saying: "an overwhelming majority of British Muslims oppose the use of violence against people publishing images of the Prophet Muhammad," referring to the Charlie Hebdo attacks. This sounded reassuring. Promising even. The results?

Twenty-seven percent of British Muslims were "sympathetic" with the Charlie Hebdo attacks and a further 11 percent thought the magazine deserved it.

That's one in three. That translates to roughly nine hundred thousand Muslims in London alone. Imagine if one in three Christians were either "sympathetic" with abortion clinic bombings or thought they deserved it. I dare say the headline would not read: "An overwhelming majority of Christians oppose the use of violence." No, we would hear about the potential terrorists in our midst. As these figures demonstrate, Muslim extremists have a substantial fan base.

You see, whether or not so-called "radical Islam" represents the majority of those practicing the Islamic faith is irrelevant; that it is representative of many who do practice that religion is undeniable. It simply won't do to characterize ISIS, the Taliban, Boko Haram, al-Qaeda, Hamas, the Fulani herdsmen militia, the Muslim Brotherhood, Hezbollah, and so on as fringe elements of Islam. These groups occupy *whole countries*, not just a mosque or two. The prevailing notion, implied in Hay's article above, that Muslims are the meek and mild of this earth who need the protection of the West, does not conform to the reality of the geopolitical situation.

I have lived in Europe and I have traveled all over it. My work takes me there an average of twice a year. The steady Islamization, which is to say the steady degradation, of Europe, is hard to miss. I recall driving through a small French village a few years ago when suddenly a table from a sidewalk café was tossed into the street in front of my car. At that moment, a man unsheathed a sword—*A sword!*—from a cane and began chasing another man down the street. I later learned from the café owner that both men were Moroccan Muslim immigrants. Such incidents are increasingly common in Europe, and in this case, it was never reported. As with the Rotherham rape cases in Britain, people are often afraid not only of Muslim retaliation, they are fearful of being labeled racist.

Islam is a religion, not a race, and the majority of Swiss don't want it in their country. The Left, for all of their championing of diversity and multiculturalism, frequently do not appreciate this very legitimate aspect of national identity. Progressives are married to globalism and anyone who is opposed to it or is remotely suspicious of its effects is damned as xenophobic and racist. One is not allowed to prefer his own culture above others; he must affirm them all as equally valid.

But they aren't equally valid.

The Swiss quite rightly recognize their values are Christian in origin and their culture is superior to what Muslim immigrants would bring. The fact that millions of Middle Eastern and African Muslims are seeking to immigrate to Europe and America is a tacit admission these people see their destination countries as superior in some sense, too. And they are. According to the Pew Forum:

> There are 49 countries in which Muslims comprise more than 50 percent of the population. A total of 1.2 billion Muslims live in these nations, representing 74 percent of the global Muslim population of 1.6 billion…. All Muslim-majority countries are in less-developed regions of the world with the exception of Albania and Kosovo, which are in Europe.[10]

This is a nice way of saying almost all Muslim-majority countries are third world. According to the Global Terrorism Index, there has been a fivefold increase in fatalities from terrorist acts since 9/11. Four groups are responsible for most of these. All of them are Islamic. Shocked? Of course you aren't. Ideas have consequences, and Islam is destroying many parts of the world as socialism once did. Travel the world. You will see it in Asia, Africa, and Europe. If progressives have their way, the Americas will suffer this blight too.

The great irony here is that while progressives are condemning those Europeans and Americans who want to stop or greatly curtail immigration from the Islamic world to their own countries, they fail to recognize no countries are more conservative than Islamic ones. In 2012, I debated a Muslim woman on the question of free speech on CNN International. One might have thought CNN International, based in London, could have found a *real* Muslim to debate me on this subject. They are there. Trust me. I have debated them in Hyde Park. Instead, I found myself opposite a woman who was something of a hippie from North Carolina. Raised Baptist, she had only lately converted to Islam. Naïve about her new religion, she argued Islam encouraged free speech. When I challenged her to name a single Islamic country that championed freedom of speech and equality, she was stumped. But she must be forgiven. There isn't one.

Allowing Muslims to flood into Western countries may fit with progressives' short-term goals—namely, a desire to overthrow Christianity's much-hated influence on cultural values as expressed in what they derisively refer to as "populism"—but they do not fit with their long-term objectives. So blinded are they by their hatred of Christianity they have become de facto apologists for this absolutist, intolerant, and perpetually violent religion. Don't like the Christian view on LGBTQ issues? Feel a deep concern for gender equality? Wait until you get a load of the Muslim view should that religion ever gain ascendancy in the West.

The West is engaged in a soft war with Islam for control of Western civilization. The religion is invading the West and remaking it into something altogether different—*and worse*. To let such people into Western countries is to bring the Trojan Horse within the walls of the city.

After a few sophomoric jokes, Christopher and Zachary decided to take a gondola up Mount Titlis. Since I had been up the mountain before, I opted for a relaxing boat tour of Lake Lucerne and the various villages on the lake. The boat—really a substantial ship—had a café on the main deck with floor-to-ceiling windows. Stretching out before me were the crystal waters of the lake, its shores framed by snowcapped Alpine mountains.

Everything here spoke of wealth: the automobiles, the hotels and restaurants, the shopping districts, the people, and especially the sketchy Russian mafia-types. Historically, Switzerland has endeavored to stay out of the politics of other nations. On the other hand, the Swiss have, like the Swedes, made their neutrality an object of worship and profit. They have accepted monies plundered from the Jews and hidden money for criminals. Hence the Russians.

I say I was on a tour boat/ship, but the vessel also served as a means of transportation to those Swiss who live on Lake Lucerne. Over a half dozen cups of coffee, breakfast, and lunch, I chatted with a variety of local people about their country, mine, the pros and cons of each, and Europe's problems. Affluent and proud to be Swiss, they generally asserted the greatness of their country. I respect that. One Swiss couple, retirees, were particularly interesting to me. Christian and Amelie, educated, well-traveled, and eager to show me their country, they defied the "rudest people in the world" reputation of Switzerland and sought me out repeatedly to add something to our conversation. Learning the purpose of my trip, they took each question very seriously.

"Why, in your opinion, doesn't Switzerland join the European Union?" I asked.

"Why would we want to?" Christian smiled. "And from your expression, I think you agree with me," he added playfully.

I chuckled. "I do agree. But I wanted your opinion."

"In truth, many Swiss do want to join the EU, but a majority of Swiss do not want it. Particularly those of us who are older."

If the Swiss are reluctant to surrender their culture to the mass immigration of a non-European people, they are equally reluctant to surrender their sovereignty to a non-Swiss governing body. Like Norway, Switzerland has never joined the EU. And to Christian's point, why would they? After the United States, Switzerland boasts the highest per-capita net worth of any country in the world.[11] They also have the lowest average income tax in Europe.[12] However beneficial it might be to other countries for Switzerland (or the United States) to surrender its sovereignty, it is of no benefit to the Swiss (nor to Americans). Great countries don't mimic or surrender sovereignty to inferior ones.

"What is your opinion of Europe's migrant problem?"

"I understand why they want to leave their own countries," Amelie said. "I would want to leave Africa, too. But the complexion of Europe is changing in a very bad way. We should not take them here."

"We need some as laborers," Christian said to Amelie. "Swiss youth won't take those jobs." He turned to me. "But it's a Faustian bargain. I think a better solution is helping them improve their own countries—if that's possible."

The conversation turned to the United States.

"We have traveled in America many times," Christian said. "It's so fascinating, so enormous. We hear your politicians refer to us as model sometimes. That amuses us."

"Why?" I was genuinely curious.

"Switzerland is such a small country. We are the size of some of your cities. America is vast. That brings with it problems we have never had to contemplate. We are always amazed by how different America is from region to region. I don't think such comparisons are meaningful."

But there are some interesting comparisons. Like America, Switzerland is a curious mixture of policies, traditions, and attitudes. Animal rights laws were enacted (1978) before there was universal female suffrage in national elections (1990).[i] In defiance of the whole of Europe, the Swiss love their guns, having one of the highest rates of gun ownership in the world, shooting competitions for children as young as twelve, and mandatory military service for those eighteen to thirty-four, but the country has almost no gun-related violence and has been neutral since 1815. Switzerland was the first country in the world to legalize physician-assisted suicide[13] but has one of the lowest abortion rates in Europe, almost three times lower than the United States.[14] This is typically Swiss, marching to the beat of their own drum.

The ship made a brief stop at Rütli and that offers us an appropriate place to bring our evaluation of this interesting country into the harbor. But not before we consider a story that makes up part of the mythology of this remarkable country and its people.

It was here at Rütli, in 1291,[ii] when Switzerland as an independent nation was born. For the Swiss, it is the stuff of legend and it involves a shadowy, probably purely fictitious figure named William Tell, the Braveheart, so to speak, of Switzerland.

According to the legend, the wicked Bailiff Gessler, an Austrian and a Habsburg[iii] magistrate charged with ruling the Swiss people

---

i   Women were given voting rights in 1971, but a few cantons held out; the last relented in 1990.

ii   1307 according to some versions.

iii   This is often Americanized as "Hapsburg."

of Altdorf, put a Habsburg hat on a pole and ordered all Swiss passersby to remove their own hats and bow before it. Everyone did—until William Tell didn't.

Dragged before Gessler, Tell's punishment was to shoot an apple off of his son's head at 120 paces with his crossbow. He would be given one chance to do it. Tucking two arrows (also called bolts) into his coat, Tell walked off the distance and split the apple.

"Your life will be spared!" Gessler pronounced. "But why did you put two bolts into your coat?"

"Had I missed with the first, I would have shot you with the second," Tell said defiantly.

Gessler, outraged, sought to imprison Tell, but the cross-bowman and his son escaped. Pursued by Gessler and his Habsburg agents across Lake Lucerne, Tell killed the Austrian with that second bolt he so cleverly kept handy. He then met at Rütli with representatives of the Swiss cantons of Uri, Schwyz, and Unterwalden. Together they took an oath and united against the Habsburgs, creating the Swiss Confederation.

It is a story every Swiss child knows. A country's mythology, be it Romulus and Remus or Washington's cherry tree, tells you a lot about its people, how they see themselves, and what they value. In this case, it speaks to their independent spirit. William Tell is a story almost any American would instinctively love.

We left impressed. This is a great country. It is also a genuine contender for our title.

CHAPTER 24

Germany: Ideas Have Consequences

"History gives one weapon to truth which it denies to the lie: lies have many versions, truth only one."[1]

—Alexander Weissberg in *The Accused*

Many years ago, it was my good fortune to be awarded a research grant that sent me to Europe to study the intellectual origins of the Holocaust. On that occasion, my eldest son Michael, then only twelve, joined me. We visited Berlin; Munich; a variety of concentration camps in Germany, Austria, and Poland; museums; libraries; and archives.

We did it all in a rented Škoda Octavia. I vividly recall leaving the car rental parking lot and turning onto the famed Autobahn. With determination, I accelerated the shaky Škoda to 110 mph. I felt like I was German Formula 1 ace, Michael Schumacher. Briefly. Almost instantaneously a big Mercedes was on my bumper flashing its lights, the international signal for "Get that junk out of my way!"

This time was different.

"What do you have available?" I was standing at the car rental desk at the Munich airport while a woman behind the counter looked at the inventory on her computer screen.

"Let's see—we have an Opel—"

"No."

"We have a Škoda—"

"Definitely not."

"And we have a promotion on a BMW M140i."

My heart skipped a beat. "And how much is that?"

"It's the same price as the Škoda."

"I'll take it!"

Among all of the letters and numbers in that make and model, the most significant is the second M. That designation means it is a product of the high-performance division of Bayerische Motoren Werke—otherwise known as Bavarian Motor Works. In the words of BMW: "M. The most powerful letter in the world." I quite agree.

Germany is famous for its work ethic, efficiency, and engineering. There's an old joke about Europeans that goes like this:

In Heaven:

    The cooks are French.

    The policemen are English.

    The mechanics are German.

    The lovers are Italian.

    And the bankers are Swiss.

In Hell:

    The cooks are English.

    The policemen are German.

    The mechanics are French.

    The lovers are Swiss.

    And the bankers are Italian.

If you have ever been to these countries or know even a little of their histories, you know the stereotypes have more than a little validity. Unfortunately, while the Germans are known for their superbly engineered automobiles, they are also known for genocide. How did a country that produced Johann Sebastian Bach author the Holocaust?

To answer that question, I pointed the sporty little BMW to the small town of Berchtesgaden in the Bavarian Alps. This time I was well-equipped for the Autobahn. One can, of course, drive a minivan on the Autobahn if he wants to. But where's the fun in that? The boys, who will rejoin our story in France, did not accompany me to Germany. But at this moment, I was grateful for their absence. Their collective weight would have made the car handle like a UPS truck. Instead, it had all the liveliness the M was meant to give it. No more scooters, rickshaws, tuk-tuks, or elephants for me.

The landscape of northern Germany, to my eye anyway, is not attractive. But Bavaria, like Switzerland, is simply breathtaking. The sun glinted off the snow-dusted Bavarian spruce trees. A river, unfrozen, cut a winding deep blue line through the white valleys, and increasingly mountains spread out across the horizon. It was a perfect backdrop for a Christmas postcard. Only it was the backdrop, the birthplace, for one of the world's greatest evils. How could a place so beautiful give rise to something so monstrous?

My first stop was at the foot of the Kehlstein. Some 6,017 feet high, atop this mountain sits Kehlsteinhaus. Known to the world as the Eagle's Nest, Hitler's famous Alpine retreat, it was part of his so-called "southern capital." Built with slave labor and given to Hitler by Martin Bormann and the Nazi Party elites for his fiftieth birthday, the Eagle's Nest was visited by the Fuhrer a mere fourteen times. Afraid of heights, he preferred the less grandiose Berghof at the bottom of the Kehlstein.[i]

Getting to the Eagle's Nest is a thrill in itself. You board a specially equipped bus that powers up a 27 percent gradient, swinging precipitously around high mountain single-lane switchbacks and, just when you think a head-on collision will be your fate, with perfect German timing the coach pulls into what is little more than a bus-length nook in the rocky cliff as another coach, moving down the mountain, passes without braking. Are you a nervous passenger? This isn't for you.

Arriving at a parking lot, passengers disembark and walk 413 feet through a marble-lined tunnel and board an elevator finished in polished brass and Venetian mirrors. The elevator takes them the remaining 430 feet to the top of the mountain, where there is a restaurant and spectacular views—but no mention of Hitler. I was here before, too, and each time it is the same. It was as if 1933–1945 never happened and any question or reference to it made people nervous.

Except at the Documentation Center in nearby Obersalzberg. There, one finds a history of National Socialism and its abuses. But the museum's presence is a source of resentment for some. Many simply do not want to be reminded of the past. They need to be. According to a 2019 poll, 40 percent of German high schoolers do not know what happened at Auschwitz. That's more than a little alarming.

I drove two hours across the Austrian border to the picturesque village of Mauthausen. Sitting on the outskirts of the town like a medieval citadel of stone is the Mauthausen concentration camp. Only prisoners marked for death were sent there. That said, it was

---

i   The US government destroyed what remained of the Berghof and turned the area into a US Armed Forces Recreation Facility. It was not returned to the German government until 1995.

not a "death camp" in the same sense as Auschwitz or Treblinka. It was a level three work camp. But the effect was the same. Prisoners died at a rate of more than 50 percent at Mauthausen—"annihilation through work," as the Nazis called it. Unlike Dachau (just outside Munich), most of what you see at this concentration camp is original: the gas chamber, the crematorium, and the enormous calcified ash heap at the bottom of a nearby cliff.

I visited other concentration camps, too. Dachau, Buchenwald, Mittelbau-Dora, and Auschwitz. In Nuremberg, I stopped at Room 600 of the Courthouse, site of the Nuremberg Trials. Finding them is not easy if you need signage. In the town of Dachau there are almost none, and at Room 600, still a functioning courtroom, I found none. Were it not for international pressure I am confident these memorials would not exist. The Germans want to forget—and they want you to forget, too.

Now is an appropriate time to return to a story I mentioned in passing—the old Nazi woman with whom I stayed in Innsbruck, Austria.

As a college student backpacking through Europe, I arrived at Innsbruck by train. I called a bed and breakfast that was recommended to me. A pleasant older woman answered the phone. Her name was Katy, she said, and she owned the bed and breakfast on the outskirts of the city in the mountains. She would come and pick me up at the train station.

Operating a chalet full of other students, Katy was a delightful grandmotherly hostess to us all. She was, that is, until—

"Katy, who is this in the photo?" I was looking at a framed newspaper clipping hanging on the wall. Yellowed, it appeared to be very old.

"That is me, young man!" she said proudly. "I was a nurse in the war."

A student of history, I was fascinated. "Wow!" I said. "I bet you have a lot of stories to tell."

"Yes, those were very hard times. The things the Russians did were just awful. They are evil people the Russians. I lost my brother in the fighting in Russia. *I hate Russians.*"

Do you sense my mistake coming?

"But Katy," I said naively, "Germany invaded Russia with four million men. Were the Russians not supposed to defend their own country?"

She erupted and began shouting at me incoherently. The grandmother veneer was gone, replaced by a woman who proudly served the Third Reich. Some Austrians opposed the Nazis. Not her.

Another student walked in and she regained her composure. "You must understand," she was speaking quietly, passionately, "what the Russians did. They murdered, raped, destroyed *everything!* And the British and Americans bombed our village!"

"I've read many stories of what the Russians did, Katy. Unspeakable evil. I can't imagine. But Germany started the war and did that stuff all over Europe, to say nothing of the Holocaust and—"

She glared speechlessly.

"We fought the war because we had to fight it! We were surrounded by enemies!"

I ignored the remark and tried to change the subject. I was determined to extricate myself from this international conflict.

The next morning when I came down for breakfast, I found her going through piles of old photographs. With apparently no one else up yet, it was just the two of us in her kitchen. She turned, holding a handful of photos she selected and began laying them out in front of me one by one.

"This is our village after the British bombed it.... This is what it looked like before the bombing.... This is what our house was like after the war...."

She was trying very hard to win me over. What was I supposed to say? "You're right, the Allies were wrong to go to war with the Nazi regime"?

"But the Holocaust," I began slowly. "Eight million people. *Eight million.*" To my young, naïve mind, this was reasonable and rational and she would surely acknowledge that whatever her country suffered, it was the consequence of a war they provoked.

"Hitler did some good things!" And with that, as they say, the cat was out of the bag. "He made us a great nation again! I will not believe all of the things they say about him and the Jews!"

I said nothing.

"You're an American," she pleaded. "I like Americans. The Americans gave each of us a cow after the war for milk. And they gave us food. But the Russians! Last week I threw a student out of this house! He said he was a Pole, but I discovered he was lying!"

To judge modern Germany in the light of the Holocaust may seem unfair, and in a sense it is. Today, Katy's generation is all but gone. Germany's current leadership was born well after the war and had nothing to do with the Nazi subjugation of Europe or the Holocaust that followed. Ideologically, German Chancellor Angela Merkel and the people who elected her are deeply embarrassed by their Nazi forebears and are determined to rehabilitate their nation.

But they live in the shadow of the Nazis.

We have seen how, in postwar Japan, MacArthur, recognizing that the Japanese people, having been failed by both their Shinto religion and their faith in their emperor, were left with a void. What faith would sustain them now? He sought to fill that void with Christianity and while the Japanese did not convert en masse, they did enthusiastically adopt the fruit of it, thus throwing off a backward feudalism and becoming a free society and a modern industrial power.

Terrified by their past, Germany has rushed to embrace fascism's ideological opposite. Having been failed by their faith in Nazism's hyper-militarism, racism, and utopian nationalism, the void left in the German mind by that secular, pagan religion has been filled with hyper-passivism, indiscriminate multiculturalism, and utopian globalism. In his book *Leftism Revisited*, Erik von Kuehnelt-Leddihn writes:

> The world is indebted to Germany in a terrifying way, because she demonstrated to everyone what the ultimate conclusions of negative and destructive ideas really are. Ideas which in London or New York are repeated as seemingly harmless abstractions have been shown up by the Germans in all their blood-chilling finality.[2]

Ideas have consequences. We have seen it all over the world. The societal consequences of Islam, atheism, socialism, fascism— we have seen them all. And while Germany is no longer the bloodthirsty militaristic state created by Adolf Hitler, it is a soulless, guilt-ridden country populated by a people who are fearful of asserting any sense of national identity lest it raise the specter of their fascist past. On the contrary, eager to prove how un-Nazi they are, Germany has accepted more immigrants than any other European country.[3] There have been startling consequences. According to *Newsweek*:

> A German university found that a 10.4 percent increase in violent crime was linked to an influx of migrants into the country's southern region.... Between 2010 and 2016,

Germany accepted 670,000 refugees and 680,000 more nonrefugee migrants from outside of the E.U., according to Pew Research data from November. Eighty-six percent of refugees who entered Germany in that time were Muslim.[4]

This report is one of the few to mention the source of the violence. Most do not mention Islam at all but instead speak vaguely of "migrants" or "refugees." This, too, is in reaction to their Nazi heritage. Germany, like a man who once attacked and killed his neighbors on the basis he was racially superior, now, to prove he is a changed man, refuses to lock his front door—and that door is now open to fascism's religious manifestation: Islam. It should be no surprise there has been a corresponding 10 percent increase in anti-Semitism in Germany.[5] But the German government, fearful of the dreaded racism charge, is keen to denounce "Islamophobia," but simply won't call a spade a spade.[6]

My final destination before returning to Munich was Berlin. The difference between northern and southern Germany, as well as between the former East and West Germany, is striking. The former East Bloc is still characterized by bad Soviet architecture of the Khrushchev era and attitudes that went with it. And where Munich is a very German city, Berlin is quite cosmopolitan. Stopping for a cup of coffee along the fashionable Kurfürstendamm, I had to keep reminding myself I was not in Paris.

I stopped at Checkpoint Charlie, the Berlin Wall Memorial, the Reichstag, and the famous Brandenburg Gate. Using a map of the city dating from the 1940s and some information gleaned from the internet, I even found Hitler's Reich Chancellery and the site of the bunker where he committed suicide, April 30, 1945. As with elsewhere in Germany, there are no signs marking the spot. Nothing. Today an apartment building stands unassumingly in the Reich Chancellery's former location and a playground has been built on top of the bunker.

Returning my car to Munich, I was met with horrendous traffic and a surge in hotel prices. The annual Munich Security Conference, I was told, was in session and various dignitaries, staff, and media commandeered the city's hotels and its main boulevards. That night, in need of some lighthearted entertainment, I went to the Viktualienmarkt beer garden. Although I don't drink beer, these things are fun. Large picnic tables fill the square and people move from one to another drinking enormous glasses of beer—what else?—and meeting people.

As I walked through the center gallery, a woman grabbed my arm and beckoned me to join their table. This is common at these gatherings.

"Sit down, sit down!" she ordered.

Upon learning I was American, she became even friendlier. "Where's your beer? Here's money. Go get one for both of us!"

Dutifully, I did as I was told. I came back and the table of eight bid me sit in the center so they could all ply me with questions.

"Your former vice president, Biden, I think, is his name, just called your country an embarrassment."

My face must have registered my confusion. I didn't know what she was referring to.

"Yeah, he did. Just right over there," she pointed back toward the city center. "Today."

"Really?" I said. "I didn't see that headline."

"Well, he did," said another in perfect English. "What a f**king embarrassment he is to be calling your country that!"

"I like America," said a third. "I would live there if I could. Los Angeles, I think."

"You like Los Angeles?" another asked in disbelief. "New York, man. I'd live in New York, the center of the f**king universe."

This alcohol-infused conversation lasted for another thirty minutes or so and was rapidly followed by a sing-along led by a group of amusing men in lederhosen.

As I made my way to the airport the next morning, Biden's remarks were on my mind. By that time, I had read the full text of his address. Said Biden:

> The America I see values basic human decency, not snatching children from their parents or turning our back on refugees at our border. Americans know that's not right. The American people understand plainly that this makes us an embarrassment. The American people know, overwhelmingly, that it is not right. That it is not who we are.

This was clearly a shot directed at President Trump's immigration policy. It was also cheap sensationalism. Whose immigration policy would Biden have us model? Britain's? Sweden's? Germany's? Let's pray not. This was the very thesis I was refuting on my world tour. America has many things for which it should be embarrassed, but this was not one of them.

Germany is a great country in a number of ways. It has great natural beauty, friendly people, strong social services, a strong work ethic, and the most powerful economy in Europe. But it is spiritually dead.

In speaking of the French Revolution, Irish philosopher and statesman Edmund Burke warned the French people, "in throwing off that Christian religion which has hitherto been our boast and comfort, and one great source of civilization amongst us, and many other nations, we are apprehensive (being well aware the mind will not endure a void) that some uncouth, pernicious, and degrading superstition might take the place of it."[7]

The mind will not endure a void. Some uncouth, pernicious, and degraded superstition is replacing Christianity—all over Europe.

CHAPTER 25

Egypt: "Wonderful Things"

"As my eyes grew accustomed to the light, details of the room within emerged slowly from the mist, strange animals, statues, and gold—everywhere the glint of gold. For the moment—an eternity it must have seemed to the others standing by—I was struck dumb with amazement, and when Lord Carnarvon, unable to stand the suspense any longer, inquired anxiously, 'Can you see anything?,' it was all I could do to get out the words, 'Yes, wonderful things.'"

—British archaeologist Howard Carter upon opening the tomb of
King Tutankhamun November 26, 1922

My flight from Munich to Cairo was a comfortable four hours. As we approached our destination, the pilot made a slow turn just below cloud level offering a panoramic view of this country's capital. Now near midnight, the lights of the city center and suburbs were visible. Highways, flanked by illuminated billboards, stretched out to the desert horizon. I looked for the famed Pyramids of Giza. If the Eiffel Tower gives orientation to those flying over Paris, the pyramids, dominating the skyline on the southern outskirts of Greater Cairo, provide it here. But it was just too dark to see them.

I was excited to be here. Were children to have "bucket lists," and we may thank God they don't, Egypt would have been on mine. The long-slumbering imagination of the boy—fired by Sunday school lessons of hardhearted pharaohs, adventure stories that pivoted on some aspect of ancient Egyptian history and lore, and, finally, bolstered by a decent Western civilization curriculum forming the bedrock of a solid education—was awakened in the man as the plane touched down at Cairo International Airport.

Prior to departing Munich, I had arranged for a hotel car to pick me up just outside baggage claim. This is always a good idea in places where foreigners, Americans in particular, make lucrative targets for scammers or worse. Better to trust a reliable hotel than surrender your fate to a dubious Uber or taxi driver of unknown quality or intentions, especially at night.

Leaving the largely empty airport and hitting an equally empty highway, my driver chatted affably about his impressions of America and Americans. Thinking it would please me, he increased the volume of the luxury sedan's stereo. The *thump-thump* bass of some sort of 90s American pop remix seemed to announce my arrival to the whole of Cairo. Sitting in the backseat, I rolled down the window and let the surprisingly cool air revive me.

We crossed the Nile on the 6th of October Bridge. An east-west artery used by more than half-a-million people daily, the bridge commemorates the date of Egypt's attack on Israel initiating the Yom Kippur War in 1973. A bloody and futile effort by Egypt and Syria to regain territory lost to their hated enemy in 1967, Israel repelled the attack at great cost. But since when have propagandists been deterred by historical truth?

At the hotel's porte-cochère, retractable bollards blocked our entrance as security, equipped with fully automatic weapons, stopped us. My passport was inspected by one guard while another rolled a mirror on something akin to a wheeled carjack beneath the undercarriage. A third guard held a leashed German shepherd loosely, allowing it to wander around the car at will, leaping into the trunk, sniffing luggage, the wheel wells, doors—everything— with an admirable sense of purpose. Before entering the hotel lobby, I passed through an airport-style metal detector and my bags were x-rayed.

None of this is out of the norm for much of the world. This routine, or one similar to it, is repeated a thousand times a day in South America, parts of Asia, Eastern Europe, and everywhere in Africa. They are, of course, looking for car bombs, suitcase bombs, suicide vests, and weapons that might be used to kill their guests and employees. It is all an unfortunate byproduct of life in the third world—and completely necessary. On a trip to Israel some years ago, I was staying at a Tel Aviv hotel when a suicide bomber detonated himself across the street. Even at that distance, the explosion rattled the hotel's windows. These security measures would be repeated every time I entered the hotel grounds, be it on foot or in an automobile.

I used some of the many points I accumulated on my journey to get a room upgrade. I wanted a view of the Nile and got it. At some 4,160 miles long, the Nile is generally regarded as the longest river in the world.[i] Flowing north through the desert from Lake Victoria in Uganda to the Mediterranean, it has given life to Egyptians for millennia. Some say it is where life itself began. And with 95 percent of Egypt's 100 million people living within a few miles of its muddy banks, very little has changed from then to now.

---

i   The Brazilian Institute for Geography and Statistics disputes this. They claim the Amazon is sixty-five miles longer. One might have thought this debate would be easily settled in the age of satellite mapping. Not so. The dispute centers on exactly where the Amazon begins and ends.

This expedition aside, I have traveled so much, I long ago lost the thrill of it all. It is simply an unavoidable consequence of a lifetime on the road. Even before my life as a writer, I developed a bit of travel fatigue. With my mother a native of Vancouver Island, Canada, and my father a career soldier from South Alabama, I grew up between cultures and countries, supplemented by frequent moves from one military base to another. It wears on you after a while. Wonder is usurped by weariness.

But this was different. My room opened to a small balcony overlooking the Nile. The mythical river sparkled in the moonlight, and feluccas, the little wooden sailboats common to this part of the world, glided across the dark waters that concealed countless mysteries. It wasn't hard to imagine Cleopatra, who for me always looks like Elizabeth Taylor, sailing along in the Thalamegos, her massive pleasure barge, with one of her many—and I do mean *many*—lovers, his head in her lap as she feeds him grapes. To say the setting was romantic is an understatement. But not in the way of a Valentine's Day card and dinner out or a walk in the surf at a Sandals resort in the Caribbean. No, this was romantic in the way only a truly ancient city can be; where the history is stacked layer upon layer, and even the shadows have the patina of antiquity.

This, however, is the Traveler's Fallacy of which I have warned throughout this book. Had we undertaken our mission to discover the world's greatest country in, say, circa 1550 BC, Egypt might have been a worthy recipient of our award. Her wealth, power, science, art, architecture, centers of learning—in short, her sophistication—were renowned throughout the Mediterranean. But not now. Egypt today is a decidedly third-world country struggling with the problems common to such nations: systemic corruption, instability, poverty, high mortality and crime rates, revolutionary forces within, enemies without, and no clear path forward. From my balcony, none of this was visible.

All these problems were exacerbated by the onslaught of the Chinese coronavirus pandemic. I arrived in Cairo just as the panic began. Passengers on my flight were greeted by people in something like hazmat suits. A few days later I stood in the Sahara Desert surrounded by North African men who daily face dangers inconceivable to the typical Westerner. I cannot begin to tell you the number of ways you can die, and die badly, in Africa.

Malaria alone kills more than 800,000 Africans each year, and the world barely notices. The mortality rate for children is sixteen times that of the developed world. That is to say nothing of other pestilences, civil war, violent crime, automobile accidents, and things of which you can barely conceive. And yet, here they were, afraid of contracting coronavirus! I have since encountered the same phenomenon all over North Africa. It was almost funny given the prevalence of dangers compared to which coronavirus was insignificant.

With the entire world suffering the consequences of a pandemic, one can guess how it would ravage a fragile Egyptian economy that derives 12 percent of its GDP from tourism. Add to this Egypt's very real concerns about terrorism destroying that industry and you get a glimpse of how fragile the economy really is. Indeed, the tourist industry suffered near annihilation when, in 1997, terrorists killed sixty-two tourists at Luxor in a single attack. Since that time, the government has taken aggressive measures to protect and attract tourists. By law, tour buses and groups must be accompanied by armed escorts who either board the buses or follow them like state troopers in hot pursuit.

Even so, sporadic attacks have continued. The U.S. State Department warns: "Terrorist groups continue plotting attacks in Egypt. Terrorists may attack with little or no warning, and have targeted diplomatic facilities, tourist locations, transportation hubs, markets/shopping malls, Western businesses, restaurants, resorts, and local government facilities."[1] Suddenly, a Sandals resort in the Caribbean sounds better, doesn't it?

Not to me. I booked a series of tours with an Egyptologist who, like the guides and hotel personnel in Asia, took a name more easily pronounced by Westerners: Olivia. For the next few days, Olivia and driver Ahkmad would be my constant companions.

Olivia was an elegant, attractive thirtysomething of distinctly Western tastes in fashion. In a country where many women wear burqas (total body coverage), niqabs (eyes visible), or hijabs (face exposed), Olivia stood out among Egyptian women in a consciously rebellious manner, embracing her femininity in an unmistakably Western style.

Walking into the Khan el-Khalili souk (i.e., bazaar), a snaggle-toothed old man shouted at her in Arabic. She turned and shouted back, never breaking her pace.

"What was that about?" I asked.

"He's a traditional Muslim man. He doesn't like the way I dress."

Then again, maybe he did. Men like this are all over the Islamic world, waving their fingers or a short stick. Detractors of the Christian faith often speak of Christians as legalistic. This is inaccurate. Legalism is a product of human nature and no religion gives expression to that nature like Islam. Legalism is always ugly, be it environmentalists or the "social distancing" Nazis, but this has an especially unsavory quality to it, accompanied as it is by leering and an attempt to humiliate while inciting others to abuse the targeted woman. Former CBS reporter Lara Logan was publicly assaulted and gang raped in Cairo's Tahrir Square while covering the Arab Spring in February 2011. That attack began with just this sort of public shaming. Islam's contempt for women is ever near the surface.

And Olivia was dressed modestly by Western standards. Her only offenses were wearing pants, jewelry, and not covering her head and face. She carried herself with the cosmopolitan air of a well-traveled woman. Only she wasn't well traveled. She had, in fact, never been out of Egypt. Olivia's sophistication was the result of a career that brought her into constant contact with people from all over the world.

"My father is a lawyer, but law can be a difficult profession in Egypt for a woman," she said as vendors hawked their wares. "He encouraged me to get a degree in Egyptology and then a job as a tour guide. It pays well by our standards."

The Khan el-Khalili souk, situated in Old Cairo, is like bazaars found all over the Arab and Middle Eastern worlds. Labyrinthine places where a GPS is utterly useless and vendors are ready to produce, like genies sprung from lamps, whatever you wish. If you've seen the Medina of Marrakesh or the Grand Bazaar in Istanbul then you have some idea what the Khan el-Khalili, which is reputed to be the oldest of them all, is like.

These markets once held treasures, sometimes quite literally, of artistic excellence. Superb leather and woodwork; beautiful brass décor and fine china; exquisite jewelry, handwoven pashmina, and silk fabrics—they were all there, and much more. But today, craftsmanship, even in these places, has been supplanted by cheap knockoffs from China.

In the following days, Olivia and Ahkmad would take me to the Al-Azhar Mosque, which doubles as a university, and the very impressive Egyptian Museum where I spent hours exploring the wonders contained in it. But this was just an appetizer for what I really wanted to see: the Pyramids of Giza.

The Giza Necropolis was almost deserted. The fact is, the Egyptian tourism industry has never fully recovered from the Arab Spring, which brought revolution and upheaval to the entire Arab World. And now that fear of the Chinese coronavirus was growing, these places were ghost towns. That suited me just fine. It was a bit like being in an amusement park without the long lines.

No photograph does the three grand Pyramids of Giza justice. They are astonishing in scale. The Great Pyramid, Khufu, also known by the Greek name Cheops, is 481 feet tall and 13.5 acres at its base. To put this in some perspective, in my hometown of Birmingham, Alabama, the tallest building is 454 feet. Stonehenge, so celebrated (and overrated) as a marvel of engineering, looks like it was built by monkeys in comparison. Consider: it is believed Stonehenge originally consisted of eighty-three stones with the bluestones—those stones laid as a kind of crossbeam—weighing about three tons each; Khufu alone is comprised of 2.5 *million* hewn granite stones ranging in weight from two to fifteen tons each. Had Stonehenge been built on the Plains of Giza you would have never heard of it. But standing out in a pasture in Wiltshire without so much as a tree nearby, it looks more imposing than it really is.

The Great Pyramid of Khufu was constructed over the course of thirty years as a royal tomb for King Khufu, the second pharaoh of the fourth dynasty. It is the only surviving wonder of the ancient world and was completed circa 2560 BC. Theories abound regarding how the ancient Egyptians did it, from clever, long-forgotten construction techniques to space aliens. But I agree with the Greek historian Herodotus who thought the answer was much simpler and a great deal less exciting: slave labor.

It's amazing what you can do when labor is cheap and you're not overly concerned about occupational safety. Need a hundred thousand laborers? *Use slaves!* And if some die? *Press gang more!* The Egyptians reject this theory for obvious reasons. Regardless of how they did it, the fact they did, indeed, do it is a remarkable testimony to the extent some men will go to be remembered.

The irony, of course, is we remember almost nothing of Khufu the man beyond the tomb bearing his name.

I wanted to explore it. Olivia, who had undoubtedly done so many times, decided to grab a cup of coffee while I went spelunking in the Great Pyramid. Stale air hung heavily in the dimly lit corridor as I climbed upward 161 feet through the narrow passage leading to the King's burial chamber at the pyramid's center. There one finds a large red granite sarcophagus. Khufu's mummy, never found, is presumed to have been stolen by tomb robbers long ago. For some reason, I felt compelled to climb into his stone coffin. Wherever he is, he's better off than in there. *Yikes.*

Pyramids were massively expensive state-funded projects, especially the Pyramids of Giza. The best architects, engineers, and artisans of the day were hired to design and build them. Some of these builders were tasked with something similar to the cybersecurity experts of today: to keep those who wanted to penetrate them out. Externally, a pyramid spoke of a king's greatness and glory, thus the granite exterior was covered with white limestone, polished until it gleamed brilliantly in the North African sun.[ii]

But a pyramid's primary purpose was more than just an awe-inspiring tombstone. It was to protect the king's body, his possessions, and to help him reach the afterlife in a manner befitting a king. This meant creating a floorplan, so to speak, an interior, so complex, so deceptive, so impregnable, the king's body would be safe for all eternity. People would know the king's body and all of his earthly wealth lay somewhere within, but that knowledge would be worth no more than knowing Fort Knox houses the U.S. gold reserves.

If pyramids were expensive to build, they were also expensive to maintain. In all probability, they were initially guarded.

---

ii   The limestone is gone today. It was later stolen to build mosques and fortresses.

But like gravesites the world over, there came a time when they were neglected. As Egypt fell into civil war and ruin, funds and personnel were directed elsewhere, and tomb raiders seized their chance. It was only a matter of time until someone succeeded in finding the pearls hidden within this stone shell. Like the building of the pyramids, no one knows exactly how they pulled off this epic theft. You might call them hackers but in a much more literal sense of the word. These were not thieves of the smash and grab variety. Such a theft would have required planning, sophistication, a sizable labor force, and considerable determination.

I imagine some ancient equivalent of Hans Gruber, dressed in a fine suit of Egyptian cotton and topped off by a red fez, attacking it with a team of dastardly and daring thieves as if it were the Nakatomi Plaza. And with no barefooted John McClane shouting "Yippee-ki-yea!" on his way to stopping them they made good their escape. The treasures then being sold to eccentric collectors to fund Gruber's and his gang's life on a Mediterranean island where they drank exotic cocktails with those little umbrellas in them.

The truth is, however, we have no idea who did it or how. As Jesus warned, "Do not store up for yourselves treasures on earth, where moths and vermin destroy, and where thieves break in and steal." (Matthew 6:19) Let that be a lesson to all of you would-be pyramid builders.

With this in mind, many later kings were buried in the less ostentatious Valley of the Kings near Luxor. But even here the thieves had their way, stealing the contents of every burial chamber but one: that of an obscure king named Tutankhamun, known best to history by his diminutive, King Tut. After years of searching for the tomb, British archaeologist Howard Carter, a socially acceptable tomb raider but a tomb raider nonetheless, made the remarkable discovery, and on November 26, 1922, he entered the tomb's anteroom where many of the treasures of this king were located. Upon seeing the glint of gold within, Carter exclaimed the now-famous words "Yes, wonderful things" to the sponsor of his expedition, Lord Carnarvon.

Can you imagine being there on that momentous occasion? How exhilarating it must have been to not only make one of the greatest archeological discoveries of all time but just to see something so extraordinary that lay hidden from human eyes for more than 3,000 years. Speaking of it later, Carter called it, "The day of days, the most wonderful that I have ever lived through, and certainly one whose like I can never hope to see again." Though frequently on tour, much of the Tut Collection can be seen at the Egyptian Museum in Cairo.

In addition to the Pyramids of Khufu, Khafre, and Menkaure, the Giza Necropolis is home to the Sphinx, a temple, a museum, and more pyramids. Just as Stonehenge is but one example of "circus stones" in Britain, there are more than a hundred pyramids in Egypt, though the rest are not as overwhelming as the three Pyramids of Giza. Before leaving the site, I would explore the interior of others, ponder Sophocles' Riddle of the Sphinx, and, visit the museum. All along the way, Olivia entertained me with her considerable store of knowledge and her questions about my life as a writer, which seemed to captivate her as much as the Pyramids captivated me. It was a fair exchange—her knowledge for mine.

Egypt might reasonably blame China for the pandemic, but it can blame only itself for the country's plague of instability and fear of terrorism keeping so many tourists away. Like so much of the Middle East, one senses the veneer of civilization might evaporate at any moment and explode into violent demonstrations—or worse. I arrived in Cairo only days after Egypt's longtime president and strongman Hosni Mubarak died. The government declared three days of national mourning in his remembrance, but Mubarak, while loved by some, was hated by many more, not the least of which is the current Egyptian president Abdel Fattah El-Sisi. Sisi's government, threatened by Mubarak supporters on the one side and the Muslim Brotherhood on the other, cracked down on both brutally. Sisi appears to be in control, but it is as I say, the whole country could erupt into violence and civil war at any moment.

Finding I had an open evening, I took a taxi back to the Pyramids of Giza for a light show, and why not? It was a clear night under the desert stars and I might never see them again. I wanted to make the most of it. As the narration began, it all felt so strangely familiar: the narrator's voice, the dated soundtrack, and the ambiance they together created. Then it hit me. I knew where I heard it before. The first James Bond film I ever saw was *The Spy Who Loved Me* with Roger Moore and Barbara Bach. As a boy of ten, I sat wide-eyed as "Jaws," a notorious assassin, killed a man in the very shadow of Khufu when he attended the same presentation I was now viewing. Bond, too late to save this unfortunate fellow, nonetheless kicks some KGB butt. All the while the narrator's voice can be heard in the background. Nothing has changed. The narration and narrator are exactly the same. But where that movie depicts a large crowd gathered for the evening's program, I looked out upon perhaps two acres of empty seats.

I briefly considered a flight to Luxor in Upper Egypt[iii] to see the Valley of the Kings but I simply had too much to do in the time remaining to me before flying to France. How does one score

---

iii   Upper Egypt is in the south. This can be very confusing to foreigners, but the orientation is given by the Nile's northerly flow. Thus, upriver is Upper Egypt and downriver is Lower Egypt.

a country like Egypt? I pondered the question one day as I walked alone through the southern outskirts of Cairo where one finds the abject squalor many of the city's poor must endure. These places are dangerous to foreigners, yes, crime-ridden as they are, but beneath the poverty that assaults your senses in the smell of raw sewage and the sight of vulnerable people who Jesus might have called "the least of these," one can, from time to time, encounter an unexpected grace in those same people and places.

On my last evening, I paid an old sailboat owner ten dollars to take me out on the Nile in his felucca. He waved me aboard, unfurled the sail, and swiveled the boom portside before walking the gunwale with startling catlike agility to the stern where he manned the tiller. The Nile has a beguiling quality. There was no Cleopatra in our little craft and no grapes were being fed to me. There wasn't even an especially comfortable place to sit. No matter.

The enchanted waters were made more beautiful by the moon casting flickering ribbons of light upon the barely percep-tible waves. A gentle breeze pushed us along. I might have taken a nap right there but for the occasional party boat, their speakers blasting pulsating dance music for their Middle Eastern tourists, which served to remind me that not everyone was deterred by fear of terrorism or viruses.

I loved Egypt. But I readily acknowledge I am not the typical traveler and I came to the country to "plunder" its historical trea-sures. Modern Egypt is a mess for all the reasons cited above. It has no history of anything we might call freedom and democracy, or, for that matter, economic, social, or political stability. In sociopo-litical terms, Egypt is at the bottom of the pyramid.

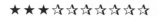

CHAPTER 26

France:
Living in the Ruins

"How can you govern a country which has 246 varieties of cheese?"[1]

—Charles de Gaulle

Political satirist P. J. O'Rourke once said the only good thing about the Germans is "they kill a lot of French." O'Rourke, I think we can safely assume, was not a Francophile. For my own part, I could only say I was not a fan of the available automobiles at the airport car rental desk. All of French make—you're better off with a rickshaw.

I arrived by air. Christopher and Zachary rejoined me. They had been in France many times and enjoyed it immensely, Paris in particular. It is a beautiful and interesting city. At the time of the French Revolution in 1789, only one in fifty Frenchmen lived in this capital; today that number is closer to one in six. This accounts for this city's dominance in French politics and culture. When an American says he has been to France, he almost always means Paris, as few Americans bother with Lyon, Montpellier,

Pau, or even Bordeaux.[i] Once you get beyond Paris's city limits, the country is mostly rural.

I have often thought of the striking contrast this city makes, historically speaking, with London. Both are beautiful cities, yet even the most ardent Anglophile would have to acknowledge Paris is a much more bewitching city. But I far prefer London's history. More accurately, I have greater respect for London's (Britain's) history. While London was once a great Christian city, and quite consciously so, with Queen Victoria sending her missionaries all over the world to bring the civilization of which Nelson Mandela spoke, Paris held fast to her paganism and no principle so much as pleasure. Historian Andrew Hussey summed it up well: "The well-known and sneering complaint of those who work in religious orders is that Paris 'is not a Christian city.' Perhaps it never truly was."[2]

Paris is also historically unstable, with social unrest and strikes common. Indeed, the French need little provocation before they're screaming *"Aux barricades!"*—to the barricades!—and someone is being beheaded and property is being destroyed. Since the St. Bartholomew's Day Massacre in 1572, the French have rioted over everything from flour and champagne to gasoline and pensions. The rule of thumb seems to be burn and behead now, ask questions later. For this reason, King Louis XIV hated Paris and built his palace at Versailles. Having suffered at the hands of the Parisian mobs in his youth, he vowed he would never be at their mercy again. The much-celebrated French Revolution, perhaps the most overrated event in history, deteriorated into mob rule and the Reign of Terror. It was only when Napoleon gave the rabble his

---

i   This is also true in reverse: when a European says he has been to America, he generally means New York City. I remind such people that although NYC is certainly an extraordinary American city, he should be careful when assuming what he encountered there is representative of the whole country.

famous "whiff of grapeshot"—that is, a blast of something like metal debris fired from a cannon—that they were brought to heel. Today, the mobs wear yellow vests instead of the famed cockade of the French Revolution.

In short, London's story is one of courage, resolve, and principle; Paris's is one of cowardice, collaboration, and self-indulgence. Following France's capitulation in June 1940, Marshal Philippe Pétain nailed it: "Our defeat was a result of our laxity. The spirit of enjoyment destroyed what the spirit of sacrifice had built."

History aside, in no city does one fall prey to the Traveler's Fallacy more than in Paris. Christopher, who is very studious, loves the museums and reading a good book in one of its coffee shops; Zachary, a social butterfly, enjoys the nightlife and the city's vibe. Whatever your preference, be it a stroll along the banks of the Seine on a nice evening, the lively atmosphere of the Latin Quarter, the stained glass of Sainte-Chapelle, or dinner in one of the city's innumerable wonderful restaurants, Paris has these and many other treasures to offer you. Paris is seductive.

But it is an illusion. As the French have reminded me many times, that is not how most French live.

Each year, Francois, a French friend of mine, visits a different part of the United States. Taking lengthy road trips—east and west coasts; the Rockies and the Mississippi Delta; Bourbon Street and Fifth Avenue—he tries to explore as much of America as possible just as Alexis de Tocqueville once did. But not to study the penal system. Francois has a very different agenda from his French predecessor. He is scouting out where he would like to live and raise his family.

Yes, he has had enough of Europe. *Entrepreneur* might be a French word, but its meaning has been eclipsed by other French words like *bureaucracy*. Indeed, so crushing is the tax burden, the highest in the industrialized world,[3] some of the government inspectors responsible for issuing business licenses will tell you (strictly off the record, of course) that for an entrepreneur to succeed he must must not report all his income. How would you live? Don't be so naïve, they say. Stash a bit of it away and out of the government's reach! Imagine the IRS giving you *that* advice.

"You can enjoy Europe," Francois often tells me, "because you aren't subject to our income tax and business laws."

His point is well taken. He understood I enjoyed a degree of freedom he only sampled while visiting America.

"Can you buy a gun in America?"

"Yup."

"What an amazing country!"

But Francois isn't actually a gun enthusiast. He is a businessman who is frustrated by a diminishing work ethic and a government that takes an adversarial view of business.

Both of these things were a matter of national humiliation when, in 2013, the French government tried to get American manufacturer Titan Tire Company to buy a defunct tire factory in Amiens to help an ailing French economy. Titan Tire CEO Maurice Taylor Jr. was less than diplomatic in his reply to French industry minister Arnaud Montebourg. Wrote Taylor:

The French workforce gets paid high wages but works only three hours. They get one hour for breaks and lunch, talk for three and work for three. I told this to the French union workers to their faces. They told me that that's "the French way"…Your letter states that you want Titan to start a discussion. How stupid do you think we are?[4]

Taylor went on to say that although France has "beautiful women and great wine," no, he was not interested in buying the factory or employing any French. The letter, given to the media by the French government, sparked something of an international incident with French workers and Montebourg offering a few insults of their own. Why Taylor didn't just say "*non, merci*" is not clear. Regardless, he was absolutely right in his assessment. He didn't even mention strikes, a favorite pastime among French workers almost as popular as wine during those two-hour (mandated by law) lunch breaks.

French workers don't like to work, and, unfortunately, French law reinforces it. In 2000, France adopted a thirty-five-hour work week. The pension system is generous and problematic with the retirement age at sixty-two, increasing pressure to move it back to sixty, and people living longer. As of October 2019, the unemployment rate in the US is 3.6 percent. In France, it is 8.5 percent. It is an unsustainable economic model and likely to drive the nation into insolvency.[5] As one French lawyer told me, "For the French, austerity means laying off the bearnaise sauce."

Trying to get anything done in France is a maddening process for an American. Most businesses do not open until 10 a.m. and they close with startling alacrity between 12 p.m. and 2 p.m. no matter what. Need something? You'll just have to wait.

More alarming to Francois, however, is his country's current immigration policy. He packed up his family and fled the big city some years ago when violence, theft, and poverty spilled over into his once-fashionable neighborhood. Islamic terrorist attacks like the Charlie Hebdo massacre, the mass shooting in Paris, and the Nice truck rampage have become common to France and Europe. Francois feels triangulated in his own country. Though the largest country in Western Europe, France is a country considerably smaller than Texas. His options there are limited.

Bear in mind this is no third-world migrant seeking political asylum. This is a man who is a productive citizen of a country that is, for many on the Left,[6] a model of what America should be. So far, Francois's efforts to obtain visas for himself and his family have been unsuccessful. Stories like Francois's intrigue me because I encounter them regularly. American exceptionalism is precisely what appeals to him. It is an exception in every way he perceives to be a barrier to his own economic success and the security he hopes to provide for his own family generationally: a reasonable tax burden, a hardworking people, a free-market mindset, a lack of government intrusion, and the ability to live among likeminded people who share his values.

But France's problems go well beyond an immigration policy that has led to sharply increased crime rates, poverty, social unrest, and terrorism. The French, quite simply, are not the great people they once were. You see it in daily life all over France in the grandeur of a bygone era: gorgeous stone-lined canals and rivers; plane tree-lined roads stretching out for miles under a green canopy; ancient city walls and beautiful churches, castle ruins and chateaux here and there—all of it speaks of a glorious past. But that's just it. It is the past. That was a much different generation of Frenchmen who built that France and their heirs aren't rebuilding it. They are living in its literal and metaphorical ruins.

General Norman Schwarzkopf Jr. once said, "Going to war without France is like going deer hunting without your accordion." Jokes like Schwarzkopf's are common among American soldiers. But as I am sure Schwarzkopf, a product of West Point, knew that joke doesn't hold for the whole of French history. Between the Battle of Agincourt in 1415 and the Battle of Blenheim in 1704, a period spanning more than the history of the

United States, the French did not lose a significant land battle. And in World War I, the French fought valiantly, suffering more casualties in the ten-month bloodbath of Verdun than the United States lost in the entire war.

The Second World War, however, is another matter. Outmanned, outgunned, and outflanked, France fell in a mere forty-six days. Adding to the national humiliation, the German occupation was eighteen months old before the first German soldier was killed. Adding still more to this once-proud nation's dishonor, many French women, known as "horizontal collaborators," fraternized with the occupiers enthusiastically. This seems hardly anomalous since almost all of the French did.

This sort of history reverberates down through decades, centuries perhaps. The Second World War, the source of such national pride for Americans and British alike, is a source of national disgrace and strife for the French. Old family animosities persist in the once seemingly innocent French penchant for telling on one's neighbors; a habit that manifested itself with such ruthlessness during the occupation, with family ratting out family.

In the Midi-Pyrénées hamlet of Col de Serrières, one finds along the roadside a handful of crosses erected to the memory of local members of the Maquis, that is, mountain fighters who were part of the French Resistance. Poorly equipped and untrained, they mostly contented themselves with small operations to disrupt German activities in the region: demolition, theft, pulling up the railway line, and so on. Betrayed by French collaborators, they were summarily rounded up and shot, their bodies pushed over the hillside near where the crosses stand.

One of the crosses reads: ROGER GAUBIL. With a bit of research, I managed to locate his surviving brother, Claude. Only five years old at the time of his twenty-three-year-old brother's death, he has since conducted extensive research.

"People get nervous with you asking questions about all of this," he said, raising his eyebrows. The warning was genuine, but he appreciated my interest in his largely forgotten brother and those who died with him.

"Why are they nervous?"

"Because that family," he pointed, "betrayed my family. And that family," he pointed again, "got rich during the war stealing money dropped by the Allies in the forest to aid the Maquis. They were also well-paid Nazi collaborators. Many people were."

The crosses, he told me, were repeatedly vandalized, knocked over, and altogether destroyed until a permanent concrete structure could be placed there. "They don't want to remember. I am determined they will never forget."

One day in the local archives, I decided to take the matter up with the mayor. Seeing the mayor of a French village isn't like trying to see New York City Mayor Bill de Blasio. They are generally friendly and available. In this case, the mayor was a communist. Quite literally. (Roughly 1,500 French mayors are members of the Communist Party.[7])

"Do you know the story of Roger Gaubil?" I asked.

He went stiff. "Oui."

"Why not honor him somehow? There are streets all over France honoring Jean Moulin.[ii] Why not honor a local boy?"

"*C'est compliqué.*" It's complicated.

He went on to say essentially the same thing Claude said but from the perspective of a mayor who knows on which side his croissant is buttered. The dead hero, betrayed by a French informant in his own village for thirty pieces of silver, was still being betrayed by his own people.

---

ii   A genuine hero of the French Resistance, he was beaten to death by Gestapo thug Klaus Barbie.

On June 6, 1944, Operation Overlord—D-Day—the much-anticipated cross-channel invasion of northern France, took place. Not quite six weeks later, on August 19, the Allied Armies liberated Paris. Supreme Allied Commander Dwight Eisenhower, at the request of Charles de Gaulle, allowed the Free French Forces, with de Gaulle at their head, to lead the way into the rapturously celebrating city and down the Champs-Élysées to the Arc de Triomphe. At the Hotel de Ville, de Gaulle gave a now-famous speech, saying:

"Paris, liberated by her own people, with the help of the armies of France, with the help and support of the whole of France, that is to say of fighting France, that is to say of the true France, the eternal France."[8]

This was, of course, a great lie. Only one French division participated in the Overlord landings and it was equipped from boots to helmet, rifle to tank, by the United States Army. The Americans suffered 6,603 casualties on D-Day; the British, 2,700; and Canadians, 946.[9] The French? Nineteen.[10] According to historian Ian Ousby, less than 3 percent of the French resisted during the German occupation. The famed French Resistance is a national myth, consciously created by de Gaulle to restore a measure of self-respect to a defeated people. But for a brave few, the whole of France played horizontal collaborator to the German conqueror. There were genuine resisters like Gaubil, but they were never numerous enough to make any real difference in the war's outcome, their grand exploits becoming the stuff of postwar movies.

So eagerly did France collaborate with the Germans that the Nazis could hardly keep up with them in their fervor to inform on one another. The Milice, a police force established by the Germans and consisting entirely of Frenchmen, outdid the Germans in their enthusiasm to round up and deport French Jews.

Prior to the Allied invasion of France, M. R. D. Foot, the famed historian, was parachuted into France. Then a member of the Special Operations Executive (SOE), he was dropped into the hands of the Germans and rapidly captured. Escaping from his POW camp, he sought assistance from French farmers working in their fields. They attacked him with pitchforks, broke his neck, and then turned him over to the Gestapo. Today, that same French farm, owned by the same family, prospers. There were never any consequences.

No good walking tour of Paris is complete without a stop in the Latin Quarter and St. Michel. There, one finds a baroque fountain featuring the Archangel Michael slaying a demon. The tour guide will likely—and proudly—show you a few places in the stone to the right of the statue where gunfire left pockmarks. From these slender indications, we are told a fanciful tale of the French Resistance. This is impressive only to those who know nothing of Warsaw and Stalingrad, cities flattened by the German Luftwaffe and Wehrmacht, and yet their citizenry fought on in the rubble.

The Parisians, to preserve Paris's fine skyline, declared it an open city to the advancing German army. While the French were (and still are) proud of having spared their city, the Poles are proud of having sacrificed theirs for the cause of freedom. While the Paris cabaret, opera, theaters, and restaurants welcomed their conquerors, the Russians drove them out. This kind of history is not irrelevant. The French have not yet slain their demons.

In every French city, town, and village you will find a sizable monument to the First World War. These enormous memorials—usually an obelisk—list the names of that community's fallen heroes. The Second World War? Typically, a plaque has been added to the previous war's memorial. Perhaps they were just too exhausted by world wars to build more monuments. But the Americans weren't. The British weren't. Even the Russians weren't. If the Germans haven't properly processed their own mid-twentieth-century crisis, and they haven't, the French haven't either. This is modern France.

On every visit to Paris, I make something of my own pilgrimage to the eleventh arrondissement. Here, on January 7, 2015, armed Muslim gunmen entered the offices of Charlie Hebdo magazine and killed twelve people, shouting "Muhammad has been avenged!" and "Allah is great!" This was a reprisal for the magazine's unflattering depictions of Muhammad. One might have thought Muhammad's life was unflattering enough, being the murderous brigand he was. But to Muslims, he is a "prophet" and "blessed." Today there is a mural of the victims and a small plaque placed there in their memory.

A five-minute walk north and one finds the Bataclan concert venue. On November 13, 2015, heavily armed gunmen proclaiming allegiance to ISIS entered as some fifteen hundred people danced to the loud, pulsating music of the California rock band Eagles of Death Metal. They killed ninety and injured more than one hundred. An additional forty people died in other attacks across the city that same day. A similar plaque hangs here, but there is no mention of Islamic terrorism beyond a brave graffitist who spray-painted "F**k ISIS" on the window of the Bataclan. Of the two, I prefer the graffiti.

Spiritually, this is the same country the Germans conquered. The French, so ready to respond with outrage at the remarks of a Taylor or a Schwarzkopf—or President Trump, who essentially said that without the United States, the French would be speaking German—expressed very little outrage when their entire country was overrun in 1940 or now that it is being overrun by a subtler, but no less subversive element.

Indeed, the week following the attack on Charlie Hebdo, Fox News said there are "no-go zones" in Paris—that is, places where non-Muslims fear to go and where the rule of law in that country has been replaced with something closer to Sharia. (This is true of many cities across Europe.) Paris Mayor Anne Hidalgo threatened to sue the network.[11] Such a move smacks of profound insecurity. Regardless, she might have done her nation greater service by directing her energy to more important matters, namely, the terrorists within, but this is all so typically French: cowardice coupled with indignation.

Today, victims of Charlie Hebdo and the Bataclan are betrayed by their government just as Roger Gaubil and those who were shot with him were once betrayed and their bodies dumped over a hillside. Modern France simply does not want to acknowledge the policies and the ideologies that caused their deaths. Fox News and Donald Trump, however insulting the French might regard their comments, are not killing French people. Their great offense in this instance is in speaking the truth bluntly. But then again, it requires no courage to attack the (sometimes) conservative network or this president. Quite the opposite, one may be sure to receive much public affirmation for doing so. The French are afraid to name the real enemy, to oppose it, just as they were once afraid to oppose another occupier. They instead aid and abet it while tilting at windmills and saving their energy for their next holiday.

France, a country so lovely to visit—and so lovely to live in if you are a one-percenter—is no place to live if you are middle class or below. But to vacation on the Riviera, to sip champagne on the Champs-Élysées? Well, those are experiences not to be missed—unless, of course, the whole country is on strike.

If the Swiss are arrogant as it is often alleged, there is at least some reason for it.

The French? Not so much.

The United States of America: "The Last Best Hope on Earth"

"America is great because she is good. If America ceases to be good, America will cease to be great."

—Alexis de Tocqueville

As the plane touched down at Atlanta's Hartsfield-Jackson International Airport, I felt a deep sense of relief. After almost two years, we had done it. If this story were a movie, this is the part where they cue the music, and the rhythmic beat of Neil Diamond's "Coming to America" starts to play. It had been a long journey. We had hit twenty-eight countries in all, doing evaluations on a grand total of twenty-six. (Austria and Uruguay were merely incidental to the trip.)[i] We were glad to be home, and I was excited to see Lauri and the rest of the family, my friends, my beloved dog, and, a triviality perhaps, to eat my favorite foods.

---

i   You will recall that we did not include reviews of Uruguay or Austria. China denied my visa.

We saw and experienced a lot on our journey:

- Zachary BASE jumped from Auckland's Sky Tower, ran from would-be thieves in Delhi's Khari Baoli spice market, got in trouble (sort of) with the local militia at the Taj Mahal, climbed Hacksaw Ridge, and enjoyed the hospitality of a Chilean family;

- Christopher and Zachary rocked out at Oslo's Hard Rock Cafe, climbed a mountain in Switzerland, explored the ancient ruins of Rome (yes, we went to Italy, too), and chilled in the coffee shops and museums of Paris; and

- I shot AK-47s with an old Viet Cong in Vietnam, rode an elephant and the Railway of Death in Thailand, had to be hidden from Fulani herdsmen militia in Nigeria, debated capitalism with Marx and Stalin impersonators in Moscow's Red Square, and visited the sites of Muslim terrorist attacks in London, Stockholm, and Paris.

As expected, some countries captivated us while others did not. India, for example, was endlessly fascinating. So, too, were Brazil, South Africa, and Russia. And I will never forget the extraordinary Christians of Nigeria. But I wouldn't recommend living in any of these countries (hear me, Cardi B?) unless you are very wealthy and are thus able to insulate yourself from the dangers and difficulties of everyday life.

Then there are those countries considered "safe" and "healthy"—Britain, France, Sweden, Switzerland, and Germany—but where life has been so regulated by nanny-state governments you can *feel* the lack of freedom. Is a society with less crime and good healthcare by definition a better society? I once thought so. I don't anymore. Progressives, in the name of safety, security, and healthcare have been steadily paring down the freedoms of everyday people. Freedom of speech and the right to bear arms are the first casualties, but others quickly follow. Former New York City Mayor Mike Bloomberg thinks it is the government's responsibility to regulate your sugar intake. The underlying assumption in all of this is the government can be trusted to make wise decisions, but you cannot. In Aldous Huxley's *Brave New World*, John "the Savage" chooses to live outside the borders of the safe and controlled environment of utopia because he values human freedom and dignity more than modern comforts and healthcare. If forced to choose, I am with John. Being free carries individual responsibility with it. There are risks. At no time have I believed this more than in the post-Chinese coronavirus world where government overreach, hyper-regulation, and polizeistaat tactics were normalized in countries traditionally thought to be free.

As we traveled around the world, we explored the question of national greatness. We discovered it can manifest itself in a variety of ways. A form of government and way of life incompatible with the American national character might work very well for citizens of another country. (Singapore comes to mind.) That said, we also discovered certain critical ingredients are necessary for a nation to be truly great: rule of law, a strong sense of national identity, a history of stability and freedom, advantageous geography, and work ethic, among other ingredients. America compares favorably in all these categories.[ii] Upon hearing he was rumored to be dead, Mark Twain quipped, "Reports of my death are greatly exaggerated." So it is with America. When you travel around the world, you quickly discover reports of America's death have been greatly exaggerated.

---

ii   See appendices for a fuller discussion of these.

Is America the Greatest Country in the World?

In a word, *yes*. Eminent historian David McCullough thinks so, too: "We are still the strongest, most productive, wealthiest, most creative, most ingenious, most generous nation in the world, with the greatest freedoms of any nation in the world, of any nation in all time."

But we have seen how many on the Left don't think so. In a 2019 article titled "Please Stop Telling Me America Is Great,"[1] *The New York Times* declared: "Comparing the United States of America on global indicators reveals we have fallen well behind Europe—and share more in common with 'developing countries' than we'd like to admit."

We have seen the "global indicators" used by the likes of the NYT, but there are others joining them in this chorus of self-hatred:

In an interview on Russian television, Hollywood director Oliver Stone said the United States is now "the evil empire."

Valerie Jarrett, a senior advisor to President Obama, said America is no longer "a beacon of hope."

And we have already seen how Ashley Judd, Michael Moore, Alec Baldwin, Rose McGowan, and many other Hollywood liberals share those negative views of America.

But the claim America is no longer great isn't just coming from the Left. In a column for *The Blaze* titled, "No, America Is Not a Great Nation," Matt Walsh wrote: "I am not happy with this country, and you shouldn't be, either. I am disappointed in it. It disgraces itself. It turns from God. It kills its young. It attacks the family."[2] Walsh goes on to cite a litany of evils presently occupying space in American culture: abortion, the rapid advancement of the LGBTI agenda, the welfare state, and illegal immigration among them.

At last! Someone who criticized America for all the right reasons!

I began this chapter with a quotation from Alexis de Tocqueville's *Democracy in America*: "America is great because she is good. If America ceases to be good, America will cease to be great." Walsh is, in effect, saying, "Well, we've reached that moment when America has ceased to be good, therefore, she is no longer great."

I am more than a little sympathetic to Walsh's point. But this is naïve idealism. Furthermore, this argument unwittingly plays into the progressive narrative. Trump's rallying cry, "Make America Great Again," is, to progressives, offensive for one word: *Again*. This is because they don't think America was ever great. In their version of things, America's freedom and prosperity are merely historical accidents and they are the agents of retribution.

By Walsh's definition, this is true, if for different reasons. That is because evil has never been successfully eradicated from America or any other country you care to name. Yes, long before the very real American sins Walsh laments, there was segregation, the internment of Japanese Americans during World War II, Jim Crow, civil war, and slavery. America has never been a perfect country. As historian Paul Reid has written: "[America's] history was often vile, often violent, and during the Civil War, catastrophic. It's not always an uplifting story, but it's a story that must be told and *understood* in order for this republic to survive."[3]

To properly understand America and its history, we must measure it against *something*. In this book, we are measuring it against its global alternatives. With this in mind, what alternative would Walsh give us? By his standard, we might as well try to colonize the moon, because Planet Earth is a lost cause. I have bad news for Mr. Walsh: no country in the world is superior to America in the moral categories he cites *other than* Islamic countries, and those countries do not recognize freedom, and they sure don't recognize the God he believes America has forgotten.

But for the sake of argument, let's accept Walsh's America-is-not-great premise and change the name of our theoretical award to the Least-Worst Country in the World. We then reconsider our ranking—grading on a curve, of course—and America still wins, and it wins for the very reason Walsh sees lacking in America:

Christianity.

Why America Is Great

The prevailing worldview of a given country is the single most important factor in determining not just national greatness, but a country's overall destiny. If human nature is the same the world over, and it is, how do we account for the fact America isn't like some of the "sh*thole countries" to which Trump so bluntly referred and we visited on our tour? Fascists attribute the difference to race. Socialists reduce it to impersonal economic forces. Still, others would say it is just an accident of history. None of these are correct.

Lord of the Flies author William Golding argued that the problems of human society are the problems of human nature. Let that sink in. It is a profound observation and it is true of every society. As we have observed, some religions and philosophies restrain the darker aspects of human nature while others exacerbate them. So, whether a country is predominantly Christian, aggressively secular, Muslim, fascist, Hindu, Buddhist, socialist, Confucian, or obsessed with Kim Kardashian *matters*. For America, a country with the largest Christian population in the world, the prevailing worldview has historically been guided by that religion above all others.

Margaret Thatcher once said, "Europe was created by history. America was created by philosophy." Bono, the lead singer of the Irish band U2, said something very similar: "America is not just a country; it is an idea." Sociologist Seymour Martin Lipset observed, "Being an American is an ideological commitment. It is not a matter of birth. Those who reject American values are un-American." But it was G. K. Chesterton who identified the philosophy, the idea, the ideology to which Thatcher, Bono, and Lipset referred: "America is the only nation in the world that is founded on a creed. That creed is set forth with dogmatic and even theological lucidity in the Declaration of Independence...."

I will not here include the entire text of that document—though I encourage you to read it and ponder its meaning—only this key passage:

> We hold these truths to be self-evident, that all men are created equal, that they are endowed by their Creator with certain unalienable Rights, that among these are Life, Liberty and the pursuit of Happiness.—That to secure these rights, Governments are instituted among Men, deriving their just powers from the consent of the governed, —That whenever any Form of Government becomes destructive of these ends, it is the Right of the People to alter or to abolish it, and to institute new Government, laying its foundation on such principles and organizing its powers in such form, as to them shall seem most likely to effect their Safety and Happiness.

That is powerful, and therein lies the "theological lucidity" to which Chesterton referred. The principles expressed here—"endowed by their Creator with certain unalienable rights...life, liberty, and the pursuit of happiness"—are not principles that spontaneously generated in the Philadelphia air of 1776. They are not principles observed in socialist regimes. They are not principles observed by Islamic regimes. They are principles that could only have been produced by those who have breathed deeply the ethos of a Christian culture.[iii]

But this is, I know, very difficult for some readers to accept. We take this idea for granted and assume other cultures believe it, too. They don't.[iv] Outside those countries where Christianity was instrumental in forming their governing institutions, we visited no country where it would be assumed I (or you or anyone else) have either intrinsic value or unalienable rights. When I made this point to John Stossel during a Fox News interview, Stossel, who is an agnostic, said:

"You even go on to say that in the Declaration of Independence where it says, 'We hold these truths to be self-evident that all men are created equal,' the only way a statement like that makes sense is if man is endowed by his creator with certain unalienable rights."

"Yes, a statement like that only makes sense within a Christian context, that is to say—"

"Why?" Stossel interrupted.

"Well, what is self-evidential about the equality of man?" I asked.

"It's … *just right.*"

"But it isn't…we believe that because we have been heavily influenced by a Judeo-Christian worldview because the only thing that is self-evidential about man is his *inequalities*—social, physical, intellectual, economic—there are *massive* inequalities. So, what does a statement like that mean? It means that in some spiritual sense men are equal, and that, of course, only makes sense if there is a God."

---

iii   See appendices for a fuller discussion of these.

iv   This assumption has gotten many a naïve American killed while traveling abroad. It has also been intermittently disastrous to American foreign policy. Truman, for instance, never understood the Russian communist mindset, and mistakenly believed Stalin to be trustworthy.

The point, however, wasn't mine. It takes an outsider to our culture to help us see what we, like Stossel, take for granted. Indian scholar Vishal Mangalwadi provides us with that missing perspective. In his superb book, *The Book that Made Your World: How the Bible Created the Soul of Western Civilization*, Mangalwadi says this very line in the Declaration of Independence makes not a bit of sense in the context of his native India or anywhere else other than a culture imbued with Christian principles:

> Are these truths self-evident to the human mind?... These "truths" are not "self-evident." Human equality is not self-evident anywhere in the world—not even in America. Women and blacks were not treated as equal in America. Equality was never self-evident to Hindu sages. For them, inequality was self-evident. Their question was, why are human beings born unequal? Hinduism taught that the Creator made people different.... The Buddha did not believe in the Creator, but he accepted the doctrine of karma as the metaphysical cause for the inequality of human beings. Nor were unalienable rights self-evident to Rome. During Jesus' trial, Pilate, Rome's governor and chief justice over Israel, declared: "I find no basis for a charge against this man." Pilate then said to Jesus, "You will not speak to me? Do you not know that I have authority to release you and authority to crucify you?" Wait a minute! Do you have the power to crucify someone whom you declare to be innocent? Isn't it self-evident to you that he has an unalienable right to life? Revelation is the reason why America believed what some Deists ascribed to "common sense." To be precise, these truths appeared common sense to the American Founders because their sense was shaped by the common impact of

the Bible—even if a few of them doubted that the Bible was divinely revealed.[4]

To summarize Mangalwadi's point, the belief that men are created equal is not innate, it is a result of Christian influence. And that religion, when taken seriously, has an ennobling effect in a way no other worldview does, even on those who are beneficiaries of its light but do not acknowledge the source.

Since the fall of man, there has never been a Christian nation. What there have been are nations reflecting varying degrees of Christian influence, and among them, none have been more deeply influenced by the Christian faith than the United States of America. Our laws, art, literature, moral sensibilities, and institutions all find their meaning in a rich Christian heritage. As T. S. Eliot observed: "If Christianity goes, the whole culture goes."

The problem, however, is the consensus among secular elites seems to be that Christianity is a bit like smoking: *It is harmful, but if you must do it, do it in the designated areas only.* That view increasingly defines the entire Democratic Party, who have set themselves against the Christian faith on just about every key cultural issue, from abortion to marriage. They should be more careful. Like many others, they grossly underestimate the degree to which their moral and intellectual sensibilities have been informed by the Judeo-Christian worldview.

Furthermore, progressives have unwittingly adopted a set of Christian concepts—tolerance, diversity, ethical treatment of animals, freedom, concern for the poor, love, environment stewardship—while amputating them from the Book and the Man that give them meaning. Lacking a fixed point, they have become all sail, no anchor. Thus, tolerance becomes tolerance of anything, and freedom becomes doing what I want to do whenever I want to do it. The first has led to moral chaos and the second is taking us toward anarchy. We are currently engaged in a dangerous experiment that is, as history demonstrates, doomed to fail.[v]

Proponents of a society free from religious influence can point to no nation or civilization founded upon atheism we might call even remotely good. The story of those regimes is well documented and may be summarized in a word—*murderous*. No, what they can point to are secular societies still running off of their accumulated Christian capital. But beware. When the fumes in that tank run out, tyranny cannot be far away. As Edmund Burke warned, some "uncouth, pernicious, and degrading superstition might take the place of it."

There are two superstitions currently filling the void left by the gradual abandonment of Christianity in Britain and continental Europe: socialism and Islam. With the Christian faith little more than a rotting corpse there, these two now dominate the continent. The first is promoted by Europe's indigenous population, the second by successive waves of immigrants. It is unlikely they will coexist indefinitely as Muslims gain greater influence in government and society.

So far, America has been spared the ruin wrought by political correctness, multiculturalism, mass immigration, the environmental panic, and the self-loathing that has engulfed the rest of the Western world. At this point, some readers will gasp at this statement, thinking we have been spared nothing of the sort. To that I can only say, *See the world!* America has been spared.

---

v   Some argue the ideals I have enumerated here do not spring from Christianity but from the so-called Enlightenment. But this is not so. The European continent was as barbarous as any Islamic state prior to the rise of Christianity that served to civilize it. The English and French Enlightenments were of a very different character: the former was rooted in Christianity; the latter was a wholesale rejection of it. Of the two, it was the English Enlightenment that had the greater influence on America while the French Enlightenment, untethered from absolute morality, degenerated into the Reign of Terror.

Why?

Because Christianity, still vibrant in America, has served as a bulwark against it. Secularism is no match for an absolutist ideology like Islam because it lacks a theology of evil. From a strictly secularist worldview, almost nothing is worth dying for because this life is all you get. Therefore, Islamic terrorists, it is often assumed, are just plain crazy.

Only they aren't.

Terrorism is perfectly rational given their worldview. I mean, if you believed, as many of them do, in Allah, his "prophet" Muhammad, and his will as it is expressed in the Quran and Hadith, then dying for your faith in the cause of Allah is an honor—and it also guarantees you eternal life and bliss! Christians understand this because we, too, believe in a God, eternity, a final judgment, punishment, reward, and that some things are indeed worth dying for. We just believe they have missed the rightful object of their worship, and with it, the whole trajectory of their societies goes dangerously awry.

But we have already dealt with Islam extensively. Not even the most fervent progressive, in spite of his open border advocacy, would have us model our society after an Islamic state. Socialism, however, requires a bit more attention. Let's remember that the country rankings most favored by progressives always put the democracies of Western Europe at the top, Scandinavia in particular. Their appreciation for socialism, which they (wrongly) perceive to be the source of these countries' secular (drug-induced) bliss is due to the fact they have only vague notions of what socialism really is.

Commenting on the 2020 presidential race, MSNBC's (now fired) Chris Matthews, hardly to be confused with a conservative, offered his own views on socialism:

The issue of this campaign, it is that word "socialism." Some people like it, younger people like it, those of us like me, who grew up in the Cold War and saw some aspects of it, if they're visiting places like Vietnam, like I have, [and seeing countries] like Cuba, being there, I've seen what socialism's like, I don't like it, OK? It's not only not free, it doesn't frickin' work!...I don't know who Bernie [Sanders] supports over these years. I don't know what he means by "socialism." One week, it's Denmark, we're going to be like Denmark. Okay, that's harmless. That's basically a capitalist country with a lot of good social welfare programs. Denmark's harmless.[5]

I am sure Matthews lost a few fans with that statement, but he is absolutely right. Just as we have done throughout this book, he is drawing on his experiences in socialist countries: "I've seen what socialism's like."[vi] We have, too. It is a broken, unworkable, utopian, bankrupt secular religion.

But what about America's sins? What about, for instance, the past evil of slavery and the present evil of abortion?

I will neither ignore America's sins nor airbrush them out. Every country, just like every individual, has committed some sort of evil. But they are not all ideologically equipped to address it, or, in some cases, to even recognize it. As we have seen, some, like China and Russia, don't acknowledge wrongdoing because they don't believe in the unalienable rights of their citizens. We don't even need to look to the distant past to find an example of this. In recent months China has failed to acknowledge responsibility

---

vi   I like Matthews. No doubt this is partly due to the fact that he loved my previous book. I am grateful for his lavish praise. But Matthews is a well-educated Catholic who often reflects the views of classic liberalism. His brand of liberalism has nothing in common with Bernie Sanders or Alexandria Ocasio-Cortez.

for a virus born (developed?) in the Chinese city of Wuhan and spread around the world resulting in a global catastrophe. Others, like France and Germany, either pretend the evil of the past didn't happen or, on the other extreme, they descend into a kind of self-flagellation that imperils their futures. Progressives, be they American or European, are utterly possessed by this self-loathing spirit and cannot stop talking about historical wrongs, both real and imagined.

By contrast, America's faith has traditionally provided her with the antidote to her sins: to see them for what they are, to repent of them, and to move forward. The evils Matt Walsh enumerated are real. But to our forebears that simply meant there was work to be done, and they constructed a country and a constitution that provided the mechanism to do it. Every great American reform movement—and reform movements, it should be noted, are not the global norm—has been led by Christians, be it the abolition of slavery or the civil rights movement. The church, imperfect as it is, remains vibrant and influential in American public life in a way it is not in the rest of the world.[vii] This alone makes America exceptional.

Alexis de Tocqueville—one of the two Frenchmen who inspired our journey (Jules Verne being the other)—was deeply impressed with the religious spirit of the American people, and he believed America's goodness had everything to do with her Christian faith:

> Religion in America takes no direct part in the government of society, but it must nevertheless be regarded as the foremost of the political institutions of that country....

---

vii   In Europe, the Christian faith has been tamed, domesticated, and robbed of its radical society-transforming power. In Asia, though it is rapidly growing, it is largely suppressed. In Africa, it is persecuted. In South America, it is either of the same toothless variety as in Europe or it is driven from public view.

Thus, whilst the law permits the Americans to do what they please, religion prevents them from conceiving, and forbids them to commit, what is rash or unjust.[6]

Writing to a French audience, he knew his readers, largely irreligious and condescending in their opinions of this young democracy and its unusual people, would turn their noses up at this. He insisted they were wrong to do so:

Such are the opinions of the Americans, and if any hold that the religious spirit which I admire [in the American people] is the very thing most wrong with America.... I can only reply that those who hold this opinion have never been in America, and that they have never seen a religious or a free nation. When they return from their expedition, we shall hear what they have to say.

Others have recognized America's exceptionalism, too, even when we have not. I remind you of Gallup's global survey of potential migrants. It is a de facto ranking of the world's greatest countries by ordinary people around the world who were asked, if they could immigrate, where would they go? Fourteen percent of the world's population would like to migrate permanently to another country. Of that number, 21 percent—or one hundred forty-seven million people—would like to move to the United States of America. The next highest country was Germany with 6 percent.[7] This is a powerful indicator of how the world perceives America. It reminds me of Chick-fil-A: no matter how much smug progressives trash it, there is always a line to get in.

Reflecting on our expedition and what it taught him about his own country, Zachary made this astute observation: "America is two things: there is the idea of America and its present reality. When we say, 'America is great,' we mean the idea."

Exactly. It is the idea of America, inspired and sustained by her Christian faith, that gives hope to so much of the world. And the reality should always be striving for the ideal.

America has faced and overcome greater challenges than any currently before us. This is not to minimize the depth of our problems. Political correctness is as much a threat to freedom in our generation as fascism and communism were to previous generations. But we have been well supplied spiritually and materially to defeat it as previous generations defeated those existential threats.

On December 1, 1862, President Abraham Lincoln prepared to give his annual State of the Union address to Congress. He had a difficult task. A civil war raged, tearing the country apart, and it was going badly for his side. Determined to save the union, the embattled president had to find the words to inspire his people to fight on, to preserve the idea of America. The alternative was grim. The concluding words of that speech echo down through the ages:

"We shall nobly save, or meanly lose, the last best hope of earth."

America teeters on a precipice over which many nations have toppled. Deep social and political divisions threaten to destroy her without the assistance of a single Islamic extremist or missile fired from the arsenal of North Korea.

America needs to repent of her present sins just as she once repented of her past sins. America needs a third Great Awakening. For it is only in Jesus Christ our souls, both as individuals and as a nation, will find healing of all that ails us as a people. And it is in turning to him we save the last best hope on earth.

Jules Verne ends his great novel with these words:

> Phileas Fogg had won his wager, and had made his journey around the world in eighty days. To do this, he had employed every means of conveyance—steamers, railways, carriages, yachts, trading-vessels, sledges, elephants. The eccentric gentleman had throughout displayed all his marvelous qualities of coolness and exactitude. But what then? What had he really gained by all this trouble? What had he brought back from this long and weary journey?

I have long pondered the same question. I brought back memories of some wonderful people and places (and some unpleasant and frightening ones). Perspective. More than a few bumps and bruises. A bit of wisdom, one hopes. And some odd coinage Lauri found in my pockets.

But mostly an appreciation for home.

ACKNOWLEDGMENTS

A book is seldom the work of a single person, and in my case, I am indebted to a number of people. First and foremost is my wife, Lauri, who believed in the book, gave me the space to write it, read it and reread it, and kept all distractions at bay. Without her, I could not have written anything. My boys, Christopher and Zachary, who were not only part of the journey but also contributed to the overall concept. Christopher, a budding author in his own right, spent many afternoons proofing the text and offering helpful suggestions. There are many others: Sharon, who made herself available, read every chapter, edited them, prevented me from many missteps, and encouraged me to keep going; Judy who read the manuscript and offered her reactions; Steve, Bew, and Brian, who did much to make the journey it is based on possible; Benjamin Wiker and Jay Smith, who lent valuable expertise to the argument; Dr. John Lennox and Melanie Phillips, who offered insights on key chapters; fellow author Eric Metaxas, who loved the concept for this book and insisted that I write it before writing anything else; and my dear mother who read the manuscript and bequeathed to me a love of knowledge and a desire to see the world.

I am grateful to them all.

ENDNOTES

Chapter 1

1   Barbara Wertheim Tuchman, *The Guns of August*, Hardcover (New York, NY: MacMillan, 1989).

2   Sebastian Modak and Katherine LaGrave, "10 Best Countries in the World to Live In," Condé Nast Traveler, June 26, 2017, https://www.cntraveler.com/gallery/best-countries-to-live-in.

3   United Nations Development Programme (UNDP), "Human Development Report 2016 Human Development for Everyone," 2016, http://hdr.undp.org/sites/default/files/2016_human_development_report.pdf.

4   Pew Research Center, "The Size and Distribution of the World's Christian Population," Pew Research Center's Religion & Public Life Project, December 19, 2011, https://www.pewforum.org/2011/12/19/global-christianity-exec/.

5   John L-Allen-Jr, "The War on Christians," *The Spectator*, October 5, 2013, https://www.spectator.co.uk/article/the-war-on-christians.

6   ACLJ.org, "A Cold Heart: Iceland 'Cures' Down Syndrome with Eugenics & Abortion," American Center for Law and Justice, August 21, 2017, https://aclj.org/pro-life/a-cold-heart-iceland-cures-down-syndrome-with-eugenics-abortion.

7   Sam Roberts, "Forrest McDonald, Historian Who Punctured Liberal Notions, Dies at 89," *The New York Times*, January 26, 2016, https://www.nytimes.

com/2016/01/22/us/politics/forrest-mcdonald-his-
torian-who-punctured-liberal-notions-dies-at-89.
html?utm_source=Fixed+Point+Foundation&utm_
campaign=188f3a403d-Daily+Blog+RSS+Email&utm_
medium=email&utm_term=0_7b195d4eb3-188f3a403d-
97510213&mc_cid=188f3a403d&mc_eid=3c81cf6344.

8 Neli Esipova, Julie Ray, and Anita Pugliese, "Number
of Potential Migrants Worldwide Tops 700 Million,"
Gallup, June 8, 2017, https://www.mybib.com/#/
projects/4KDMJk/citations/new/webpage.

Chapter 2

1 David Reid, "Almost 40% of the World's Countries Will Witness Civil Unrest in 2020, Research
Claims," CNBC, January 16, 2020, https://www.cnbc.
com/2020/01/16/40percent-of-countries-will-witness-civil-
unrest-in-2020-report-claims.html.

2 Ryan Ong, "10 Things Not to Do in Singapore," Wander-
Luxe, June 22, 2017, https://wanderluxe.theluxenomad.
com/10-things-not-to-do-in-singapore/.

3 Kirsten Han, "How Singapore Elected a President without
a Vote," CNN, September 12, 2017, https://edition.cnn.
com/2017/09/11/asia/singapore-race-presidential-election/
index.html.

4 Eleanor Ross, "Singapore PM Called 'Big Brother Omnipresent' by Siblings Worried about Surveillance State,"
Newsweek, June 14, 2017, https://www.newsweek.com/
singapore-pm-called-big-brother-omnipresent-siblings-wor-
ried-about-625610.

5 Bruce Einhorn, "Singapore and Australia
Hit by Latest Snowden Spying Leak," www.
bloomberg.com, November 27, 2013, https://

www.bloomberg.com/news/articles/2013-11-26/
singapore-and-australia-hit-by-latest-snowden-spying-leak.

6   Nectar Gan, "Has China Outgrown Its Need for
Singapore as a Role Model?" *South China Morning
Post*, May 24, 2017, https://www.scmp.com/
news/china/diplomacy-defence/article/2095310/
has-china-outgrown-its-need-singapore-role-model.

7   Kishore Mahbubani, "Why Singapore Is the
World's Most Successful Society," *HuffPost*,
August 4, 2015, https://www.huffpost.com/entry/
singapore-world-successful-society_b_7934988.

8   Shane Harris, "The Social Laboratory," Foreign
Policy, n.d., https://foreignpolicy.com/2014/07/29/
the-social-laboratory/.

9   Palash Ghosh, "Singapore: Drug Laws and The
Death Penalty," *International Business Times*,
June 22, 2011, https://www.ibtimes.com/
singapore-drug-laws-death-penalty-292911.

Chapter 3

1   Prince Charles Quotes. BrainyQuote.com, BrainyMedia
Inc, 2020. https://www.brainyquote.com/quotes/prince_
charles_383693, accessed June 1, 2020.

2   Francis Schaeffer. AZQuotes.com, Wind and Fly LTD,
2020. https://www.azquotes.com/quote/718636, accessed
June 01, 2020.

Chapter 4

1   Mark Twain, *The Innocents Abroad, or, The New Pilgrims'
Progress* (Orinda, Ca: Seawolf Press, 2018).

2   World Nomads, "15 Things I Wish I Knew Before Going
to Argentina," www.worldnomads.com, n.d., https://www.

worldnomads.com/explore/south-america/argentina/15-things-i-wish-i-knew-before-going-to-argentina.

3   "MRD Foot, obituary," *The Telegraph*, February 20, 2012, https://www.telegraph.co.uk/news/obituaries/culture-obituaries/books-obituaries/9094496/MRD-Foot.html.

4   Toshikazu Kase, "Vanquished Felt That Nobler Ideal Won World War II," *The New York Times*, September 2, 1970, sec. Archives, https://www.nytimes.com/1970/09/02/archives/vanquished-felt-that-nobler-ideal-won-world-war-ii.html.

5   Rupert Wingfield-Hayes, "Why Does Japan Have Such a High Suicide Rate?" BBC News, July 3, 2015, https://www.bbc.com/news/world-33362387.

6   Marco Stahlhut, "Orthodox Islam and Violence 'Linked' Says Top Muslim Scholar," *Time*, September 8, 2017, https://time.com/4930742/islam-terrorism-islamophobia-violence/?source=dam.

Chapter 5

1   J. R. R. Tolkien, *The Fellowship of the Ring* (New York, NY Ballantine Books 1967).

2   Business, "Rich Silicon Valley Doomsday 'preppers' Buying up New Zealand Land," *The Sydney Morning Herald*, January 24, 2017, https://www.smh.com.au/business/rich-silicon-valley-doomsday-preppers-buying-up-new-zealand-land-20170125-gty353.html.

3   Carol Pinchefsky, "The Impact (Economic and Otherwise) of Lord of the Rings/The Hobbit on New Zealand," *Forbes*, December 14, 2012, https://www.forbes.com/sites/carolpinchefsky/2012/12/14/the-impact-economic-and-otherwise-of-lord-of-the-rings-the-hobbit-on-new-zealand/#2da79e8731b6.

4   Institute for Economics & Peace, "Global Peace Index 2019: Measuring Peace in a Complex World," Sydney, June 2019, http://visionofhumanity.org/indexes/global-peace-index/.

5   Michael Trimmer Fri 13 Dec 2013 13:33 GMT, "Christians No Longer a Majority in New Zealand," www.christiantoday.com, December 13, 2013, https://www.christiantoday.com/article/christians.no.longer.a.majority.in.new.zealand/35053.htm.

6   Michael Gryboski, "New Zealand University Students Vote to Disaffiliate Pro-Life Student Group," www.christianpost.com, August 30, 2017, https://www.christianpost.com/news/new-zealand-university-students-vote-disaffiliate-pro-life-student-group-197348/.

7   Maya Kosoff, "Americans Are Applying to Move to New Zealand at an Astounding Rate," *Vanity Fair*, March 14, 2017, https://www.vanityfair.com/news/2017/03/americans-are-applying-to-move-to-new-zealand-at-an-astounding-rate.

Chapter 6

1   Peter Singer Quotes. BrainyQuote.com, BrainyMedia Inc, 2020. https://www.brainyquote.com/quotes/peter_singer_390024, accessed June 1, 2020.

2   Kevin Toolis, "The Most Dangerous Man in the World," *The Guardian*, November 6, 1999, https://www.theguardian.com/lifeandstyle/1999/nov/06/weekend.kevintoolis.

3   Fyodor Dostoevsky, The Brothers Karamazov (public domain).

4   Kirby Spencer, "Outrage as Father's Day Ad Is Pulled Ahead of Gay Marriage Vote," *Mail Online*, September 1, 2017,

https://www.dailymail.co.uk/news/article-4844502/Father-s-Day-ad-pulled-ahead-gay-marriage-vote.html.

Chapter 7

1   Douglas MacArthur. AZQuotes.com, Wind and Fly LTD, 2020. https://www.azquotes.com/quote/346260, accessed June 01, 2020.

Chapter 8

1   Ho Chi Minh Quotes. BrainyQuote.com, BrainyMedia Inc, 2020. https://www.brainyquote.com/quotes/ho_chi_minh_162586, accessed June 1, 2020.
2   A Vietnamese language version of it with subtitles is available here: https://www.youtube.com/watch?v=ChhHiSr_2D8
3   National Public Radio, "Learning from Vietnam, 30 Years Later," NPR.org, March 20, 2006, https://www.npr.org/templates/story/story.php?storyId=5290976.

Chapter 9

1   Timothy Rice, Miles Bindon, Göran Bror Benny Andersson, Björn K. Ulvaeus, 1984.
2   Tom Hewitson, "How to Beat Bangkok's Scams," Lonely Planet, January 25, 2013, https://www.lonelyplanet.com/articles/how-to-beat-bangkoks-scams.

Chapter 10

1   Sholto Byrnes, "Creeping Islamisation," *New Statesman*, September 6, 2007, https://www.newstatesman.com/society/2007/09/malaysia-religious-muslim.
2   Department of Statistics Malaysia, "Population Distribution and Basic Demographic Characteristic Report 2010

(Updated 05/08/2011)," Dosm.gov.my, July 29, 2011, https://www.dosm.gov.my/v1/index.php?r=column/ cthemeByCat&cat=117&bul_id=MDMxdHZjWTk1S-jFzTzNkRXYzcVZjdz09&menu_id=L0pheU43NWJwR-WVSZklWdzQ4TlhUUT09.

Chapter 11

1   Rudyard Kipling, "A Quote from Plain Tales from the Hills," www.goodreads.com, n.d., https://www.goodreads. com/quotes/181817-now-india-is-a-place-beyond-all-oth-ers-where-one.

2   Jules Verne, "Jules Verne Quotes (Author of Twenty Thou-sand Leagues Under the Sea)," www.goodreads.com, n.d., https://www.goodreads.com/author/quotes/696805. Jules_Verne?page=2.

Chapter 12

1   Oliver Smith, "Aeroflot: From World's Deadliest Airline to One of the Safest in the Sky," *The Telegraph*, February 10, 2016, https://www.telegraph.co.uk/travel/news/ Aeroflot-from-worlds-deadliest-airline-to-one-of-the-safest-in-the-sky/.

2   Oliver Smith, "Aeroflot: From World's Deadliest Airline to One of the Safest in the Sky," *The Telegraph*, February 10, 2016, https://www.telegraph.co.uk/travel/news/ Aeroflot-from-worlds-deadliest-airline-to-one-of-the-safest-in-the-sky/.

3   Adam M Olearius and Samuel Haskell Baron, *The Travels of Olearius in Seventeenth-Century Russia*, (Stanford: Stanford U.P, 1967).

Chapter 13

1   George Pitcher, "Practising Muslims 'Will Outnumber Christians by 2035,'" *The Telegraph*, May 7, 2008, sec. News, https://www.telegraph.co.uk/news/1936418/Practising-Muslims-will-outnumber-Christians-by-2035.html.

2   Andrew Norfolk, "Police Files Reveal Vast Child Protection Scandal," *The Times*, September 24, 2012, https://www.thetimes.co.uk/article/police-files-reveal-vast-child-protection-scandal-ffrpdr09vrv.

3   Martin Robinson, Steph Cockroft, James Tozer, Jaya Narain, and Daniel Martin, "Shame of grooming cover-up: Cynical councillors could be going to jail after report says they systematically hid truth," *Daily Mail*, February 4, 2015, https://www.dailymail.co.uk/news/article-2939129/Two-local-councillors-corrupt-police-officer-accused-having-sex-victims-Rotherham-abuse-scandal.html.

4   BBC News, "Policeman among 16 Charged with Child Sex Offences," BBC News, December 18, 2019, sec. Leeds & West Yorkshire, https://www.bbc.com/news/uk-england-leeds-50838823.

5   Daniel Greenfield, "Cops: Muslim Sex Grooming Gangs "Didn't Understand That It Was Wrong," *FrontPage Magazine*, January 23, 2020, https://www.frontpagemag.com/fpm/2020/01/cops-muslim-sex-grooming-gangs-didnt-understand-it-daniel-greenfield/.

6   Helen Pidd, "Rotherham Council Told to Apologise to Abuse Whistleblower," *The Guardian*, April 18, 2018, sec. UK news, https://www.theguardian.com/uk-news/2018/apr/18/rotherham-council-apologise-abuse-grooming-jayne-senior-whistleblower.

7   Victoria Friedman, "Sikhs Ask Media to Stop Calling Pakistani Muslim Rape Gangs 'Asian,'" *Breitbart*, August

8, 2019, https://www.breitbart.com/europe/2019/08/08/sikhs-call-media-stop-referring-pakistani-muslim-rape-gangs-asian/.

8   Ella Hill, "As a Rotherham Grooming Gang Survivor, I Want People to Know about the Religious Extremism Which Inspired My Abusers," *The Independent*, March 18, 2018, https://www.independent.co.uk/voices/rotherham-grooming-gang-sexual-abuse-muslim-islamist-racism-white-girls-religious-extremism-a8261831.html.

9   NHS Rotherham Clinical Commissioning Group, "Key Statics for Rotherham 2011 CENSUS," 2011, http://www.rotherhamccg.nhs.uk/Downloads/Publications/Equality%20and%20Diversity/2011_CENSUS_ROTHERHAM.pdf.

10   Daniel Greenfield, "Cops: Muslim Sex Grooming Gangs "Didn't Understand That It Was Wrong," *FrontPage Magazine*, January 23, 2020, https://www.frontpagemag.com/fpm/2020/01/cops-muslim-sex-grooming-gangs-didnt-understand-it-daniel-greenfield/.

11   Alexis Jay Obe, "Independent Inquiry into Child Sexual Exploitation in Rotherham," 2014, https://www.rotherham.gov.uk/downloads/file/279/independent-inquiry-into-child-sexual-exploitation-in-rotherham.

12   Lizzie Dearden, "Almost 19,000 Children Sexually Groomed in England in Year, Official Figures Suggest," *The Independent*, December 28, 2019, https://www.independent.co.uk/news/uk/home-news/grooming-child-sex-abuse-exploitation-rotherham-rochdale-police-a9215261.html.

13   One might have thought that marrying into and being welcomed by the Royal Family; being given a $45 million

wedding, compliments of the British taxpayer; and a gift of noble titles were fairly strong indicators of a lack of discrimination.

14   Telegraph Reporters, "Rotherham Child Sex Abuse: Woman Made Pregnant Aged 12 Believes Child Was 'Product of Pure Evil,'" *The Telegraph*, February 2, 2017, https://www.telegraph.co.uk/news/2017/02/02/rotherham-child-sex-abuse-woman-made-pregnant-aged-12-believes/.

15   Sam Tonkin, "Child Sex Gang Members Shout 'Allahu Akbar' in Court as They're Jailed," *Mail Online*, February 2, 2017, https://www.dailymail.co.uk/news/article-4184966/Child-sex-gang-members-shout-Allahu-Akbar-court.html.

16   Sandy Tolliver, "#MeToo Madness Could Destroy Male College Athletes," *The Hill*, October 6, 2018, https://thehill.com/opinion/civil-rights/409947-metoo-madness-could-destroy-male-college-athletes.

17   Paul Bischoff, "Surveillance Camera Statistics: Which City Has the Most CCTV Cameras?" Comparitech, August 15, 2019, https://www.comparitech.com/vpn-privacy/the-worlds-most-surveilled-cities/.

18   Adam Satariano, "London Police Are Taking Surveillance to a Whole New Level," *The New York Times*, January 24, 2020, sec. Business, https://www.nytimes.com/2020/01/24/business/london-police-facial-recognition.html.

19   Martin Evans, "London Now More Dangerous than New York City, Crime Stats Suggest," *The Telegraph*, October 20, 2017, https://www.telegraph.co.uk/news/2017/10/20/london-now-dangerous-new-york-crime-stats-suggest/.

Chapter 14

1   Scripture taken from the New King James Version®. Copyright © 1982 by Thomas Nelson. Used by permission. All rights reserved.

2   Camila Domonoske, "D.C. Couple Killed In Tajikistan Attack Were Biking Around The World Together," NPR.org, July 31, 2018, https://www.npr.org/2018/07/31/634373403/d-c-couple-killed-in-tajikistan-attack-were-biking-around-the-world-together.

3   Chantal Da Silva, "Headteacher 'Murdered' on Amazon Trip Joked about Being Killed Days Before," *The Independent*, September 20, 2017, https://www.independent.co.uk/news/world/americas/british-teacher-amazon-brazil-kayak-murder-emma-kelty-killed-names-joked-days-london-a7956636.html.

4   John L-Allen-Jr, "The War on Christians," *The Spectator*, October 5, 2013, https://www.spectator.co.uk/article/the-war-on-christians.

5   Connor Adams Sheets, "'Deadliest Drive In Africa': The Harrowing Bus Ride From Abuja To Lagos, Nigeria," *International Business Times,* November 8, 2013, https://www.ibtimes.com/deadliest-drive-africa-harrowing-bus-ride-abuja-lagos-nigeria-1461296.

6   Joseph Conrad, *Heart of Darkness* (New York, NY W. W. Norton & Company; Fifth edition 2016)

7   nigerianstalk, "How to Travel in Nigeria – Salisu Suleiman," NigeriansTalk, October 14, 2013, http://nigerianstalk.org/2013/10/14/how-to-travel-in-nigeria-salisu-suleiman/.

8   Larry Alex Taunton, "The Forgotten Christians of Nigeria – Faithful While Enduring Incredible Persecution," Fox News, October 13, 2017, https://www.foxnews.com/opinion/

the-forgotten-christians-of-nigeria-faithful-while-endur-
ing-incredible-persecution.

Chapter 15

1   Religion, "Nelson Mandela's Religious Worldview In His Own Words," *HuffPost*, December
6, 2013, https://www.huffpost.com/entry/
nelson-mandela-religion-spirituality-_n_4399847.

2   The World Bank, "Intentional Homicides (per
100,000 People) | Data," data.worldbank.org, n.d.,
https://data.worldbank.org/indicator/VC.IHR.PSRC.
P5?name_desc=true.

3   Richard Sprenger, Mustafa Khalili, and Alex Purcell,
"Nelson Mandela, 1964: 'I Am Prepared to Die' - Audio
Recording of Speech at Sabotage Trial," *The Guardian*,
December 5, 2013, https://www.theguardian.com/world/
video/2013/dec/05/nelson-mandela-1964-speech-audio.

Chapter 16

1   Uki Goñi, "The Long Shadow of Argentina's Dictatorship,"
The New York Times, March 21, 2016, https://www.nytimes.
com/2016/03/23/opinion/the-long-shadow-of-argenti-
nas-dictatorship.html.

2   Transparency International, "Corruption Perceptions Index
2019," www.transparency.org, 2019, https://www.transpar-
ency.org/cpi2019.

3   Transparency International, "One in Five People in Latin
America and the Caribbean Experiences…," Transparency.
org, September 25, 2019, https://www.transparency.org/
news/pressrelease/one_in_five_people_in_latin_america_
and_the_caribbean_sexual_extortion.

4 ethnic, "Gisele Bündchen," Ethnicity of Celebs | What Nationality Ancestry Race, October 6, 2008, http://ethnicelebs.com/gisele-bundchen.

Chapter 17

1 C. S. Lewis, *The Screwtape Letters* (New York, NY, Harper One 2013).

2 The Holy Bible, English Standard Version (ESV) is adapted from the Revised Standard Version of the Bible, copyright Division of Christian Education of the National Council of the Churches of Christ in the U.S.A. All rights reserved

3 Scott Stinson, "From Unpaid Workers to Barren Arenas, Rio's Olympic Legacy Has Quickly Become One of Regret | National Post," googleweblight.com, May 24, 2017, https://googleweblight.com/?lite_url=http://news.nationalpost.com/sports/olympics/from-unpaid-work-ers-to-barren-arenas-rios-olympic-legacy-has-quickly-be-come-one-of-regret&s=1&f=1&ts=1580081889&re=1&sig=ACgcqhom7ztpTj0yNJR3hNJEFcwWZAM-xQ.

4 France 24, "Rio Police Suspected of Using Snipers in Favela," France 24, February 21, 2019, https://www.france24.com/en/20190221-rio-police-suspected-using-snipers-favela.

Chapter 18

1 Jon Lee Anderson, "The Dictator," *The New Yorker*, October 12, 1998, https://www.newyorker.com/magazine/1998/10/19/the-dictator-2.

2 Daniel Zovatto, "The State of Democracy in Latin America," Brookings, September 15, 2014, https://www.brookings.edu/opinions/the-state-of-democracy-in-latin-america/.

3   Peter Beinart, "How Trump Wants to Make America Exceptional Again," *The Atlantic*, February 2, 2017, https://www.theatlantic.com/politics/archive/2017/02/how-trump-wants-to-make-america-exceptional-again/515406/.

4   Lisa Yulkowski, "Evangelicals Gain Following among Chile's Poor," Reuters, January 15, 2007, https://www.reuters.com/article/us-chile-evangelicals/evangelicals-gain-following-among-chiles-poor-idUSN0340332120070115.

5   Martin Arostegui, "Extremist Links Undercut Chile's Image of Stability," *The Washington Times*, January 30, 2017, https://www.washingtontimes.com/news/2017/jan/30/chile-image-of-stability-undercut-by-extremist-lin/.

Chapter 19

1   Herman Melville, *Moby Dick* (CreateSpace Independent Publishing, 2015).

2   William Neuman, "Peru Forced to Confront Deep Scars of Civil War," *The New York Times*, May 26, 2012. https://www.nytimes.com/2012/05/27/world/americas/peru-confronts-wounds-of-civil-war.html?r-ref=collection%2Ftimestopic%2FShining%20Path&action=click&contentCollection=timestopics&region=stream&module=stream_unit&version=latest&contentPlacement=6&pg

Chapter 20

1   Heritage History, "Story of Theodore Roosevelt by J. W. McSpadden," www.heritage-history.com, accessed June 1, 2020, https://www.heritage-history.com/index.php?c=read&author=mcspadden&book=roosevelt&story=panama.

Chapter 21

1 Ryan Cooper, "Bernie Sanders Wants the U.S. to Be More like Norway. Is That Even Possible?" theweek.com, August 6, 2015, https://theweek.com/articles/570205/bernie-sanders-wants-more-like-norway-that-even-possible.

2 Patricia Reaney, "Norway Unseats Denmark as World's Happiest Country: Report," www.yahoo.com, March 20, 2017, https://www.yahoo.com/news/norway-unseats-denmark-worlds-happiest-country-report-060821781.html.

3 Royal Norwegian Embassy, "Energy and Marine Resources," Norgesportalen, n.d., https://www.norway.no/en/usa/values-priorities/energy-marine-res/.

4 Luca Ventura and Pham Binh, "Global Finance Magazine - Richest Countries in the World 2019," *Global Finance Magazine*, April 15, 2019, https://www.gfmag.com/global-data/economic-data/richest-countries-in-the-world?page=12.

5 The Local, "Danish PM in US: Denmark Is Not Socialist," Thelocal.dk, November 1, 2015, https://www.thelocal.dk/20151101/danish-pm-in-us-denmark-is-not-socialist.

6 Jeffrey Dorfman, "Sorry Bernie Bros But Nordic Countries Are Not Socialist," *Forbes*, July 8, 2018, https://www.forbes.com/sites/jeffreydorfman/2018/07/08/sorry-bernie-bros-but-nordic-countries-are-not-socialist/#6c3c3f2c74ad.

7 Oliver Smith, "How to Beat the Falling Pound – the World's Cheapest Countries, Mapped," *The Telegraph*, July 24, 2019, https://www.telegraph.co.uk/travel/maps-and-graphics/mapped-the-cheapest-and-most-expensive-countries-to-live-in/.

8 Fraser Nelson, "Norway's Tough-Love Approach to the Refugee Crisis," *The Spectator*, November

25, 2017, https://www.spectator.co.uk/2017/11/norway-is-hard-on-migrants-but-tough-love-works/.

9   James Traub, "The Death of the Most Generous Nation on Earth," *Foreign Policy*, February 10, 2016, https://foreignpolicy.com/2016/02/10/the-death-of-the-most-generous-nation-on-earth-sweden-syria-refugee-europe/.

10 Katia Hetter, "World's Happiest Country for 2019 Revealed," CNN Travel, March 26, 2019, https://www.cnn.com/travel/article/worlds-happiest-countries-united-nations-2019/index.html.

11 Gallup, "2016 Global Emotions Report," 2016, http://www.ecoclimax.com/2016/03/gallup-2016-global-emotions-report.html

12 The Nordic Page Norway, "One in Four Use Drug in Norway Capital," *The Nordic Page*, September 2, 2016, https://www.tnp.no/norway/panorama/5364-one-in-four-use-drug-in-norway-capital.

13 Will Hagle, "The World's Happiest Countries Take The Most Antidepressants," Opposing Views, March 2, 2018, https://www.opposingviews.com/health/worlds-happiest-countries-take-most-antidepressants.

Chapter 22

1   Title of a song from the album ABBA Gold: Greatest Hits · Copyright: Writer(s): Benny Goran Bror Andersson, Bjoern K. Ulvaeus, Aleksej Anatolevich Kortnev.

2   Fraser Nelson, "Norway's Tough-Love Approach to the Refugee Crisis," *The Spectator*, November 25, 2017, https://www.spectator.co.uk/2017/11/norway-is-hard-on-migrants-but-tough-love-works/.

3   K. A. Geier, "EVERYTHING YOU THINK YOU KNOW ABOUT SWEDEN IS WRONG," The American

Prospect, June 3, 2008, https://prospect.org/article/
everything-think-know-sweden-wrong./.

4   Paulina Neuding, "Sweden's Violent Reality Is
Undoing a Peaceful Self-Image," *POLITICO*,
April 16, 2018, https://www.politico.eu/article/
sweden-bombings-grenade-attacks-violent-reality-undo-
ing-peaceful-self-image-law-and-order/.

5   James Traub, "The Death of the Most Generous Nation
on Earth," *Foreign Policy*, February 10, 2016, https://
foreignpolicy.com/2016/02/10/the-death-of-the-most-gen-
erous-nation-on-earth-sweden-syria-refugee-europe/.

6   Paulina Neuding, "Sweden's Violent Reality Is
Undoing a Peaceful Self-Image," *POLITICO*,
April 16, 2018, https://www.politico.eu/article/
sweden-bombings-grenade-attacks-violent-reality-undo-
ing-peaceful-self-image-law-and-order/.

Chapter 23

1   The Third Man (London Film Productions, 1949).

2   Kevin Drew, "Switzerland and Japan Are the World's Best
Countries," US News & World Report, June 10, 2019),
https://www.usnews.com/news/best-countries/articles/
us-news-unveils-best-countries-rankings.

3   Sean Mowbray, "This Country Has Been Named One of the
World's Most Unfriendly Places," Culture Trip, September
14, 2017, https://theculturetrip.com/europe/switzerland/
articles/this-country-has-been-named-one-of-the-worlds-
most-unfriendly-places/.

4   Mark Hay, "Does Switzerland Have a Problem with Diver-
sity?" Expat Guide to Switzerland | Expatica, May 25,
2020, https://www.expatica.com/ch/about/culture-history/
does-switzerland-have-a-problem-with-outsiders-840047/.

5   swissinfo.ch, "Swiss against Islam as an Official Religion,"
    SWI swissinfo.ch, November 7, 2016, https://www.
    swissinfo.ch/eng/society/religious-integration_swiss-against-
    islam-as-an-official-religion/42572738.

6   Jeffrey Manley, "Waugh's Religion," The Evelyn Waugh
    Society, February 18, 2016, https://evelynwaughsociety.
    org/2016/waughs-religion/.

7   Pfander, "The Siege of the Banu Qurayza," Pfander UK,
    February 20, 2014, https://www.pfander.uk/debate-topics/
    historical/siege-banu-qurayza/.

8   Larry Alex Taunton, "Islam and Christianity Not
    Comparable: Column," *USA TODAY*, March 18, 2015,
    https://www.usatoday.com/story/opinion/2015/03/18/
    christianity-isil-islam-religion-column/24847699/.

9   Sima Kotecha, "UK Muslims 'Oppose Cartoons Reprisals,'"
    BBC News, February 25, 2015, https://www.bbc.com/
    news/av/uk-31617940/british-muslims-oppose-cartoons-re-
    prisal-attacks-bbc-poll-finds.

10 Pew Research Center, "Muslim-Majority Countries," Pew
    Research Center's Religion & Public Life Project, January
    27, 2011, https://www.pewforum.org/2011/01/27/
    future-of-the-global-muslim-population-muslim-majority/.

11 The Local, "US Takes 'richest Nation on Earth'
    Crown from Switzerland," Thelocal.ch, September
    19, 2019, https://www.thelocal.ch/20190919/
    us-takes-richest-nation-on-earth-crown-from-switzerland.

12 Peter Siegenthaler, "Do the Swiss Really Pay so Little Tax?,"
    SWI swissinfo.ch, April 30, 2018, https://www.swissinfo.
    ch/eng/business/oecd-staaten_do-the-swiss-really-pay-so-lit-
    tle-tax-/44084950.

13 Pacific Standard Staff, "How Physician-Assisted
    Suicide Happens Around the World," Pacific

Standard, July 7, 2016, https://psmag.com/news/how-physician-assisted-suicide-happens-around-the-world.

14   Maggie Fox, "Abortion Rates Go down When Countries Make It Legal: Report," NBC News, March 21, 2018, https://www.nbcnews.com/health/health-care/abortion-rates-go-down-when-countries-make-it-legal-report-n858476.

Chapter 24

1   Alexander Weissberg, *The Accused* (New York, NY Simon and Shuster 1951)

2   Erik von Kuehnelt-Leddihn, *Leftism Revisited* (Washington, DC Gateway Books 1991).

3   U.S. News Staff, "10 Countries That Take the Most Immigrants," US News & World Report, December 18, 2019, https://www.usnews.com/news/best-countries/slideshows/10-countries-that-take-the-most-immigrants?slide=10.

4   Grace Guarnieri, "A German Study Has Linked Increases in Violence and Crime to Migrants in Europe," *Newsweek*, January 3, 2018, https://www.newsweek.com/migrants-europe-violence-crime-germany-study-770105.

5   The Associated Press, "Shooting in Germany Is Latest Indication of Increasing Anti-Semitism," *Longview News-Journal*, October 12, 2019, https://www.news-journal.com/features/shooting-in-germany-is-latest-indication-of-increasing-anti-semitism/article_9132e8e4-ec78-11e9-b6af-07c9ea115d0c.html.

6   Jonathan S Tobin, "Don't Blame the Surge of European Anti-Semitism on the Populists," *National Review*, May 29, 2019, https://www.nationalreview.com/2019/05/anti-semitism-europe-muslim-immigrants/.

7   eNotes, "Reflections on the Revolution in France 'Man Is A Religious Animal,'" eNotes, n.d., https://www.enotes.com/topics/reflections-revolution-france/quotes/man-religious-animal.

Chapter 25
1   Travel.State.Gov, "Egypt Travel Advisory," State.gov, 2019, https://travel.state.gov/content/travel/en/traveladvisories/traveladvisories/egypt-travel-advisory.html.

Chapter 26
1   Charles de Gaulle Quotes. BrainyQuote.com, BrainyMedia Inc, 2020. https://www.brainyquote.com/quotes/charles_de_gaulle_398023, accessed June 1, 2020.

2   Andrew Hussey, *Paris: The Secret History* (New York: Bloomsbury USA, 2008), p.17.

3   Paul Hannon, "France Tops OECD Table as Most Taxed Country," *Wall Street Journal*, December 5, 2018, sec. Economy, https://www.wsj.com/articles/france-becomes-the-worlds-most-heavily-taxed-country-1544004004.

4   Antonio Perez, "Titan Tire CEO in Work Ethic Spat With French Minister," *The Epoch Times*, February 22, 2013, https://www.theepochtimes.com/titan-tire-ceo-in-work-ethic-spat-with-french-minister_1477170.html.

5   Alexander Stille, "Why the French Are Fighting Over Work Hours," *The New Yorker*, October 3, 2013, https://www.newyorker.com/business/currency/why-the-french-are-fighting-over-work-hours.

6   Mona Charen, "Obama: President of France," *Townhall*, January 23, 2015, https://townhall.com/columnists/monacharen/2015/01/23/obama-president-of-france-n1946912.

7   Adrien Welsh, "Communists lead class struggle at local level in France's 'Red Cities,'" *People's World*, May 13, 2020, https://www.peoplesworld.org/article/communists-lead-class-struggle-at-local-level-in-frances-red-cities/.

8   Lauren Henry, "History Milestone: The Liberation of Paris," origins.osu.edu, August 2019, https://origins.osu.edu/milestones/the-liberation-of-paris-wwii.

9   News, "D-Day Landings: Operation Overlord in Numbers," *The Telegraph*, January 17, 2019, https://www.telegraph.co.uk/news/2016/06/06/d-day-landings-operation-overlord-in-numbers2/the-allied-casualties-figures-for-d-day-have-generally-been-esti/.

10   Bruce Kauffmann, "BRUCE'S HISTOR LESSONS: De Gaulle's Eternal Myth: The Liberation of France," *Terre Haute Tribune-Star*, August 25, 2009, https://www.tribstar.com/news/local_news/bruce-s-histor-lessons-de-gaulle-s-eternal-myth-the/article_89c4aef4-2e2a-5845-bed2-88ce0cd4e012.html.

11   Philip Sherwell, "Paris Mayor: 'We'll Sue Fox News over Muslim No-Go Zone Claims,'" *The Telegraph*, January 20, 2015, https://www.telegraph.co.uk/news/worldnews/europe/france/11358845/Paris-mayor-Well-sue-Fox-News-over-Muslim-no-go-zone-claims.html.

Epilogue

1   Times Video, "Opinion | Please Stop Telling Me America Is Great," *The New York Times*, July 1, 2019, https://nytlive.nytimes.com/video/opinion/100000006468226/america-great.html?playlistId=1194811622182.

2   Matt Walsh, "No, America Is Not a Great Nation," *The Blaze*, July 3, 2015, https://www.theblaze.com/contributions/no-america-is-not-a-great-nation.

3   Larry Alex Taunton, "Celebrated Author Paul Reid Tells Us Why Winston Churchill Thought History Was Important—and Why We Must, Too.," LAT, February 6, 2020, https://larryalextaunton.com/2020/02/winston-churchill-history/.

4   Vishal Mangalwadi, *The Book that Made Your World: How the Bible Created the Soul of Western Civilization*, (Nashville, TN Thomas Nelson Pp. 390-392)

5   Daily Wire News, "MSNBC's Chris Matthews Explodes On Democrats Over Socialism: 'It Doesn't Frickin Work!'" *The Daily Wire*, February 8, 2020, https://www.dailywire.com/news/msnbcs-chris-matthews-explodes-on-democrats-over-socialism-it-doesnt-frickin-work.

6   Alexis de Tocqueville, *Democracy in America, Part I*, The Project Gutenberg, January 21, 2016, https://www.gutenberg.org/files/815/815-h/815-h.htm.

7   Neli Esipova, Julie Ray, and Anita Pugliese, "Number of Potential Migrants Worldwide Tops 700 Million," Gallup, June 8, 2017, https://www.mybib.com/#/projects/4KDMJk/citations/new/webpage.